KT-471-238

Contents

THAMES POLYTECHNIC LIBRARY

598.29421 ATL

116385

THAMES POLYTECHNIC
LIBRARY
★ ★
VANBRUGH HOUSE, KING STREET, W

MW

ATLAS OF BREEDING BIRDS
OF THE LONDON AREA

Atlas of Breeding Birds of the London Area

Edited by
DAVID J MONTIER

for the London Natural History Society

THAMES POLYTECHNIC
LIBRARY
HERBURT HOUSE, KING STREET, W.6

WITHDRAWN
FROM
UNIVERSITIES
AT
MEDWAY
LIBRARY

London area collection

THAMES POLYTECHNIC LIBRARY

598.
2942.
1022
3
ATL

B. T. Batsford Ltd
London

First published 1977

© 1977 London Natural History Society
and the contributing authors and illustrators.

ISBN 0 7134 0876 6

All rights reserved.
No part of this book may be reproduced, stored in a
retrieval system, or transmitted in any form, or by any
means, electronic, mechanical, photocopying or otherwise, without the prior permission of the London
Natural History Society and the publishers.

Typeset by Tek-Art Ltd., London SE20
Printed in Great Britain by
The Anchor Press Ltd. Tiptree
for the Publishers B.T. Batsford Ltd,
4 Fitzhardinge Street, London W1H 0AH

598. 294 21 ATL

16385

WITHDRAWN FROM UNIVERSITIES AT MEDWAY LIBRARY

THAMES POLYTECHNIC
23 AUG 1990
LIBRARY

Text figures

Tables

Foreword
by Stanley Cramp

London's birds have been studied more thoroughly than those of any comparable area in the world. There has been a long history of ornithological observation and there are probably now more birdwatchers a square mile than anywhere else. These enthusiasts may flee from the bricks and mortar for their more exciting expeditions, but many have also devotedly studied their home areas — and London, as this book shows, offers more to interest and enthral than might at first be suspected. The London Natural History Society has for many years encouraged and published their observations, which were gathered together in an impressive volume edited by R.C. Homes — *The Birds of the London Area* (1964). Thorough as this compilation was, it suffered from the inevitable drawback that it had to be based on records available, which meant that rarely had any species been studied in one year over the whole Area, while some of the less attractive districts had received inadequate attention. The launching of the Atlas scheme by the British Trust for Ornithology provided an incentive to try to cover all breeding species of the London Area at the same time and, going one better, to do so on a 2x2-km rather than a 10-km square basis.

So, thanks to the devotion of some 450 observers and the enthusiastic guidance of David Montier and his team, we now have the most complete picture of London's breeding birds ever provided. No longer are there disturbing gaps in our knowledge because certain districts, such as many suburban areas, or some species, like the Woodpigeon or House Sparrow, had failed to arouse sufficient interest. It is now at last possible to see in detail how different birds are adapting to or retreating from urban development — a continuing and fascinating process. But if the facts are now available, the reasons are still often little understood, and this Atlas will provide endless scope for more detailed enquiries. For some species the factors involved in their distribution are clear and are given in the accompanying text, but others are more puzzling. Why, for instance, has the Collared Dove so far failed to penetrate as a breeding bird into the inner core of London when in some European cities it competes successfully with its relatives the Woodpigeon and Feral Pigeon? Why is the Lesser Spotted Woodpecker so much more restricted in its distribution than its larger relatives? And why is the Tree Sparrow able to live alongside the far more numerous House Sparrow in many areas, but not in others apparently equally suitable?

Perhaps the main value of this Atlas is that it provides a base-line to measure future changes. With the enormous increase in birdwatching in recent years, it has become abundantly clear that bird distribution is far from static — the ranges of many species are changing, often dramatically. Even within the London Area, six breeding species have been gained since 1954 and two lost. Some of these and other changes reflect events over a wider range, while others may be specifically connected with alterations in the London environment. It would be a rash man who attempted to guess what a repeat of this enquiry in ten or twenty years will reveal.

This Atlas will also, I hope, serve a third purpose — that of assisting bird conservation. As more and more people throughout the world live in cities there has been a growing tendency to press for improvements in the quality of urban life, not only in material amenities, but in the richness of the living environment. This is not a hopeless task — in Inner London itself, despite the pessimists, the number of bird species nesting regularly has almost doubled since 1900. A major reason for this has been the change in human attitudes towards living creatures, with less persecution, increased benevolence, such as the provision of food and nest-boxes, and active conservation by making sanctuaries or more varied habitats. Here the Atlas offers a guide, not only to the variety of nesting birds, but to environmental diversity for human beings — and suggests strongly that much needs to be done in some areas of London.

Preface

While there have been numerous studies of bird distribution in selected localities and wider surveys of certain species, mapping of the summer distribution of all species breeding in the London Area has never previously been attempted. The impetus for such a scheme was the launching by the British Trust for Ornithology in 1968 of its plans to produce a national Atlas based on the presence or absence of each breeding species in every 10-kilometre square of the Ordnance Survey national grid and which culminated in the publication in 1976 of *The Atlas of Breeding Birds in Britain and Ireland* compiled by Dr. J.T.R. Sharrock. Clearly the London Natural History Society had an obligation to support the project within its own recording Area, but the Research Sub-Committee of the Ornithology Section decided that the opportunity should be taken to go further and study breeding bird distribution in London more fully. Fieldwork on the national and local schemes was combined using exactly the same recording codes, so that the London Area survey not only formed the basis of returns to the British Trust for Ornithology, but also produced a local picture on a scale twenty-five times more detailed.

This *Atlas of Breeding Birds of the London Area* thus presents the results of five years of intensive work by many observers over the years 1968 to 1972. A project of this scale, covering 120 nesting or potential nesting species, has only become possible because of the much greater interest in ornithology in recent years. Perhaps its most important and lasting achievement is the establishment of a base-line against which future workers will be able to make comparisons.

Before the main section of the book, an introduction defines the London Area covered by the Society and describes the survey and the recording methods used. A brief review of the geological structure underlying the Area and the present range of habitats available to breeding birds demonstrates that, in spite of the enormous human population and the great extent of the built-up area, there is still room for a wide variety of species. A series of maps then shows the pattern of distribution for each of the 120 species and the accompanying text summarises the known changes throughout the present century, indicating some possible reasons for expansion or decline. Where appropriate, reference is made to records for years following the survey mainly up to the end of 1974, but extended to 1976 where there have been significant developments within Inner London.

The sequence of species in the main section, vernacular names and scientific nomenclature follow that of the British Trust for Ornithology's Guide No:13 — *A Species List of British and Irish Birds* (1971). Scientific names of birds dealt with in the main species accounts are given in the heading to each species; scientific names of plants and animals other than birds are given in Appendix III. A gazetteer of place-names mentioned in the text is included in Appendix IV. Records received during the Atlas survey were given simply under a tetrad (2x2-kilometre square) map reference and therefore place-names relating to the period 1968-72 for the most part indicate the location of the tetrad, unless more precise information was available in the *London Bird Reports* for those years.

Although a revision of administrative county boundaries in 1965 absorbed parts of Essex, Hertfordshire, Kent, Surrey and most of Middlesex into a new region called Greater London, this book retains the old boundaries as an aid to comparison with earlier periods. Unless otherwise stated, references to Buckinghamshire, Essex, Hertfordshire, Kent and Surrey mean those parts of the counties within the Society's recording Area.

In writing this book constant reference was made to *The Birds of the London Area Since 1900,* first published in 1957, with a revised edition edited by R.C. Homes in 1964. This has been a major influence on all species accounts and is the basis of all statements on status up to 1954 unless other references are given. Where it is referred to specifically it is given as 'Homes' without a date. For later information much use has been made of all subsequent *London Bird Reports. Breeding Birds of Britain and Ireland* by J.L.F. Parslow was also consulted and frequent references to 'Parslow' without a date relate to that work. For some species comparison is made between population changes in London localities and the British Trust for Ornithology's Common Birds Census. National population indices are based on annual sample censuses and revised tables have recently been published by Batten & Marchant (1976). For economy of space in the text this reference has been reduced to 'B & M 1976'.

For convenience a number of other abbreviations have been used throughout the book and these are listed below:

Bucks	Buckinghamshire
Herts	Hertfordshire
BTO	British Trust for Ornithology
LNHS	London Natural History Society
RSPB	Royal Society for the Protection of Birds
WAGBI	Wildfowlers' Association of Great Britain & Ireland
G.P.	Gravel Pit
S.F.	Sewage Farm

As the Atlas project was based on the metric grid system all measurements and distances are shown in metric form, i.e.

1m	(metre)	3.281 feet
1km	(kilometre)	0.621 miles
1km^2	(square kilometre)	0.386 square miles
1ha	(hectare)	2.471 acres
1 tetrad	(2x2-km square)	400 hectares

Any additions, amendments or comments on the records produced by this survey would be welcome, together with up-to-date reports. These should be sent to the Records Committee of the Ornithology Section, LNHS, c/o British Museum (Natural History), Cromwell Road, London, SW7 5BD. The more interesting records and summaries of bird distribution from year to year appear in the Society's annual publication, the *London Bird Report.*

Acknowledgements

None of these Atlas results would have been achieved had not the BTO launched its own scheme for a national Atlas survey and devised the original rules and instructions which the LNHS adopted for its own recording Area. That our London project was such a success was due to the ready co-operation of some 450 observers involved in five years of fieldwork under the enthusiastic organisation of P.J. Sellar. Help is gladly acknowledged from all those who took part and whose names are shown in the list on pages 281 to 283, kindly prepared by K.H. Palmer from about 2,500 record cards and a thick file of other returns. Apologies are offered for any names inadvertently omitted. Special thanks are due to all 10-km square organisers who shouldered much of the responsibility within their own localities. Valuable assistance was received from neighbouring Societies with which the London recording Area overlaps. The London organisers are greatly indebted to them, especially to members of the Surrey Bird Club who were not otherwise providing cover on the same 2x2-km square basis; to Herts ornithologists on whom the LNHS relied entirely for coverage of that part of the Area within their county; and to the county Atlas organisers for providing a ready exchange of records — Mrs P.V. Upton for Essex, C.J. Mead for Herts, R.H.B. Forster for Surrey and G.F.A. Munns and D.W. Taylor for Kent.

Members of the LNHS Ornithology Section Records Committee assisted on certain records and the Research Sub-Committee, firstly under the chairmanship of Stanley Cramp and latterly P.J. Sellar, provided much help and encouragement. In relating present distribution to wider ornithological studies in London, this book owes a considerable debt to R.C. Homes and the Editorial Committee of *The Birds of the London Area* and to Editors of the *London Bird Reports*.

All the work involved in the Atlas project has been carried out by amateurs in their spare time, including the production of the material for this book. The Editor is pleased to acknowledge the invaluable contributions of both members and non-members of the LNHS in this final and important stage of the project — the presentation of the results.

Contributors to the text were: R.J. Chandler, J.G. Francis, A. Gibbs, P.J. Grant, R.C. Homes, F.H. Jones, D.J. Montier, Mrs Mary Montier, P.J. Oliver, K.C. Osborne and R.F. Sanderson.

Vignettes were produced by: L. Baker, B. Bland, P.J. Grant, A.C. Parker and R.E. Turley.

The background map of the London Area and the geological cross-section were prepared with great skill by K.C. Osborne, who also gave advice on numerous technical points during preparation of the manuscript. The dot distribution maps were specially processed for the Society by the Biological Records Centre of the Institute of Terrestrial Ecology at Monks Wood Experimental Station, for which thanks are due to Miss Christine Allen, H.R. Arnold and J. Heath.

Valued criticism of the species accounts was received from P.A.D. Hollom, J.D. Magee and P.J. Oliver. In addition M.S. Andrews, K.C. Osborne, B.L. Sage and P.J. Strangeman

Acknowledgements

made constructive suggestions on the chapter on bird habitats, and the geological section benefited from the comments of R.E. Butler and R.J. Chandler, who also drew Figure 3 and whose assistance in a variety of ways, often at short notice, was greatly appreciated. Information on reservoirs in the London Area was freely given by the Thames Water Authority. All these helped to clarify and improve the text: any mistakes that remain are the responsibility of the Editor.

The unenviable job of typing several drafts was most capably undertaken by Mrs Joan Farmer, with additional help from Mrs Lesley Buckthorpe, Mrs Barbara Cook, Mrs Eunice Chandler and Miss Jean Ross. Joan Farmer and the London Polytechnics Computer Unit, Polytechnic of North London, produced the figures in Appendix 1, the apparent simplicity of which belies the great deal of work involved. Mrs Pamela Washer is thanked for compiling indexes. Copying facilities were very kindly provided by Furness, Withy & Co. Ltd.

In addition to expressing his gratitude to all these, the Editor would also like to record his special debt to his wife, Mary, who, too, has had to live with this project since 1968 and, as well as contributing to the text, has provided immeasurable help and advice throughout.

Introduction

In attempting to map the summer distribution of all breeding species in the London Area during the course of five years from 1968 to 1972, a series of definitions and rules were laid down to ensure that as far as possible all parts of the Area were covered and that all observers followed the same recording methods.

The established recording Area of the LNHS is in the form of a circle centred on St Paul's Cathedral and having a radius of 20 miles. For the Atlas survey the recording unit was the 2x2-km square, or tetrad, identified by the even-numbered lines of the Ordnance Survey national grid. This necessitated an amendment to the boundary of the Area to correspond exactly with tetrad lines. As a result, the circle became a stepped polygon of 856 tetrads, covering 3,424km^2. A rectangular area shown on the maps as enclosing the centre of London had been given the title of 'Inner London' in the 1920s (Macpherson 1929), though it was measured, not from St Paul's, but from the site of the old Charing Cross on the south side of Trafalgar Square. It stretches for four miles east and west of that point and two and a half miles north and south, giving a total length of 12.87km, a width of 8.05km and a total area of 103.6km^2. This part of central London has retained a special significance in local ornithology and is referred to frequently in the following pages.

To collect data for this Atlas, observers were supplied with instructions and a coding system describing different bird activities and were asked to fill in cards for each tetrad visited during the breeding season. Coverage of the London Area was mainly arranged through a network of local organisers, but records were also received as a result of casual observations. Exact plotting of records within the correct tetrad, and hence within the correct square on the distribution maps, was a critically important feature of the project. Details of the codes to be entered on the cards against each species are set out in Appendix II. There were three basic definitions:

- Present in the breeding season in   Shown as a small dot on the species maps
  a suitable nesting habitat though
  without any evidence of breeding

- Probably breeding   Shown as a medium-size dot

- Breeding   Shown as a large dot

Observers were not asked to count the birds or pairs present or to make any assessment of their relative densities. A dot on a map may therefore represent a single pair or many pairs. Similarly a pair shifting its nest site from one tetrad to another in different years would be included as two records, but this is unlikely to affect the conclusions significantly. The survey thus dealt only with distribution and a record from any one of the five years qualified for inclusion.

To be sure of complete accuracy in a breeding bird survey would mean accepting only records of nests found containing eggs or young. While this may have been suitable for a conspicuous species like the Grey Heron, such a basis would have made the project impracticable and caused an unacceptable degree of disturbance to nesting birds. The codes that were devised represent a level of recording that was attainable without destroying the overall value of the scheme.

Each of the three categories of records presents particular problems. Even when present in a suitable nesting habitat, a bird may possibly have been a passage migrant or simply visiting the area to feed. In the second category, some records of singing males might again include migrants or unmated males. To describe them as probably breeding could sometimes be an overstatement. The third category was designed to indicate definite breeding, but this also has limitations. Free-flying young still being fed by their parents long after leaving the nest could have wandered out of their home tetrad into a neighbouring one and some records of adults carrying food may relate to birds, such as the Kestrel, holding large territories and hunting over several tetrads. These qualifications should be borne in mind, but they do not detract from the overall pattern shown on the maps which provide much more detailed information, especially about the commoner species, than has previously been available.

An uneven distribution of birdwatchers over the London Area inevitably caused some degree of bias in the results in that some tetrads were visited more often than others, leaving small patches where coverage was less than adequate. This is mainly noticeable in parts of outer and south Essex. Organisers attempted to direct observers into areas where work was most needed and by the end of five years only 14 tetrads had not been visited at all, amounting to 1.6% of the total. The location of these blanks is shown on the map in Appendix I, which sets out in diagrammatic form the total number of records for each tetrad. A close study of the local environment would be necessary in order to judge whether any of the totals accurately represented the variety of species present. Such a detailed comparison is beyond the scope of this book, but as a rough guide, the Appendix also shows the average number of species in tetrads within four different zones. A particularly high total in any tetrad may indicate a greater diversity of habitat than is characteristic of that zone; a low total may indicate either the reverse or, in a few cases, poor observer coverage. The four zones and their different features are discussed in the following chapter.

With the exception of the Grey Heron, all species maps include records received for the three code categories, with only minor editing of apparent errors. For the Grey Heron the map is confined to definite breeding records marking the sites of all known heronries within the Area. Five species, Sparrowhawk, Hobby, Wryneck, Woodlark and Red-backed Shrike, were considered to be especially vulnerable to disturbance and at a low population level, with a particularly marked decline affecting the last three. The Sparrowhawk may be increasing, but, like the scarcer Hobby, is in danger from human predators stealing eggs or young. For security reasons, therefore, maps for these species show the numbers of records in each county within the London Area without disclosing the specific tetrads in which they occurred.

Though based on the same survey carried out over the same period, a detailed examination of the maps in this book against those in *The Atlas of Breeding Birds in Britain and Ireland* will show a number of variations. In some cases these represent records received with only a 10-km square map reference which was not sufficiently precise to identify the tetrad; in other cases minor adjustments were made as a result of more information coming to light during preparation of the text. Overall the maps are thought to give a reasonably accurate picture of distribution over the London Area in the years 1968-72. Comparison with the past is complicated by the absence of any similar previous survey. Earlier records were generally summarised either under place-names or by geographical features which are unlikely to correspond with grid lines. One or two changes since the early 1950s, however, are readily apparent.

Based on records up to 1954 available when the systematic list was prepared for the first edition of *The Birds of the London Area,* Homes indicated that there were about 100 species breeding more or less regularly in the London Area and perhaps another ten nesting occasionally. During 1968-72 a total of 112 species was recorded as nesting and a further eight merited inclusion in the study.

All but one of the species breeding during the Atlas survey and not known to do so in the earlier period were connected with water or waterside habitats. The exception was the Collared Dove, which is now so well established that it is surprising to recall that as recently as 1956 this species had never been recorded in the London Area and first nesting was not reported until 1962.

Shelduck were first proved to have nested in the Area in 1954 on the Thames marshes and have done so almost annually since 1959. They extended their range inland in 1974 when two pairs bred at Queen Mary Reservoir, which, in 1958, had provided the first nesting record in London of the Common Tern. Herring Gulls were the next colonists choosing a site at the Zoo in Regent's Park in 1961. Greylag Geese appear in the list of gains following their introduction into one site in the Area also in 1961; by the time of the Atlas survey there were breeding records from four tetrads. The only passerine to be added is the Bearded Tit, which bred successfully at a site in Herts in 1966 and 1968. Oystercatchers have been the most recent addition to the list of breeding species. A pair was seen with downy young at Swanscombe Marsh in 1971 and in the same year another pair nested at Rainham Marsh, but deserted the eggs.

Of the newcomers, only the Collared Dove has increased to any extent. Growing numbers of Common Terns have been attracted to rafts forming artificial islands at Rye Meads, but the Shelduck, Herring Gulls and Greylag Geese are present in small numbers in only a handful of localities. So far neither the Oystercatcher nor the Bearded Tit has managed to become established. The Ringed Plover almost qualifies as a new breeding species in London, as two pairs nesting in 1957 were the first to be recorded since 1901. Since its recolonisation birds have been found nesting in most years.

Two species breeding in the 1950s were not known to have done so during the present survey. One was the Cirl Bunting, which has always been scarce in the London Area and may have declined generally in south-east England. The other was the Black-headed Gull, *Larus ridibundus,* which is still a widespread species in the Area throughout most of the year, but there was no suggestion during the 1968-72 survey that any birds were holding territory or prospecting for nest sites. Breeding had previously occurred at two localities. One of the former colonies was established in the 1940s at Perry Oaks S.F. and by 1947 contained about 300 nests. This appeared to be a peak and later numbers varied from about 150 to 250, though dropping to about 125 in 1961. In that year six pairs nested at Maple Cross S.F. This colony had a very short life and was down to one nest by 1964, when Perry Oaks had also declined to only two. Neither site was reoccupied in 1965 and no further breeding attempts have been reported, though perhaps Black-headed Gulls might be tempted back by the presence of nesting pairs of Common Terns.

Introduction

Since the end of the Atlas survey the Woodlark appears to have been lost as a breeding species, while both the Wryneck, reduced to probably only one pair, and the Red-backed Shrike, down to one, perhaps two pairs at the most, seem likely to follow.

To take a more encouraging view, are there going to be any gains over the next few years? Three species that up to 1974 were not proved to have nested successfully in the London Area, but are included in this book, are the Lesser Black-backed Gull, Firecrest and Siskin. Pairs of Lesser Black-backed Gulls have taken up territories from time to time in the Inner London parks since 1966, though a first breeding record is unlikely to generate as much excitement as the other two possibilities from the opposite end of the size-scale. Firecrests are now increasingly reported in the spring and once as late as June. A few pairs nest annually beyond the boundary in Bucks and, with suitable habitat available, they will surely be found breeding within the Area before long. Siskins, too, are recorded more frequently than in the past. A pair was reported to have built a nest which was subsequently destroyed in 1901, but a record of successful breeding is still awaited. Expectations have increased since a party of fledged juveniles was found during the Atlas survey, though these birds may have wandered into the Area from elsewhere.

In many respects this Atlas survey raises more questions than it answers and some possible lines of further enquiry are mentioned in the individual species accounts. Why is it, for example, that Pochard seem to find gravel pits unsuitable as breeding habitats? If that is true, is it related to the depth of water in which they would have to dive for food? Though the Collared Dove is now regarded as a common bird in many areas, it appeared in fewer tetrads than the Turtle Dove. A study of their relative densities where they both occur might produce some interesting results. Similarly, how do the numbers of the three woodpeckers compare in different habitats in different parts of the Area? Some monitoring of the Sand Martin population might be appropriate in view of what is thought to have been a serious decline of the species in some parts of the country and a wider study of the numbers of Reed and Sedge Warblers present in selected localities would usefully expand the somewhat limited data already available.

Furthermore, blank spaces on the maps do not necessarily mean that a species is absent from a particular spot; it may have been overlooked. The distribution maps should therefore be regarded as a challenge and any corrections or discoveries should be notified to the Society so that the fund of knowledge on the birds of the London Area can be increased.

18

Geology and habitats

Londinium was established by the Romans on the north bank of the River Thames where part of the City of London now stands. At that point the higher ground gave protection against floods, and the surrounding marshes beyond the walls provided an additional measure of security. A navigable river gradually helped the growth of trade and commerce, and industry developed as man's knowledge and technology increased, the greatest changes coming in approximately the last 200 years with the beginning of the industrial revolution. Thus man has exerted more and more influence over his environment and now, nearly 2,000 years after the Roman settlement, the administrative county of Greater London, roughly corresponding to the central shaded area in Figure 2, covers some 1,600km^2 and holds a human population of seven million. Beyond what may be described as the built-up area, outlying towns and villages add to the total population. Few extensive tracts of open countryside remain entirely without human habitation and probably none of the original habitat is still in its natural state.

In any review of bird distribution in the London Area in the present day the activities of man are now likely to show the greatest impact, destroying original habitats, creating new ones and modifying others. Yet the nature of the soils and physical structure of the land continue to affect the pattern of natural vegetation and indirectly the availability of suitable breeding habitats for birds.

GEOLOGICAL STRUCTURE

The River Thames is the most immediately obvious natural feature of London, flowing eastwards from Egham on the western boundary and more or less bisecting the Area before reaching Northfleet in the east. It lies at the centre of a shallow synclinal basin composed of Cretaceous and Eocene strata laid down by seas that covered the south-east of England between 40 and 140 million years ago, and folded into their present structure during the Miocene period about 15 million years ago. This London Basin is bounded by two ranges of Chalk hills, both with outward-facing scarps; by the Chilterns in the north-west and, in the south, by the North Downs running approximately west to east. These hills comprise most of the high ground within the Area, the highest point being 269m above sea level on the North Downs between Limpsfield and Woldingham. In some places on the Chalk there is a covering of a later deposit of Clay-with-flints. Beneath the Chalk and cropping out to the south of the North Downs lie the Upper Greensand, the Gault and the Lower Greensand. Of these, the Lower Greensand reaches the surface in a line of hills stretching along the southern margin of the Area between Redhill and Brasted Chart and rising to 215m above sea level at Hosey Common. Between these hills and the Downs there is a narrow band of Upper Greensand and Gault, the latter forming a low-lying clay vale.

Above the Chalk, on the margin of the London Basin, lie the Eocene deposits of

Thanet Sands and Woolwich and Reading Beds consisting of sands and clays. These, together with the Blackheath Pebble Beds, present relatively small patches on the edge of the London Clay which floors the greatest part of the Basin between the Chilterns and the North Downs and extends over much of Essex. In places on the higher ground of the London Clay, Bagshot Beds provide a capping of fine sand and gravel, for example, at Brentwood, Hampstead Heath, Harrow and Esher Common.

Discontinuous patches of superficial or 'drift' deposits overlie the Eocene strata. Broadly speaking they consist of clays, sands and gravels laid down in the geologically recent past by ice, melt-waters and rivers and as the products of weathering of pre-existing rocks. In the London Area the most important drift deposits are the extensive flood plain terraces of gravel laid down by the Thames and its tributaries and in which many of the present gravel workings and reservoirs are situated. On the higher terrace gravels, such as at Dartford Heath, the vegetation is frequently similar to that found on the Lower Greensand. This dry heathland flora also occurs in the small pockets of earlier Pliocene sediments, the Netley Heath deposits, which can be found in a few places on the North Downs.

A cross-section of the geological structure of the London Area is shown in Figure 1 and a summary of the main strata is given in Table 1.

Fig 1. **Geological Section**

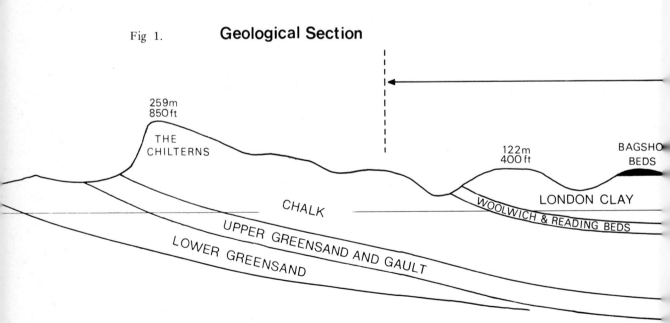

HABITATS

In considering the present physical scene in more detail it is perhaps appropriate to deal first with major water and waterside habitats which are found in all parts of the Area from the centre to the boundary. At least a quarter of the 120 species included in the Atlas survey were water-birds or birds primarily associated with wetlands during the breeding season. Clearly therefore the preservation of such habitats plays a vital part in maintaining the variety of London's avifauna.

Water and waterside

In spite of its significance as the main river of the London Basin, the Thames itself, tidal for over two-thirds of its length through the Area, is of relatively little importance to nesting birds. Except in the east, the land on both sides is mostly built-up, though for the last third of its journey, from Barking Creek on the north bank and the Plum-stead/Erith Marshes on the south, the Thames passes through stretches of more open country. On the north side of the River a belt of marshland and grazing land with rough vegetation and drainage channels remains alongside the Ford motor factory at Dagenham and the mainly industrial development between Purfleet and Tilbury. To the birdwatcher, Rainham Marsh, forming part of this area to the east of Dagenham, offers the greatest attraction. This largely reclaimed land consists of open beds of mud slurry dredged from the Thames which gradually dry out in a series of lagoons between earth banks. Shelduck and Ringed and Little Ringed Plovers have nested there successfully, Oystercatchers

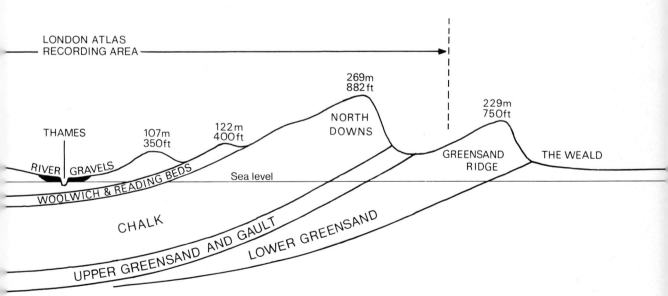

Geology and habitats

Table 1. The main stratigraphy of the London Area (most recent to oldest), with examples of present-day habitats.

Formation	Extent	Examples of habitat
RECENT and PLEISTOCENE		
Lower terraces of alluvium, sands and gravels	Flood plain of Thames and tributaries	Drained marsh, lowland farming, reservoirs, gravel workings
Higher terraces of sands and gravels	Former river terraces both sides of Thames	Mostly built over; open spaces — Hyde Park/Kensington Gardens, Clapham and Wandsworth Commons, Dartford Heath
Glacial Boulder Clay	Ice Age deposits in north Essex, extensions west to St Albans, south to Finchley	Farmland with woods; built-up nearer central London
Plateau Gravel	Isolated patches	Remnant heathland within built-up area — Richmond Park, Wimbledon Common
Clay-with-flints	Residual layer on flat tops of Chalk Downs	Oak, beech woodland on Chalk
Pebble Gravel	Isolated Cappings	Hertford Heath, highest parts of Epping Forest
PLIOCENE		
Crag deposits of sand and thin gravel	Netley Heath deposits	Heaths on North Downs above c180m — Headley and Walton Heaths
EOCENE		
Bagshot Beds of fine sand and gravel	Higher ground within London Basin	Heaths, commons — Hampstead Heath, High Beach (Epping Forest), Brentwood, Esher Common, Oxshott Heath
London Clay	Most of London Basin	Mostly built over; farmland in Essex, Herts and Surrey; oak woodland
Woolwich, Reading and Blackheath Pebble Beds, Thanet Sands — clays, loams, sands and pebble beds	Generally narrow belt between London Clay and Chalk; isolated cappings on Chalk	Pine, birch heaths — Addington Hills, Hayes Common, Petts Wood
CRETACEOUS		
Chalk	Chilterns, North Downs	Downland pasture reverting to scrub where not grazed; arable farming
Upper Greensand and Gault — sand and clay	Narrow band south of North Downs	Farmland
Lower Greensand — sandstone	Belt of high ground along southern boundary of London Area	Beech, birch, pine woodland; heaths — Limpsfield Chart, Hosey Common; sand pits — Godstone, Bletchingley

have attempted to do so and other species typical of the area include Stonechat, Whinchat, Meadow Pipit and Yellow Wagtail.

On the opposite side of the Thames, habitats again include drained marshland at Dartford, Stone and Swanscombe, some of which has been gradually lost to redevelopment. Littlebrook Power-Station stands on Dartford Marsh and the new town of Thamesmead has been built on part of the Plumstead/Erith Marshes. On higher ground, where the North Downs extend as far as the River, the Chalk has been extensively quarried for the cement industry. Abandoned quarries quickly develop a scrub habitat suitable for a variety of small passerines, while Stock Doves and Jackdaws can sometimes find nestholes on the cliff-sides. Swanscombe Marsh was at its best for birds in the early 1960s when, as at Rainham, Thames-dredged mud was pumped onto lagoons. Though the Marsh is now totally reclaimed, both Ringed and Little Ringed Plovers nested there during the period covered by the Atlas survey.

Major tributaries of the Thames are the rivers Colne, Lea and Roding in the north and the Wey, Mole and Darent in the south. Like the Thames, they all flow through parts of the built-up area, though the Roding, entering the Area at Chipping Ongar in the north-east, crosses the rural part of Essex before it reaches the suburbs near Chigwell and finally the Thames at Barking Creek. Only a short stretch of the Wey affects the London Area before it flows into the Thames at Weybridge, but the Mole, on a winding course from Mickleham to the Thames at East Molesey, passes through open country as well as the rural town of Leatherhead before reaching the outer suburbs.

The Lea, the Colne and the Darent are all closely connected with the extensive gravel pits and main reservoirs of the London Area. In the south-east, the Darent rises near Limpsfield and reaches the Thames at Dartford Marsh. There are gravel pits at Chipstead (Kent), Riverhead and between Horton Kirby and Dartford. Disused pits at Ruxley are now used to control flooding on the River Cray, a tributary of the Darent. These pits have an abundant growth of surrounding trees and bushes and provide nest sites for such species as ducks, warblers and finches. Gravel pits are also a prominent feature in the upper part of the Lea valley from Rye House Marsh, where the RSPB has recently established a reserve, south to Cheshunt. From there a series of reservoirs extends into the inner suburbs as far as Walthamstow. Their main ornithological interest lies in their attraction to wintering wildfowl, though the Walthamstow group, containing several wooded islands, holds one of the largest heronries in Britain.

In the west of the London Area the River Colne, rising near Hatfield, flows southwest past sand and gravel pits at Old Parkbury, to Rickmansworth, where it is joined by the River Gade and the smaller River Chess. From there the Colne passes Stocker's Lake, Maple Cross S.F. and a long series of gravel pits southwards to Staines. There are also numerous pits and lakes in the valley of the Thames itself on the western limits of the Area, as well as such long established reservoirs as the King George VI, Staines, Queen Mary, Kempton Park, and the Walton group south of the River. Much nearer central London, Barn Elms Reservoirs lie in a bend of the River only just outside the Inner London boundary. They provide a feeding area in the summer for Swifts and House Martins nesting in the neighbourhood and also attract breeding ducks. Often a pair of Reed Warblers and occasionally Reed Buntings breed in adjacent habitat. Another reservoir in an urban setting is the Brent, or Welsh Harp, near Hendon. It is also largely surrounded by development including high-density housing. For breeding birds the principal feature is a marshy area at its east end containing shallow pools with small islands and a considerable growth of reed and sallows. Stoke Newington Reservoir in north London is again in an urban locality, but is mainly of interest in the winter.

By 1954 reservoirs already covered over 1,200ha of the London Area. Four have been constructed since then — Hilfield Park Reservoir in 1955, Queen Elizabeth II in 1962, Wraysbury in 1971 and Queen Mother Reservoir at Datchet, right on the western boundary of the Area, in 1976. With these later additions the total is now in excess of 1,800ha.

Any large area of water tends to come under pressure from a variety of sporting and leisure interests. This is particularly true of many of the gravel pits and, increasingly of the reservoirs, which are now used for angling, sailing or water-skiing. Homes (1976), in a survey of wintering duck counts in the London Area, urged that established wildfowl sites should receive complete protection from disturbance and that boating should be based on the new reservoirs where the birds have not had the opportunity to build up a tradition of nesting or wintering. Many birds, however, will tolerate some degree of disturbance. Gravel pits, even those in commercial use, still have a considerable breeding bird population including Reed Warblers, Sedge Warblers and Reed Buntings in the surrounding reeds and scrub. Sand Martins sometimes form colonies where the pits have steep sandy banks. Little Ringed Plovers nest on more or less bare gravel in disused or working pits and also on the floor of reservoirs under construction. In recent years Ringed Plovers have shown signs of expanding into these inland habitats, but not yet in sufficient numbers for the two species to come into direct competition. Management of gravel pits to make them particularly attractive to birds can increase both the numbers and the diversity of species. As demonstrated at the Sevenoaks G.P. reserve near Riverhead, just inside the London boundary north of Sevenoaks, a planting and maintenance programme designed to ensure a varied habitat, as well as the creation of small islands, not only increases the available nesting sites, but also provides valuable wintering grounds and resting spots for migrants. This particular reserve was developed as a joint WAGBI/ Wildfowl Trust project and its success has been fully described by Harrison (1974).

Sewage Farms continue to be an important habitat for birds, though the appearance of many in the London Area has undergone a considerable change. Instead of the old-style open lagoons, flooded and dried out on a rotational basis, there are now concrete encased filter-beds and the extent of the surrounding wetland is much reduced. As a result Beddington S.F. has lost its breeding Snipe, and a large works at Crossness near the Thames at Erith has taken over from other suburban farms such as Elmers End which has closed down. Those that remain, even if reduced in size, continue to offer suitable breeding areas for Reed and Sedge Warblers, Pied and Yellow Wagtails, Reed Buntings, Tree Sparrows and sometimes Corn Buntings. Apart from the presence of workmen, birds suffer little disturbance and an abundance of insect life and seeding weeds provide a ready food supply. The same factors can apply to modern purification plants, as at Maple Cross on the River Colne and Rye Meads on the Lea valley water meadows, both of which amply demonstrate that such places can retain their ornithological attraction.

OTHER HABITATS

Away from the main waterways, four other zones can broadly be identified. Though each merges into the other without clear-cut divisions, it is convenient to discuss separately Inner London, inner suburban London, outer suburban London and rural London.

Inner London

Inner London, defined earlier on page 15, includes the most densely built-up commercial heart of London. Reviews of the birds of this special area have been published by Cramp & Teagle (1952), Cramp & Tomlins (1966) and Cramp (1975).

Here man's alterations to the basic habitat are most marked and much of the area is covered by buildings, roads and railways. Open ground, particularly in and to the east of the City, is limited and is artificially preserved and cultivated. There are several important parks — oases in a largely concrete desert — but otherwise the habitats available to birds comprise small private gardens, occasional cemeteries, waste ground and public and private squares with trees, lawns and well tended shrubberies. Feral Pigeons and House Sparrows are the dominant species present, though Blackbirds may be found in unlikely spots, Pied Wagtails sometimes breed and Black Redstarts are something of a London speciality around industrial locations. Several species increased in central London during and after the second world war when bombed sites became overgrown with plants. These sites gradually disappeared, but large redevelopment areas have sometimes remained undisturbed for many months and have provided a similar, though temporary habitat.

In the western half of Inner London several large open spaces introduce more variety into the landscape and significantly increase the range of habitats for nesting birds. Regent's Park, for example, extends to 197ha. It is partly bordered by large gardens and to the north by Primrose Hill so that this whole parkland habitat covers some 243ha. Hyde Park/Kensington Gardens comprises 257ha, Holland Park 22ha, Green Park and St James's Park, together with the adjoining grounds of Buckingham Palace, cover an area of approximately 58ha right in the centre, while just south of the Thames there is the 81ha of Battersea Park. With the exception of Holland Park and Green Park, all these have lakes, some of which owe their origin to streams that used to flow across low-lying parts of London, such as the West-bourne that supplied the Serpentine in Hyde Park/Kensington Gardens and the Ty-burn that supplied the lake in St James's Park. Though the parks consist predominantly of short mown turf with scattered trees, the lakes generally have small wooded islands where full-winged ducks nest alongside collections of ornamental waterfowl. Shrubberies, too, are sometimes fenced off as sanctuaries for wildlife, allowing passerines like the Blackcap and sometimes the Willow Warbler to find suitable breeding sites. Amongst the wide variety of birds found in the parks are other such unlikely species for a city centre as Great Crested Grebe, Grey Heron, Jay and Magpie.

Recent accounts of the birds of some of these parks have been published by Brown (1972) for Holland Park, Sanderson (1968) for Hyde Park/Kensington Gardens and Wallace (1974) for Regent's Park.

Victoria Park in Hackney, of 88ha, also possesses a lake with a small island and is the only comparable area of open ground east of the centre. In the south-east corner of Inner London, however, a man-made habitat of an entirely different character has recently become prominent. This is the site of the former Surrey Commercial Docks on the south side of the Thames. After their closure in 1970 the Docks became a mixture of open water and overgrown waste ground attracting numerous migrant species as well as providing nesting territories for birds not previously associated with densely urban localities, of which perhaps the most notable have been Red-legged Partridge, Lapwing, Ringed Plover, Little Ringed Plover, Skylark, Yellow Wagtail and Reed Bunting (Grant 1971, George 1974). While conditions in the parks, squares and cemeteries are relatively stable, changes are already taking place in the Docks and they are unlikely to remain such an important area for birds for very long.

Before leaving Inner London, one further environmental factor to consider is the possible effect on birdlife of clean air legislation introduced in the Clean Air Act 1956. Records indicate that both Swifts and House Martins have penetrated further towards the centre of London in recent years (Gooders 1968, Cramp & Gooders 1967) and that the numbers of other insectivorous species, with the exception of the Spotted Flycatcher, have generally increased (Cramp 1975). A reduction in atmospheric pollution may have led to a greater quantity of insect food becoming available, though it is clearly difficult to distinguish this particular factor from others affecting bird populations. Mild winters since 1962-63 have probably improved the survival rate amongst resident species, while in Inner London birds may also be influenced by the micro-climate of a large city centre of high-density buildings producing mean summer and winter temperatures slightly higher than elsewhere.

Inner suburban London

Beyond the boundary of Inner London, but within about 16km of the centre, the habitat continues to be largely urban, with the greater part of it given over to housing or industry. It differs little in character from Inner London, though playing fields and allotments add variety to the scenery and gardens tend to be larger. These features may not be vitally important as nesting habitats, but they are all much used as feeding areas. It is the parks and commons, breaking up the relative uniformity of these inner suburbs, that provide the main attraction for breeding birds.

In north London, Hampstead Heath, rising to about 134m above sea level, stands on one of the patches of Bagshot Beds, resulting in a light acid soil and forming a large area of heath and woodland only about 2km from Regent's Park. Wanstead Park on the River Roding is also within this zone, where it is the most southerly, though now somewhat isolated, extension of Epping Forest. A more extensive stretch of open country, however, is found in the south-west where Richmond Park and Wimbledon Common together have a maximum width of about 5km. This area retains tracts of wild undisturbed country and combines heathland and mature woodland plantations with a more open parkland landscape of scattered trees and short grass. A reedbed and scrub habitat around Pen Ponds in Richmond Park provide further variety, along with the Beverley Brook which flows through on its way to the Thames. With Kew Gardens, Putney Heath, Putney Vale, Barnes Common and Wimbledon Park all nearby, there is a remarkably large expanse of countryside within these southern suburbs. Dulwich Woods further east add to the rural atmosphere. There were breeding records of such species as Grey Partridge, Woodcock and Cuckoo from Richmond Park during the Atlas survey and Wood Warbler from Wimbledon Common.

In south London, Mitcham Common, though not as important as the other localities, still holds a pair, sometimes two pairs, of Stonechats. Greenwich Park and Blackheath are situated in the south-east of this zone where the Woolwich and Blackheath Beds cover the high ground overlooking the Thames. Blackheath and the lower ground of the park itself consist mainly of short grass, but the southern part of the park contains an ornamental lake and a wilderness area with sanctuaries for birds. The park and its bird-life have been described by Grant (1967).

Outer suburban London

The next sub-division takes in the land between 16 and 24km from London. Though here labelled suburban for convenience, this is an over-simplification, as the habitat merges with the urban inner suburbs on one side and the rural zone on the other. It is mainly covered by low-density housing, but has a more wooded appearance and a greater extent of open ground in the form of playing fields, golf courses, woods and heaths. A large part of Epping Forest lies on the London Clay within this zone and although no completely natural woodland remains, it represents one of the most valuable stands of semi-natural woodland in the London Area. Oak is the natural climax vegetation of the Clay and here it is accompanied by hornbeam, and by beech on the higher ground where there is a capping of Pebble Gravel. Redstarts and Wood Warblers are two of the species attracted to this area, though the former are now much reduced in numbers.

South of the Thames the narrow belt of sands and gravel results in woodland and heathland habitats at Petts Wood and Hayes and Keston Commons, where birch, gorse and bracken predominate. Warblers, including the Wood Warbler, are amongst the breeding birds, Yellowhammers are close to their inner limits and the Redpoll has increased considerably in recent years. Selsdon Woods, the Addington Hills and, to the west of Croydon, Banstead Downs give further open country in this part of London. On the north bank of the Thames within a great bend of the River south-west from Richmond Park are the two remaining London Royal Parks, Hampton Court and Bushy Park. Both have lakes, but whereas Hampton Court is a large formal garden with lawns and flower-beds, Bushy Park has a more rural aspect. An account of these and the other Royal Parks of the London Area has been given by Simms (1974).

Rural London

Though some of London's ribbon development spreads into parts of the rural zone, principally along the main arterial roads, this outer section is still largely protected from excessive development by restrictions on building under the Green Belt regulations. Woodland and heathland are fairly widespread between numerous satellite towns and farmland. Major centres of population are Brentwood, Harlow, St Albans and Watford north of the Thames, Staines and Weybridge in the Thames valley on the west side and Redhill on the southern boundary.

With the exception of Thorndon Park, south of Brentwood, and the northern extension of Epping Forest, much of outer Essex is given over to agriculture. In the southern part the land is relatively open with large fields and few hedges providing only limited habitat for birds. Northaw Great Wood, which has been described by Sage (1966), and Broxbourne Woods, a collective title for Broxbourne, Cowheath, Highfield and Wormley Woods, are important woodlands in Herts. The latter contain extensive conifer plantations and attract Woodcock, Nightjars and Grasshopper Warblers. The remainder of rural Herts within the London Area lies mainly in the upper valley of the Colne where farming dominates the open country, while the wetland habitats of the lower Colne valley south of Rickmansworth cover most of west Middlesex within this rural zone.

Geology and habitats

Whereas the heaths and commons of suburban London are found on the old gravel terraces of the Thames, those in the Surrey rural zone occur on Bagshot Beds at Esher Common and Oxshott Heath, on London Clay at Ashtead, Epsom and Bookham, on sandy deposits at Headley and Walton Heaths and on Lower Greensand at Limpsfield. Loss of habitat caused by the recent construction of a six-lane highway across the middle of Esher Common has seriously affected what was an important heathland for the Nightjar. Oxshott Heath, too, has suffered from man's activities as the spread of conifer plantations changes its former heathland character. Bookham Common, owned by the National Trust, has been of special interest to the LNHS since 1941. It stands on heavy London Clay covered in places by sand and gravel probably washed down from the Plateau Gravel of the higher ground. Oak woodland occupies about 112ha of the Common, which is approximately three-quarters of the area studied by the Society, with scrub, including gorse and bracken, over much of the remainder. Annual reports of ecological studies appear in the *London Naturalist* and reviews of the changes in breeding bird populations of the oakwood have been published by Beven (1963, 1976). Headley and Walton Heaths have a similar type of vegetation to that found further east on the Lower Greensand, where a well drained acid soil produces a dry heathland flora including heather as well as gorse and bracken.

Rural Kent within the London Area is dominated by the Chalk North Downs which have a thin calcareous soil with a short springy turf where the land is regularly grazed, but which quickly reverts to hawthorn and bramble scrub if grazing ceases. A comprehensive account of the flora of the Chalk Downs is given by Lousley (1969). Where the Chalk is capped by a deposit of Clay-with-flints the climax vegetation is oak and beech woodland, one of the habitats where the Hawfinch may be found. Another feature of the Chalk is the lack of surface water and the presence of dry valleys, which may be seen along the north-facing dip slope of the Downs.

It is hoped that this very broad outline of the character of the London Area will be of some help in interpreting the patterns of bird distribution shown in the species accounts that follow. Clearly both geology and physiography have a considerable effect on the distribution of breeding bird species, but in the London Area, perhaps increasingly so in recent years, man plays the decisive role. Often in the past developments were carried out with little regard for the existing flora or fauna. With the present greater public awareness of nature and more appreciation of the need for conservation, perhaps future changes will be planned with wider considerations in mind and, instead of reducing the diversity of wildlife, the effect may be the reverse.

Fig. 2. Map of the London Area, showing 10-km Ordnance Survey grid lines in full and tetrad lines on the west and south margins. Shading indicates extent of the built-up area and broken line marks the rectangle of Inner London. Old county boundaries are retained for continuity of recording. These boundaries are represented by the River Thames, providing a division between north and south, and by the dotted lines.

Numbers within Inner London indicate the position of the following localities:

1	St Paul's Cathedral	6	Buckingham Palace Gardens
2	Regent's Park and Primrose Hill	7	St James's and Green Parks
3	Holland Park	8	Battersea Park
4	Kensington Gardens	9	Surrey Commercial Docks
5	Hyde Park	10	Victoria Park

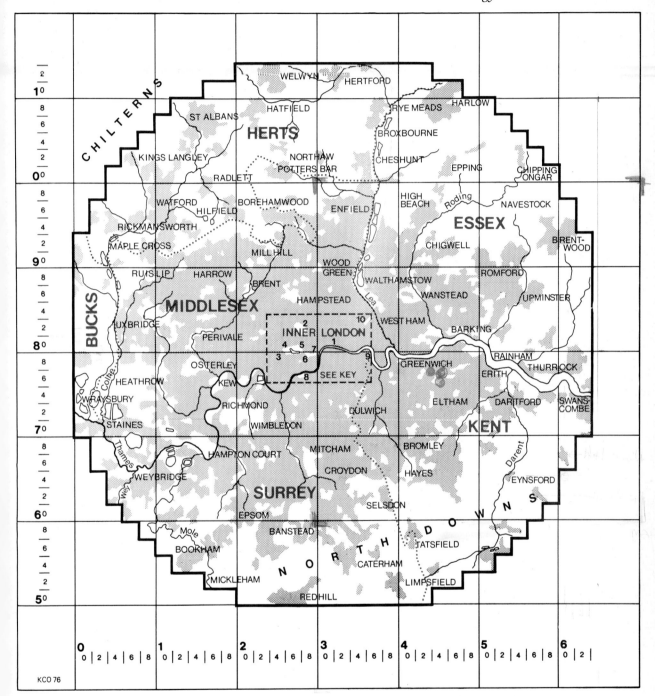

GREAT CRESTED GREBE

Podiceps cristatus

Once very scarce in the London Area, the Great Crested Grebe is now relatively abundant and breeds on most waters that have sufficient vegetation for anchoring its floating nest. It has recently spread to Inner London and will even nest occasionally on concrete-sided reservoirs.

Since the last century, when it was persecuted for its plumage, the Great Crested Grebe has increased markedly. From breeding records at only three localities in 1900, it had spread to 22 sites by 1931. Later counts have generally concentrated on numbers of adults present including non-breeding birds. On this basis, numbers during 1946-55 varied from 292 in 1947, after a very severe winter, to 635 in 1953 and 445 in 1955 (Melluish 1957). Actual breeding numbers were not known, but average figures suggested that they were about 40% of the population. By 1965 the total of birds counted was down to about 420, against the trend of the national sample census which showed an increase. Since then there has been no evidence of any major change. As a rough indication, assuming the breeding proportion is still 40%, the total of about 90 pairs present in 1972 would imply that the summer population that year was in the range of 400-500 birds, which compares closely with earlier counts.

As expected, the distribution mainly follows the lines of the major river valleys in which most reservoirs and gravel pits are situated. The greatest concentration is in the western part of the Area around Weybridge, Chertsey, Staines and northwards up the Colne valley into Herts. Records from the Darent valley show a clear association with gravel workings which now serve as an important alternative habitat to natural lakes and reed ponds. In the Lea valley the species breeds at Walthamstow Reservoirs which are shallow and have a number of small islands, but is absent from the deeper reservoirs.

In 1971 birds held territory and attempted nest-building in Hyde Park/Kensington Gardens. A pair bred there and in Regent's Park in 1972, in both cases rearing two young and becoming the first records of successful nesting for Inner London. This success was repeated in 1973 and 1974 and numbers increased to two pairs in both parks in 1975 and 1976. Although boating is allowed on the lakes, certain areas have been chained off to provide refuges where the birds can remain undisturbed.

Clearly the future of this species as a breeding bird in London depends to a considerable extent on preservation of old gravel pits and the degree to which they can be kept free of excessive pollution and disturbance from competing amenity interests such as sailing and water-skiing.

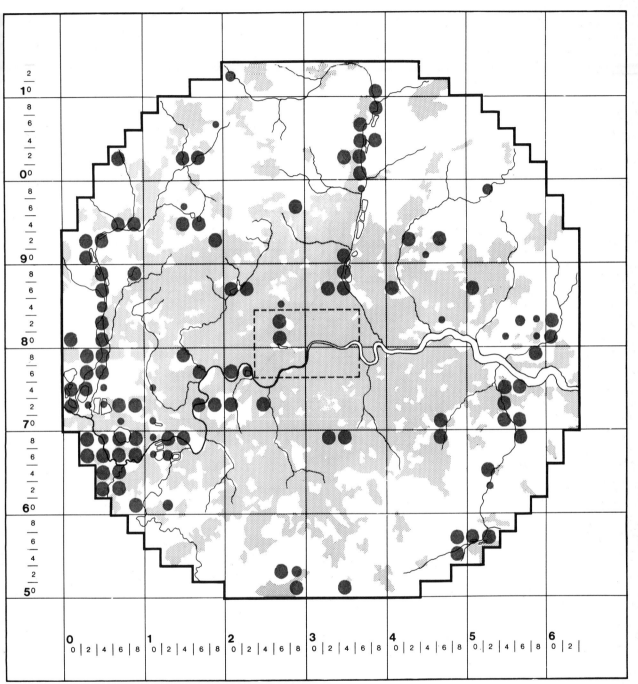

LITTLE GREBE

Tachybaptus ruficollis

This species will occupy a wider variety of habitats than the Great Crested Grebe and breeds regularly, not only on lakes and gravel pits, but also on undisturbed stretches of rivers such as the Chess, Mole and upper reaches of the Lea.

Sound evidence of fluctuations in numbers over the years has been sparse, though some reports have referred to decreases or even the abandonment of some waters like gravel pits, as habitat changes made them no longer attractive breeding localities. Drainage and changes in land use have also rendered sites unsuitable, as with the Thamesmead new town development near Erith. Numbers at Rye Meads appear to have declined; there was a report of 13 pairs there in 1961, but only four pairs were recorded ten years later. Elsewhere the records are insufficient to detect any significant increases or decreases except for Inner London. This was colonised at the end of the last century. Little Grebes nested occasionally in St James's Park and Regent's Park between 1900 and 1945 and continued to do so for a few more years in the grounds of Buckingham Palace until that, too, was deserted soon after 1950 (Cramp & Tomlins 1966). Whether these instances are indicative of the pattern over the London Area as a whole is unknown. Parslow found similar difficulty in interpreting the national situation and concluded that the species increased in the first half of the present century during the main period of climatic amelioration, but that, on rather sketchy evidence, the present trend may be downward.

Atlas records show breeding in 93 tetrads, probable breeding in 14 more and birds present in the breeding season in a further 32, a total of 139 compared with 116 for its larger relative, the Great Crested Grebe. This reflects the Little Grebe's willingness to accept smaller stretches of water and its ability to exploit sites such as the rubbish dump at Aldenham where two pairs bred in 1961 amongst boxes and pots in shallow water. As the map shows, the main distribution is again along the river valleys and the species is most widespread in the west of the Area in the region of Chertsey, Weybridge and Stoke D'Abernon and along the Colne and Lea valleys north of the Thames.

It is subject to the same pressures from human activity as the previous species and requires the maintenance of reeds or undergrowth round the margins of waters to provide it with secluded nesting sites.

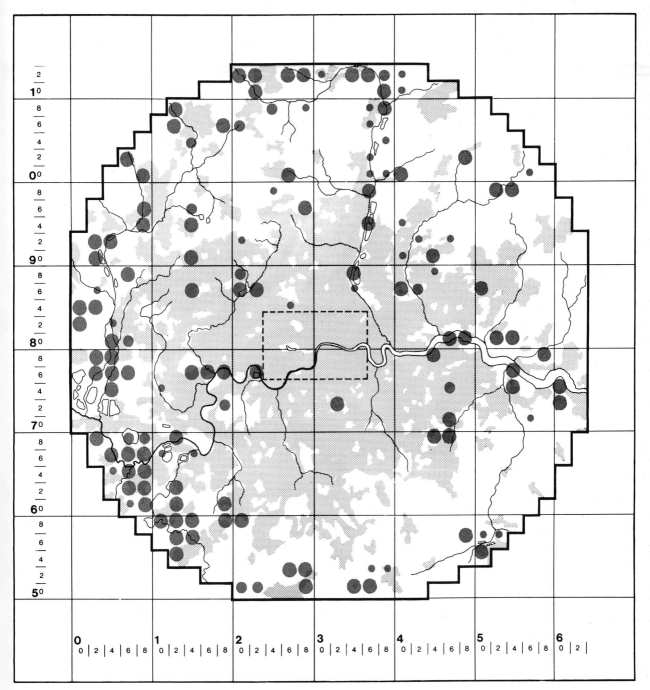

GREY HERON

Ardea cinerea

During the Atlas survey the Grey Heron nested at five localities in the London Area. Three heronries have become extinct since 1954, but two new ones were established in 1967 and 1968. The numbers of occupied nests at each known heronry for the twenty years to 1974 are given in Table 2.

In Britain the Heron population falls after severe winters and returns within a few years to its former level (Lack 1954). Numbers nesting in the London Area followed this pattern in the twenty years up to 1954, but were unaffected by the hard winter of 1955-56. Following that of 1961-62 and the much more severe one of 1962-63, however, there was a sharp decline to the lowest levels known for the Area. At Kempton Park, previously the largest London heronry, numbers have remained low, but at the Waltham-stow group, where the Herons nest on islands in the reservoirs, they had returned to their former level by 1967. Apart from a setback in 1971 related to drainage of one of the reservoirs, numbers there have continued to increase, so that a record population was present in 1974. The reasons for this are not clear, but may include a transfer of birds from Kempton Park (Oliver 1975) and a better food supply. Whatever the reasons, expansion at Walthamstow has been faster than that of the national population (Stafford 1971, Reynolds 1974), yet taking the London Area as a whole numbers have remained well below those attained before 1962.

Food supply was thought to be one of the factors that enabled this species to establish a new heronry at Regent's Park in Inner London in 1968. Birds from this site spend part of their time at the zoo nearby taking food provided for the captive collection and some may fly to the disused Surrey Docks where feeding Herons have also been recorded.

Table 2.   Numbers of occupied Herons' nests in the London Area, 1955-74
(Oliver 1975, with later revisions for Chevening)

	55	56	57	58	59	60	61	62	63	64	65	66	67	68	69	70	71	72	73	74
Walthamstow	62	65	80	62	69	62	55	48	34	34	41	39	63	84	86	82	57	83	105	113
Wanstead	1	2	1	–	–	–	–	–	–	–	–	–	–	–	–	–	–	–	–	–
Parndon	11	9	6	4	5	5	4	4	–	–	–	–	–	–	–	–	–	–	–	–
Richmond	6	6	8	7	7	7	–	–	–	–	–	–	–	–	–	–	–	–	–	–
Kempton	88	83	88	86	91	91	95	83	49	47	12	44	?	24	18	7	3	10	6	20
Gatton	9	10	12	14	16	17	18	18	12	6	6	6	4	3	5	4	5	5	7	7
Chevening	–	–	–	–	–	–	–	–	–	–	–	–	1	4	5	5	4	8	10	6
Regent's Park	–	–	–	–	–	–	–	–	–	–	–	–	–	2	2	10	2	3	5	3
Miscellaneous	–	1	–	–	–	1	1	–	–	–	–	–	–	–	–	–	–	–	–	–
Total	177	176	195	173	188	183	173	153	95	87	59	89	68+	117	116	108	71	109	133	149

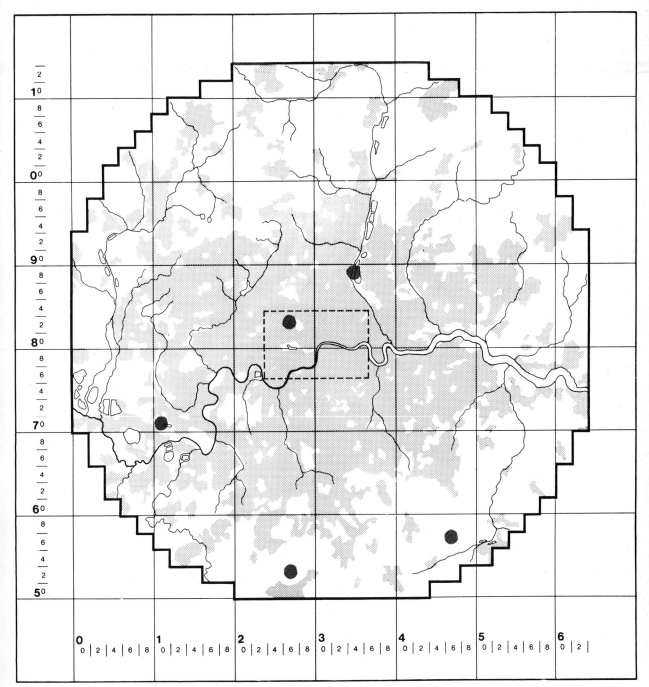

MALLARD
Anas platyrhynchos

As the commonest duck in the London Area, the Mallard breeds wherever there is any water and a safe nesting site, even in densely built-up areas. It is scarce or absent on the North Downs and on some agricultural land of the outer zone lacking suitable permanent lakes or ponds.

In favourable habitats breeding density can be high and examples of peak numbers reported during the Atlas survey are shown in Table 3.

The rapidity of colonisation in a suitable environment is exemplified by Sevenoaks G.P. reserve, where careful management of food supply and habitat has resulted in the number of pairs rising from ten in 1962 to 85 in 1973 (Harrison 1974). Two unusual breeding reports from dates well outside the Atlas definition of the breeding season were received from St James's Park, where in 1969 there was a duck with six young on 26 January and, at the other end of the year, a nest with 14 eggs on 24 November.

While there have been winter counts of wildfowl in the London Area over a long period, comparable details of breeding are not available. There is no reason to suppose, however, that there has been any overall material change in Mallard numbers, though when conditions themselves have altered there may be shifts in local populations. Breeding records during the Atlas survey came from 442 tetrads, probable breeding was reported from another 28 and birds were present in 100 more, representing two-thirds of the total area. The most important factors controlling numbers are probably food supply and climate. Hard weather brings more Mallard to the London Area in winter, but may adversely affect the breeding stock, while building developments, drainage and closure of the old-fashioned, open type of sewage farm all represent a loss of potential feeding areas, though Mallard are quick to exploit new sources and new habitats.

Table 3. Numbers of breeding pairs of Mallard at selected localities in the London Area, 1968-72

1968	Regent's Park	up to	44	pairs
1969	Hampton Court	about	50	pairs
1970	Sevenoaks G.P. reserve		75	pairs
1971	Hyde Park/Kensington Gardens	about	30	pairs
1972	Stocker's Lake/Springwell gravel pit		28	pairs

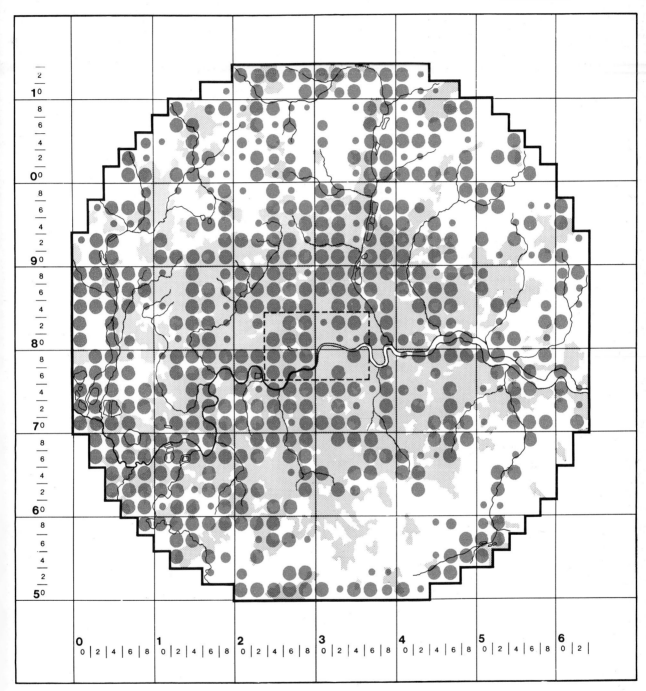

TEAL

Anas crecca

Breeding was proved during the 1968-72 Atlas survey in only two localities, both in the south-west, and this species remains scarce in the London Area in the breeding season.

There has been little change since Teal were first proved to have bred in 1930 when a nest was discovered near Cobham. From 1931 until about 1941 birds nested in the Ruislip to Harefield district, with four pairs at Ruislip in 1934. A few reports of pairs present in summer suggest that breeding may occasionally occur undetected, but the only other known nesting attempts before the present survey were at Epsom S.F. in 1951 and at Fishers Green in the Lea valley in 1959 and 1965, though in the latter year the deserted nest and eggs were not discovered until after the breeding season. With such an irregular history no trends can be established and the records depend largely on the perseverance of individual observers. On a national level Parslow found little evidence of change throughout Britain, though a slight decrease was suspected.

As well as the two breeding records during the Atlas survey, birds probably bred at three other sites and were present in the breeding season at 13 more. In this latter category the birds may have been late migrants or non-breeders making a prolonged stay in suitable habitats. Definite breeding for the Atlas was established when a female with young was found at Black Pond, Esher, in 1971. In the same locality the following year two nests were located which were thought to have belonged to two females mated to one male, but it was not known whether any young were produced. At the other breeding site a nest with five eggs was reported in 1971. Of the three records of probable breeding, one came from Hadley Wood Lake, where in 1969 a female in dense vegetation may have had young, and the other two were from sites in Bucks and Surrey. The scattering of other records was centred on the valleys of the Colne, Lea and Darent and at Rainham Marsh where birds were found in the breeding season in three of the five Atlas years.

While Teal, as a breeding species, are normally associated with moorland or woods bordering small lakes, they will also nest in rough grassland in low-lying country. Sufficient suitable habitat of this kind still exists in parts of the London Area to support more breeding birds, but the factors preventing its exploitation have not been identified.

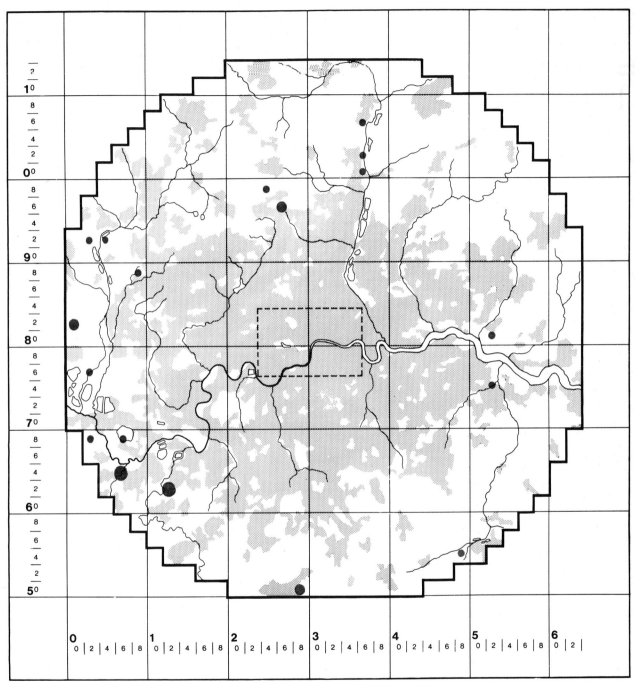

GARGANEY

Anas querquedula

Although there are records from all months from March to September, the Garganey remains a scarce passage migrant and summer visitor to the London Area. Very few breeding pairs have ever been recorded and none at all throughout the Atlas survey.

The species was not recorded in the Area until 1927 and the first evidence of breeding was from Elstree Reservoir in 1931. Since then there have been only three further reports of nesting. In 1952 a duck was seen on the River Wey at Weybridge with two small young incapable of flight; in 1959 there was a duck with seven ducklings at Broxbourne gravel pits; and the most recent report (Harrison 1974) was of breeding, though unsuccessfully, at Sevenoaks G.P. reserve in 1974. A regular series of observations, particularly from the Colne and Lea valleys and Rainham Marsh, suggest that nesting may occur rather more frequently than is reported.

In Britain the Garganey is at the western edge of its breeding range and, although varying from year to year, the present breeding population throughout the country is probably not more than 100 pairs (Parslow). There was a gradual increase until about 1952 and then, following a contraction of range during the next few years, a temporary revival in 1959. This revival was reflected in the London Area when, in that year, there were far more spring records than usual.

During the Atlas survey probable breeding was reported from Stanwellmoor where a bird was thought to be holding territory. The only remaining records were of birds present in the breeding season, but these may have referred to migrants.

Reports of successful nesting depend largely on the chances of finding downy young rather than occupied nests. Ducks' nests are very vulnerable to predation, particularly by Carrion Crows which are now extremely abundant, and therefore breeding by pairs that lost all their eggs or young would probably go undetected. On the other hand, searching for nests in itself increases the likelihood of predation, so it is important that disturbance is kept to the minimum whenever breeding is suspected and reliance placed on seeing the duck with young for providing evidence of success.

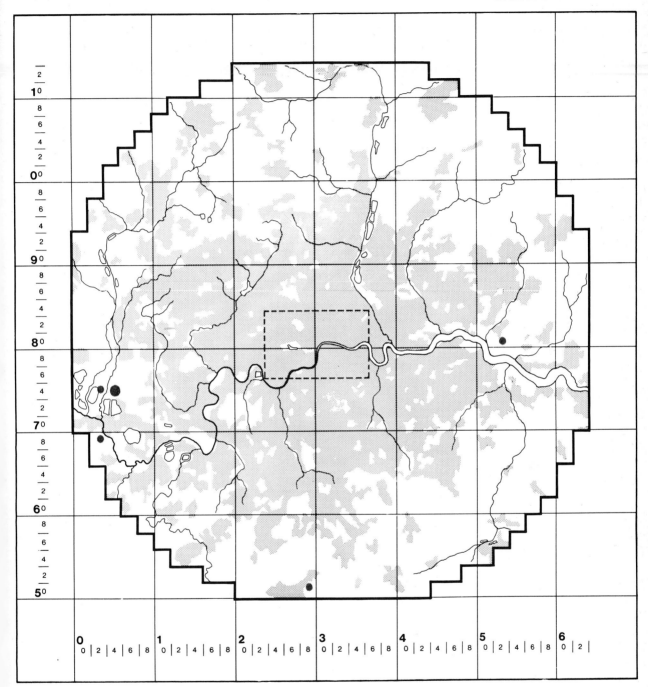

THAMES POLYTECHNIC LIBRARY

GADWALL

Anas strepera

The Gadwall continues to be a very scarce breeding species in the London Area and until recently was confined to Barn Elms where, from 1936, up to three pairs used to breed annually following the escape of full-winged birds from the collection in St James's Park. Latterly it has bred irregularly at five other localities.

In 1932 fifteen young were reared in St James's Park and remained unpinioned; then in the autumn the lake was drained, these birds dispersed and there were subsequent records from Kensington Gardens, Godstone and Staines. Breeding continued in St James's Park in the following years and there is little doubt that nesting pairs at Barn Elms and occasionally at Beddington originated from the increasing numbers of free-flying birds in the London Area. Since 1958, although birds have continued to summer in most years at Barn Elms, the only records of breeding there have been of one pair in the two years 1963 and 1969. From 1964 to 1972 a total of 131 hand-reared birds was released at Sevenoaks G.P. reserve (Harrison 1974). Subsequent breeding at Godstone, Ruxley and at the Sevenoaks reserve itself was almost certainly due to feral birds from that source. Reports of birds nesting at Cheshunt and at Walthamstow Reservoirs in the Lea valley must also be suspected of originating from there or the Inner London parks.

Any discussion of the national status, too, is confused by introductions, but there has been a northward extension of range in Scandinavia and a considerable increase in Iceland this century, both thought to be associated with climatic changes (Parslow). With the volume of local introductions, however, it is unrealistic to surmise that this natural spread of the European population has played any part in the expansion of the species in the London Area.

Reports of breeding during the Atlas survey were confined to the years 1969-72; from Barn Elms, Cheshunt and Godstone in 1969 only, from Walthamstow Reservoirs in 1971 and 1972 and from Ruxley and the Sevenoaks area in three out of the four years.

So far as is known the Gadwall's breeding habitat requirements differ little, if at all, from those of Mallard, but as its main centre of distribution is more easterly and continental, future developments will probably depend on further colonisation by feral birds, though factors elsewhere in the species' range may gradually assume greater importance, particularly if the present population trend continues.

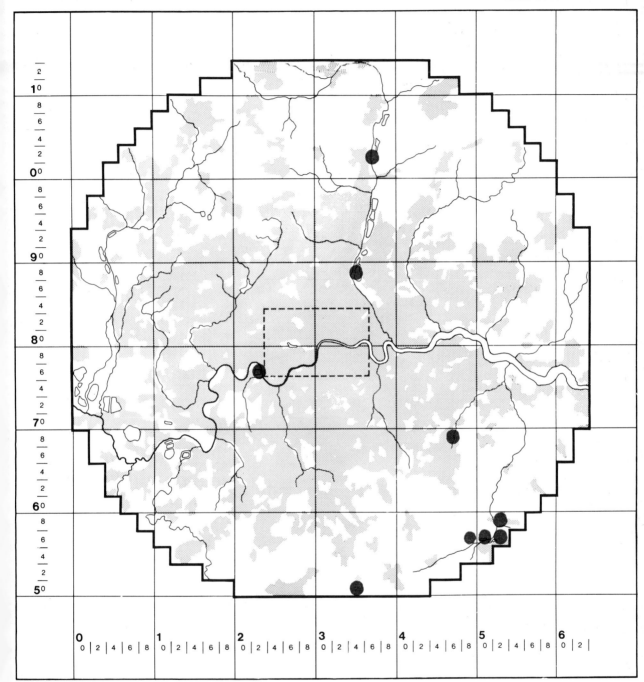

SHOVELER

Anas clypeata

As with the last three species, this is another duck that breeds irregularly in the London Area, with, at most, only a few pairs nesting annually.

There has been little change in the situation since the 1930s when definite breeding was first established, coinciding with reports of increasing numbers of migrants and winter visitors in the Area. During that decade young were seen at Beddington, Langley and at Queen Mary and Staines Reservoirs. In addition, birds were present throughout the breeding season of most years at Brooklands S.F. Later, breeding was proved or suspected in the Staines/Perry Oaks district almost annually from 1948 to 1962 with a maximum of three pairs in any one year. In the Lea valley birds summered at Fishers Green in several years in the 1950s and prior to the Atlas survey there were records of nesting at Rye Meads from 1959 to 1961 and in 1967 and also in the latter year at Walthamstow Reservoirs. The only other locality where breeding may have occurred is around Rainham and young were seen late in the season at Berwick Pond nearby in 1951.

A widespread expansion took place in other parts of the country and on the continent earlier in the century, which suggests that the absence of London breeding records before 1930 was largely a reflection of limited observations. Examining the present status of the British breeding population, Parslow found one or two cases of new colonisation in some counties, offset by decreases elsewhere due to changes in habitat, mainly drainage, but the overall trend was uncertain. As the Shoveler normally has a more southerly distribution, a recent considerable increase in wintering numbers in the London Area, possibly as a result of climatic changes, may be relevant in that greater numbers in winter could lead to more breeding occurrences, provided suitable habitat is available.

During the present survey breeding records came from three localities in the lower part of the Colne valley and from Walthamstow Reservoirs and Rye Meads in the Lea valley.

The Shoveler's main breeding habitat is on lowland marshes or in water meadows, both much reduced by drainage. It has been further affected by modernisation of sewage farms which were favoured in earlier years. Creation of nature reserves in the river valleys, however, and also freedom from disturbance on reservoir banks where it has nested on grass-covered causeways, could provide opportunities for further breeding.

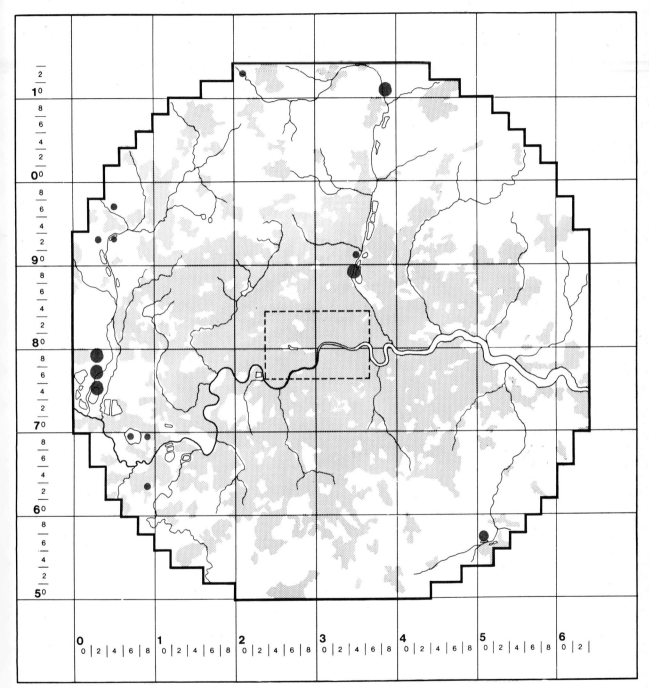

MANDARIN DUCK

Aix galericulata

Having been imported into this country earlier this century, the Mandarin now breeds not uncommonly in the river valleys in the south-west of the London Area. There are also isolated breeding records from one or two other localities.

Its chief centre of distribution is in Surrey and east Berkshire just outside the Area, where the Mandarin originally became established in wooded country around Virginia Water and Windsor Great Park. This colony was thought to have originated with escapes from a collection at Cobham and free-flying birds were first noted about 1929. Very few, however, were seen in the London Area and there were no breeding records until 1946 when a nest was found, though the eggs were taken. Since then the Mandarin has spread rapidly, even though within a relatively confined district.

Parslow reported little recent change in the British population as a whole, based on an earlier report by Atkinson-Willes (1963) who considered that a shortage of suitable habitat was a limiting factor. At the present time, records in the London Area certainly suggest that the Mandarin may be increasing and possibly extending its range slightly. Outside the breeding season flocks of over 40 have been seen.

Atlas records show that the main breeding localities within the Area are in the valleys of the rivers Bourne, Mole and Wey in Surrey extending from Thorpe and Esher to the southern boundary. In 1969 as many as 55-60 pairs were found during a thorough search along the River Mole between Mickleham and Esher. The breeding record at Wraysbury, just north of the Thames, forms part of this concentration in the south-west, but during the five-year survey there were only three reports from elsewhere, Gatton Park, Osterley Park and two broods at Wrotham Park. In all, the breeding records came from 18 tetrads, nesting probably occurred in six more and birds were present in the breeding season in a further nine.

The preferred habitat appears to be lakes and rivers bordered by woodland containing trees with holes suitable for nesting. More open country will also be occupied provided there are sufficient old trees, but the species of tree may have some importance as acorns are a feature of the Mandarin's diet.

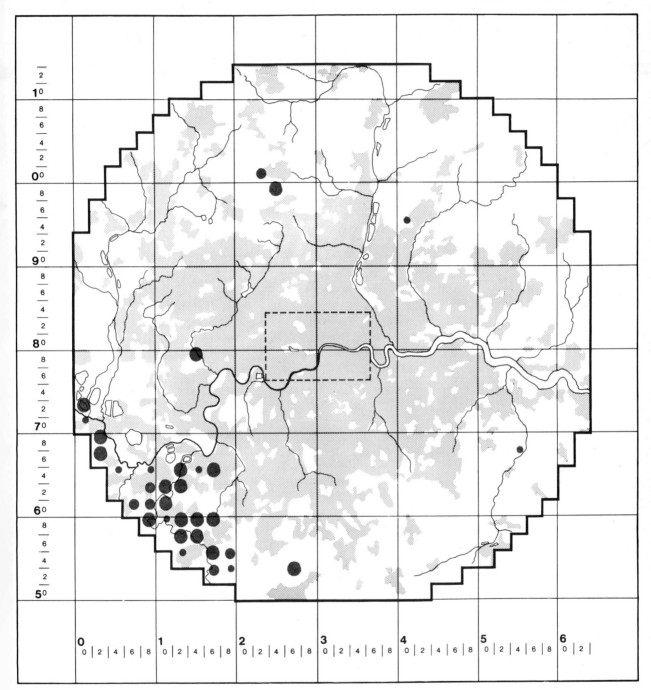

THAMES POLYTECHNIC LIBRARY

47

TUFTED DUCK

Aythya fuligula

This is a widely distributed species throughout the London Area, breeding wherever suitable conditions exist, including most parks in Inner London and the built-up suburbs. Homes described it as breeding in limited numbers in several places, probably more extensively in the twenty years up to 1954 than earlier. Since then numbers have increased further.

Tufted Ducks were first introduced into St James's Park in the middle of the last century and full-winged birds were breeding freely in 1913, before which year little is known of their status. The degree to which colonisation of the Area depended initially on this source cannot be estimated, but the enormous increase in the wintering population could well have played a more important part at a later stage. Some indication of the growth in numbers can be gained by comparing counts from sites before 1939 with more recent reports. In the 1930s Walthamstow Reservoirs were considered the main breeding locality outside Inner London with up to 12 pairs nesting. There were also 12 pairs at Gatton Park in 1935. St James's Park has continued to be a stronghold of the species with 100 ducklings in 1929 and a report of 60 nests in 1967.

During 1968-72 breeding records came from 86 tetrads, birds probably bred in another 22 and were present in the breeding season in a further 76. Distribution is closely linked with the main river valleys of the Thames, Colne and Lea and with the presence of gravel pits, but there is also a wide scatter on park lakes and reservoirs. Examples of high breeding populations reported during those five years included 35 broods comprising 183 young at Rye Meads in 1968, 25 pairs at Walthamstow Reservoirs in 1969 and 34 pairs at Broxbourne gravel pits in 1971. Though St James's Park held 50 pairs in 1969, breeding success was low and about 40% of mostly well grown young in early August were lost within three weeks.

Parslow referred to a continued marked increase in the population and suggested that more than 500 pairs now breed in England south of a line from the Mersey to the Humber. This probably understates the present position, since over 180 pairs were actually counted in the London Area in 1970 and if the many sites not visited in that year are included, the actual breeding numbers in London alone are probably of the order of 300 pairs.

Many ducklings are taken by predators, but sufficient evidently survive to sustain an increasing population. Some pairs succeed in producing young even in such apparently unfavourable habitats as Clapham Common and it is probable that the population will continue to increase.

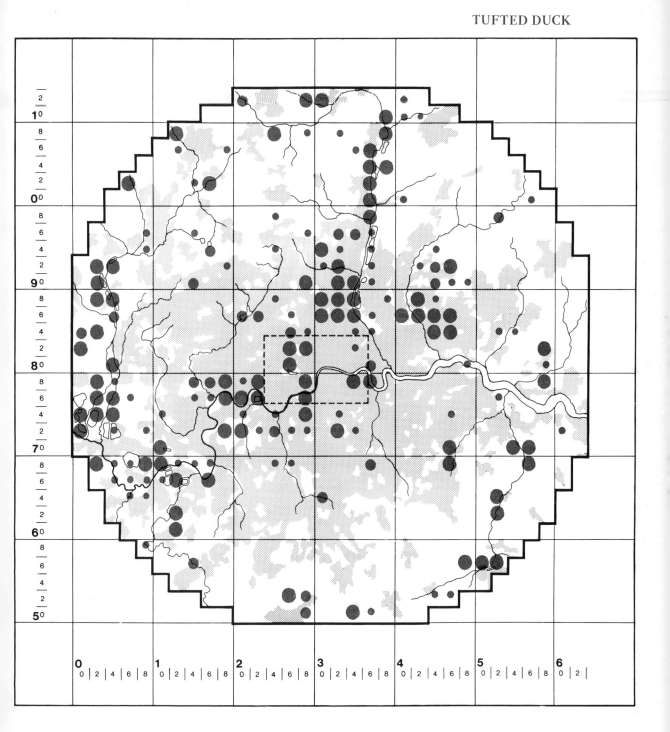

POCHARD

Aythya ferina

Records of Pochard are fewer than those of Tufted Duck, though it breeds regularly in various parks in the inner built-up zone and with less regularity in other scattered sites.

The first known breeding record in the London Area was in 1927 at Barn Elms, but up to 1940 nesting had been recorded in only six localities, in all of them inter-mittently except in St James's Park where pinioned and unpinioned birds mixed. A subsequent increase in numbers was most marked from about 1954. Before the Atlas survey the biggest recorded concentration of breeding birds was of ten pairs in Regent's Park in 1967, whereas totals in the 1930s probably never reached even that figure for the whole of the Area. A noticeable increase in the British population reported by Alexander & Lack (1944) was considered by Parslow to be still continuing. Thus the increase in the London Area may not have been entirely due to feral birds originating in St James's Park, though in all probability these were wholly or partly responsible for the colonis-ation of other London parks. Some immigration from other parts of the country also probably occurred, particularly as the only county with any sizeable population is the neighbouring one of Kent.

Atlas records of breeding came from 18 tetrads, probable breeding from five and reports of birds present in the breeding season from an additional 32. Most records were from the valleys of the Colne and Lea and from several parks in Inner and suburban London, such as Finsbury, Regent's, Hyde Park/Kensington Gardens, St James's, Battersea, Richmond and Kew Gardens. The only breeding reports outside these three main localities were at Thorpe and in the Darent valley. Numbers of pairs in the parks were generally in single figures, though 15 pairs were counted in St James's Park in 1969. One pair present in Richmond Park in 1969 provided the first breeding record there since 1932.

Gravel pits seem to be generally unsuitable for Pochard as breeding sites (Parslow). Certainly few pairs have been recorded using them for nesting in the London Area, though in 1973 as many as six pairs were reported from Tilehouse G.P. in the Colne valley. Compared with the Tufted Duck, Pochard feed more on vegetable than animal matter and tend to dive less deeply (Witherby *et al.* 1940). If the right food were avail-able, however, at an acceptable depth it might become more numerous as a breeding species, but there would appear to be scope for more research on whether gravel pits are in fact less suitable and, if so, why.

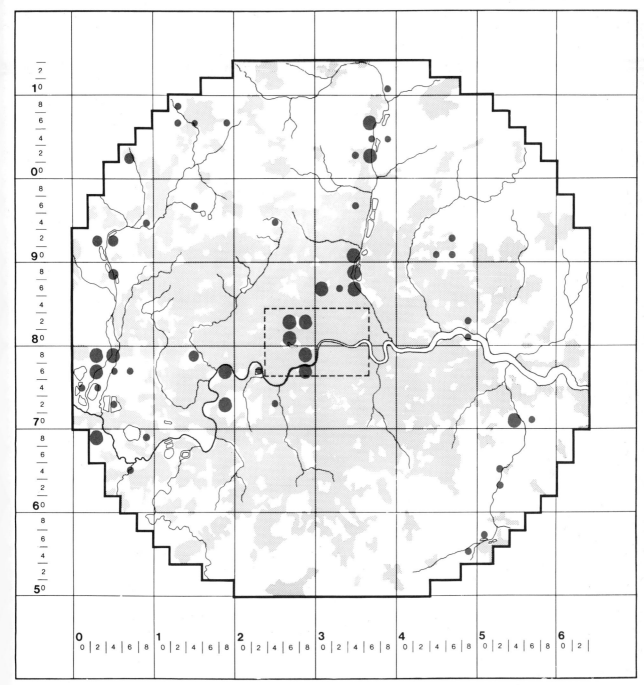

SHELDUCK

Tadorna tadorna

Breeding was proved for the first time in the London Area in 1954 on the lower Thames marshes and has been more or less annual since 1959. No more than one pair was proved to breed in each year up to 1967, except for a possible two in 1959 and 1963, but observations of birds throughout the breeding season suggest that, over the years, there may have been several other undetected attempts. All records during these years were from the Thames marshes at Aveley and Rainham on the north side and Stone and Swanscombe on the south.

Breeding records for the Atlas years 1969-72 are shown in Table 4, together with those for 1973 and 1974. In addition, there was a pair present at Rainham in June and July 1968 not included in the Table as breeding was not proved.

Inland nesting of apparently wild birds was reported for the first time in the Area in 1973, though the one pair which was at Sevenoaks G.P. reserve, was unsuccessful. In the following year, however, two pairs at Queen Mary Reservoir produced a total of nine young. This was well inland on the west side of London, but even the two pairs which almost certainly attempted to nest on Erith Marsh in 1974 were further upstream than previous breeding birds. These records, along with a report of a pair rearing one young in 1973 near Bough Beech Reservoir not far beyond the southern boundary of the London Area (Hindle 1975), fit in well with the national trend mentioned by Parslow for this species increasingly to nest inland.

Shelduck on the Thames-side marshes will frequently nest in trees, hay or straw stacks, or farm buildings, sometimes quite a long way from their territories which are established at the beginning of the breeding season on fresh water fleets and which appear to serve mainly as feeding areas (Hori 1964). This type of habitat is very limited in the London Area and any great increase in breeding Shelduck is probably unlikely, but recent records show that the Area offers some scope for expansion at reservoirs and gravel pits.

Table 4. Numbers of breeding pairs of Shelduck recorded in the London Area, 1969-74
(Brackets indicate unsuccessful pairs or outcome unknown)

	69	70	71	72	73	74
Rainham Marsh	1	2	1	3	3	1
Swanscombe Marsh	—	—	—	1	1	—
Sevenoaks G.P. reserve	—	—	—	—	(1)	(1)
Erith Marsh	—	—	—	—	—	(2)
Queen Mary Reservoir	—	—	—	—	—	2

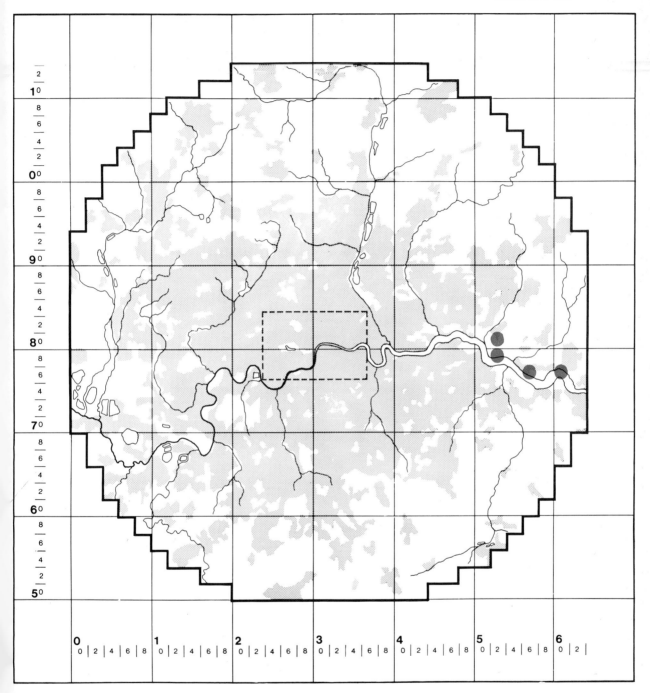

GREYLAG GOOSE

Anser anser

Following introductions in Kent, the Greylag Goose now breeds in a feral state at several localities around Sevenoaks and the recent spread to the Colne valley may possibly originate from the same or a similar source.

Greylag Geese were first introduced into the Sevenoaks G.P. reserve in 1961 and a total of 38 birds was released between then and 1966. Successful breeding has occurred annually since 1964 and the number of broods of mature young ranged from one to six in the years up to 1972. In 1973 there were as many as ten broods with a total of 44 young and by the autumn the feral flock had reached a maximum of 108 birds (Harrison 1974). Breeding reports also came from gravel pits in the Colne valley and in 1973 three broods of goslings were seen at different sites. This followed an increase in the number of reports of birds in that area during the previous year.

Introductions have been made in other places in England and Scotland and are responsible for the appearance of the species as a breeding bird in several new localities. Another important factor, however, is that on the continent and in Scotland the long-term decline of the wild breeding population is believed to have been halted by better protection (Parslow). The future seems to depend entirely on the extent to which the geese are allowed freedom from shooting should they ever become more numerous and widespread. Given favourable treatment they are likely to continue increasing around the London Area and to colonise new habitats where suitable stretches of water exist, particularly if these contain islands to provide safe nesting sites. In earlier times the species used to breed much more commonly in fenland and low-lying marshy areas than it does today and the natural habitat is not therefore necessarily akin to the moorlands of northern Scotland and the Outer Hebrides to which most of the relic British wild population is now confined.

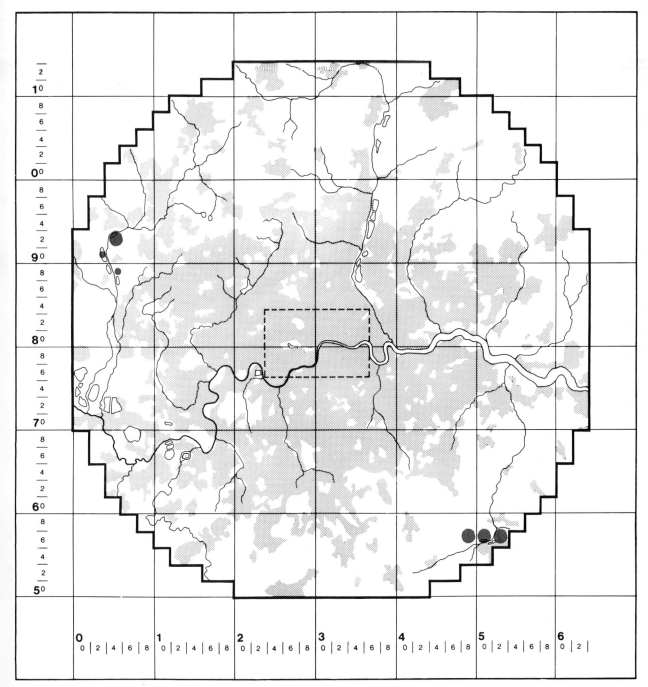

CANADA GOOSE

Branta canadensis

Originally introduced into Britain, this species now breeds in parks, both in Inner London and the suburbs, at gravel pits and lakes mostly in the valleys of the Thames, Colne and Darent and also at a series of lakes along the southern edge of the London Area. At the present time the total population is probably about 75 pairs.

The early history of this species in the London Area is little known and after breeding reports from Godstone in 1905 and Walthamstow Reservoirs in 1907-08, there is nothing on record until 1929 or 1930 when Canada Geese were first found breeding at Gatton Park. A large flock built up there and was probably responsible for birds colonising Cobham, Oxted and Reigate Priory and recolonising Godstone. The Gatton Park population, which built up to 200 birds by 1936, was reduced by control measures and the remaining birds left during the second world war because of military disturbance (Parr 1972). There were further breeding records from Walthamstow in 1936 and 1940 and from Ilford in 1953. These sketchy details are the only evidence of breeding before 1955. Since then introductions have undoubtedly hastened the spread of the Canada Goose. Birds were released in Hyde Park/Kensington Gardens in 1955 and by 1965 they were established in several localities including four Inner London parks. Nesting pairs at any one locality were few, but about ten bred in Regent's Park in 1967.

During the Atlas survey breeding records came from 50 tetrads and probable breeding from a further six. Nesting was reported from Inner London in Hyde Park/Kensington Gardens, Regent's Park, St James's and Battersea Parks and suburban localities included Wanstead, Pymmes, Gunnersbury, Bushy and Richmond Parks, Wandsworth Common and Kew. Other main areas were in the Colne and Darent valleys and around Thorpe and Weybridge. Apart from Pymmes Park, there were few reports from the Lea valley, but in the south birds continued to nest at lakes from Gatton Park to Oxted.

With the present fairly wide range of breeding localities and the existence of large autumn flocks, Canada Geese may become more common as a breeding species. Where conditions are to their liking, they will nest in large numbers, as indicated by the report of 71 adults with 31 goslings at Wraysbury G.P. in 1973.

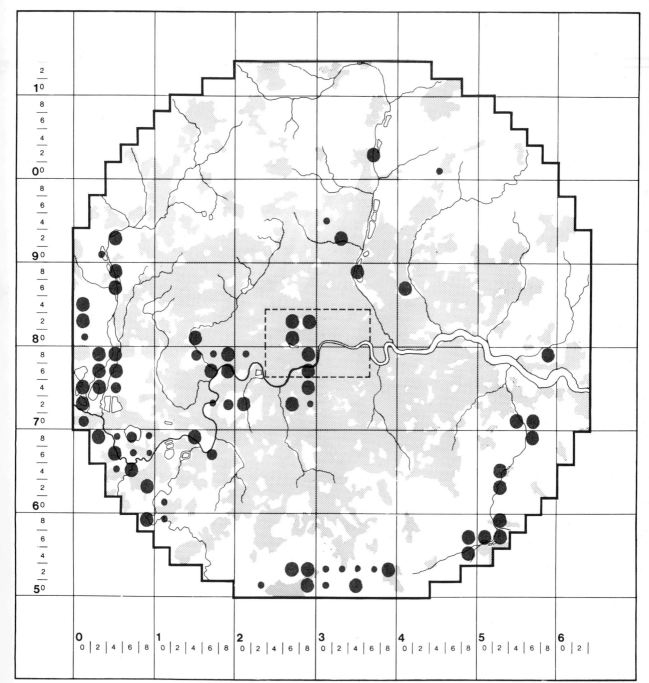

MUTE SWAN

Cygnus olor

Mute Swans commonly breed along rivers, on gravel pits and on lakes and ponds, both in the rural and built-up areas. Pairs can be found in many parks and other public spaces where the chances of successful breeding depend largely on the availability of a secure nesting site.

Censuses in London in 1955 and 1956 (Cramp 1957) recorded 173 nests in the first year and 188 in the second, though even allowing for differences in census methods between the two years, there were considerable changes in the sites occupied. In 1956 about 95% of the available waters were checked and, making an estimate for the remaining 5%, the real breeding population was probably about 200 pairs. Compared with England as a whole, the concentration in the London Area was very high, giving a density of about 1.38 nests per ten square miles in 1955 and 1.50 in 1956 in contrast to the national figure of 0.50 (0.53, 0.58 and 0.19 per $10km^2$ respectively).

Breeding records during the Atlas survey came from 163 tetrads, well spread out over much of the London Area except for the North Downs and the north-east of the Area where few suitable waters exist. As expected, most records were concentrated along the river valleys. Figures for the Atlas years are not of course directly comparable with population estimates of the earlier censuses which were based on counts of breeding pairs, whereas the present study was concerned solely with distribution and was not quantitative.

Parslow thought there was a general increase in the number of Mute Swans throughout Britain until 1959. Probably the vast spread of gravel extraction along the river valleys contributed to this, both nationally and around London. The increase, however, has been much more widespread, having been reported throughout the species' range in north-west Europe. In Sweden great moulting flocks in the Baltic were associated with increases in local breeding populations, but they reached an apparent peak in the late 1960s (Mathiasson 1973).

Though swans are large birds with few natural predators, they are subject to a number of hazards directly or indirectly resulting from man's activities. In the breeding season disturbance may take the form of egg stealing or, on occasions, removal of the birds themselves because of the public's reaction to the swans' own habit of persecuting other water birds. Such behaviour varies between different birds, related perhaps to temperament and to bird density within their territory.

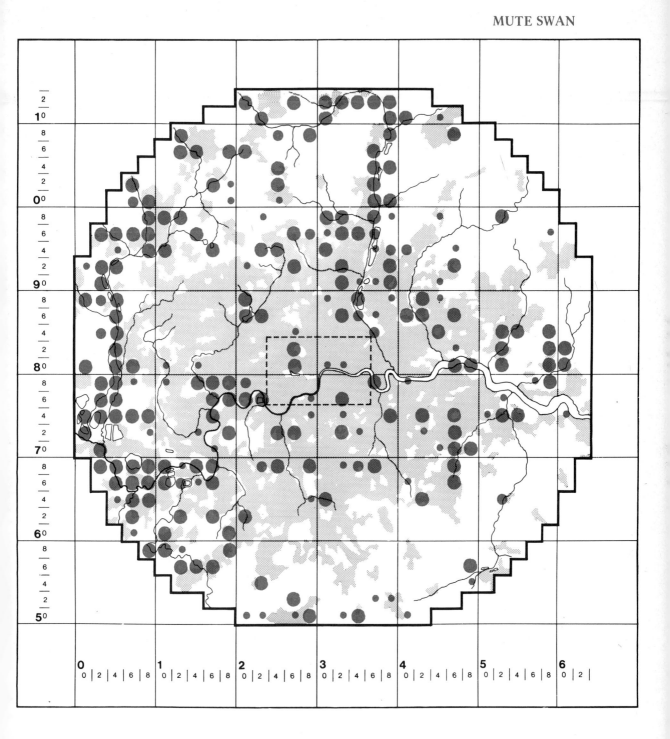

SPARROWHAWK

Accipiter nisus

Breeding records are now very sparse in the London Area and mainly confined to the south-west. Annual reports of definite breeding had not exceeded two for many years until 1974 when three pairs bred. While this may understate the real position, there is no evidence to suggest that the number now nesting in the London Area could be more than a handful.

Before the second world war the Sparrowhawk was heavily persecuted by game-keepers, but it made a considerable recovery when gamekeeping declined during the war and it was increasing from about 1940. Around Oxted and Limpsfield one observer found 18 pairs breeding in 1948, which looks a remarkably high density by present standards. About this time it became a regular breeding bird as close to central London as Richmond Park, Wimbledon Common and occasionally Greenwich Park. It also attempted to breed on Hampstead Heath and even in Inner London, at Holland Park.

Subsequently in the late 1950s a marked decline, particularly evident in eastern England, was almost certainly associated with contamination of prey by persistent toxic chemicals (Cramp 1963, Prestt 1965). By 1959 only four pairs were recorded in the London Area and the lowest ebb seems to have been reached in 1964 when only one pair was seen. Restrictions on use of the most toxic of these compounds were intro-duced in the mid-1960s and since then there has been a gradual increase in numbers of Sparrowhawks seen during the breeding season.

The pattern was similar throughout much of Britain. Parslow concluded that the greatest post-war numbers were reached in 1946 and 1947, agreeing well with the report for Oxted and Limpsfield mentioned earlier, but found little evidence of any major recovery from the subsequent widespread decline. In a study in southern Scotland, Newton (1973) found that the proportion of occupied sites increased between 1967 and 1971, but the number of young raised remained consistently low.

During the five-year Atlas survey in the London Area breeding was reported from seven tetrads, all but one in Surrey, and records of probable breeding came from a further 12. Sparrowhawks were seen in the breeding season in only 31 other tetrads and there were large sections of the Area where they appeared to be entirely absent.

In Surrey outside the London Area 21 territories were found within about $60km^2$ in 1974 (Washington 1975). Thus recovery is possible, but complete protection will be needed if the Sparrowhawk is to have any chance of becoming reasonably common again inside the London Area.

60

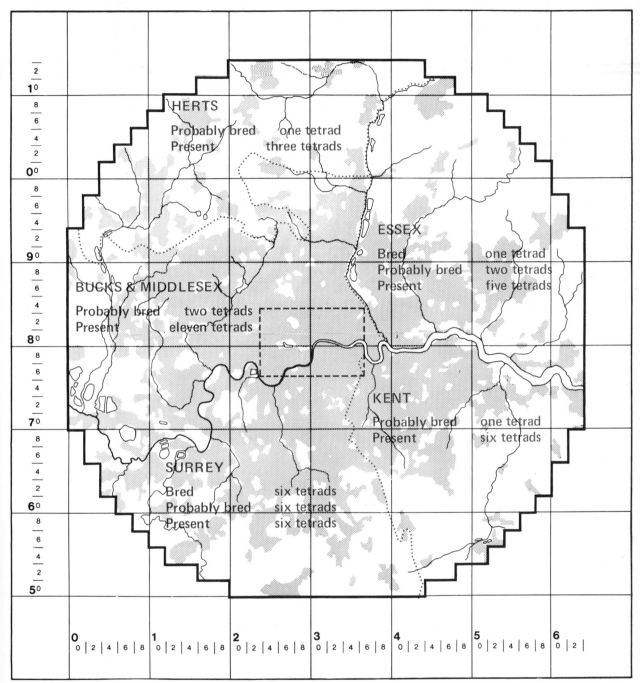

HERTS

Probably bred — one tetrad
Present — three tetrads

ESSEX

Bred — one tetrad
Probably bred — two tetrads
Present — five tetrads

BUCKS & MIDDLESEX

Probably bred — two tetrads
Present — eleven tetrads

KENT

Probably bred — one tetrad
Present — six tetrads

SURREY

Bred — six tetrads
Probably bred — six tetrads
Present — six tetrads

HOBBY

Falco subbuteo

With no evidence of more than three pairs nesting in the London Area during any one year of the Atlas survey, the Hobby ranks amongst London's rarest summer residents.

The first breeding record this century for the London Area was in 1937. Since then there has not been any sign of the population expanding to any significant extent and numbers have always been low. Most of the summer sightings of birds that might have been within breeding territories have come from Surrey, though in some years there have been regular observations in Kent, but few from north of the Thames.

Numbers during 1968-72 varied from year to year, but there were more reports than usual in 1970, when birds were seen in eight localities between the middle of May and the middle of July. Such records suggest that the size of the breeding population is generally understated and that an additional pair or two may nest undetected, or at least unreported. The Atlas survey showed that the south-west sector was still the most regularly occupied part of the London Area, contributing more than half the records. Known breeding pairs, however, totalled only five in three tetrads spread over the three counties of Surrey, Herts and Kent. Of these records, two pairs nested in 1968 and three in 1969, when two were found in the same locality in Herts. Surrey was the only county with any suggestion of additional records of probable breeding and then only in two tetrads.

In England the Hobby is on the north-west edge of its range and is almost entirely restricted to southern counties. Parslow estimated the total breeding population at about 85-100 pairs, though its elusiveness is likely to result in all estimates being on the low side. It has probably always been scarce and there is no indication of any recent change in status. As an aerial feeder, the Hobby may require summers that are somewhat hotter and drier than the general average for this country. Therefore, while the present trend of numbers nesting in the London Area is perhaps upward rather than downward, any significant increase in the population would seem to be unlikely.

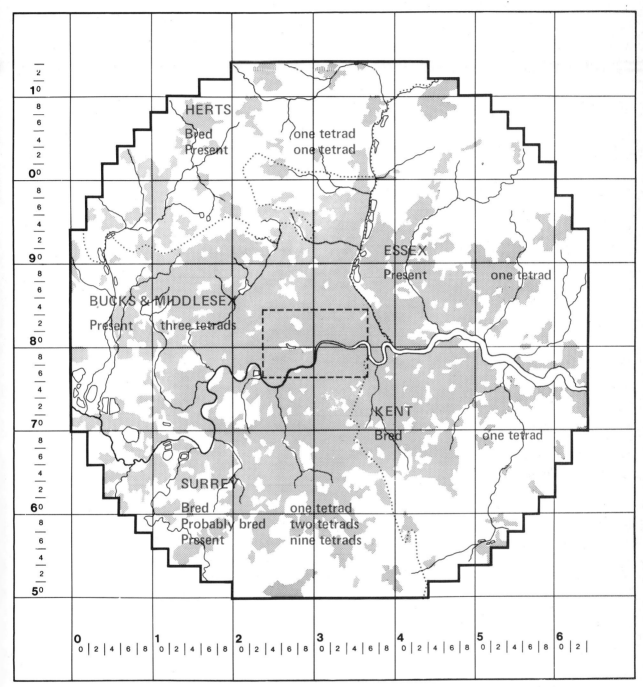

HERTS
Bred   one tetrad
Present   one tetrad

ESSEX
Present   one tetrad

BUCKS & MIDDLESEX
Present   three tetrads

KENT
Bred   one tetrad

SURREY
Bred   one tetrad
Probably bred   two tetrads
Present   nine tetrads

KESTREL

Falco tinnunculus

This is the most numerous diurnal bird of prey and breeds throughout the London Area, more commonly in wooded and built-up parts of Surrey and Middlesex than in the agricultural zones to the east and north-west.

Any comparison with breeding numbers in earlier years is difficult as better observer coverage during the Atlas survey resulted in many more pairs being reported. Clearly numbers increased during and after the second world war, probably because of reduced gamekeeping. This increase then spread to Inner London, no doubt helped by the presence of bombed sites which provided open feeding areas.

Like other predators, Kestrels declined in eastern England in the late 1950s and early 1960s, possibly through the effects of toxic chemicals (Cramp 1963, Prestt 1965, Parslow). While the reduction was evident in the London Area, the position has since improved and numbers are now markedly higher. A total of 20 pairs located in Richmond Park in 1967, even though the result of a special survey, was thought to reflect a genuine increase (Montier 1968). Kestrels also seem able to exploit human development successfully and nesting pairs, though not common, are now widely distributed in the suburbs with a few in Inner London.

The first record of a pair nesting in Inner London for fifty or sixty years was in 1931. Numbers built up to five or six pairs soon after the last war (Cramp & Tomlins 1966, Montier 1968), but had fallen again by the early 1960s. By 1972, the last year of the Atlas survey, a considerable improvement resulted in reports that year of four definite, three probable and three possible breeding pairs. In densely built-up areas with few rodents, Kestrels appear to feed mainly on House Sparrows, and nest on a variety of man-made sites such as power-stations, office buildings, churches, and even window-boxes on tower blocks.

Atlas records showed Kestrels breeding in 233 tetrads and probably breeding in 144, amounting to 44% of the Area. Birds were present in another 295 tetrads, but as a tetrad is a small territory for a bird of prey, hunting birds from proved or probable breeding pairs could account for many of these sightings. Nevertheless a total of 377, even though built up over a five-year survey, contrasts with 98 breeding pairs and 13 probables reported in 1967 (Montier 1968). At that time some three-quarters of the breeding pairs were found in Surrey and Middlesex. Though the figures are larger, the present pattern is broadly similar, with most reports again in those two counties.

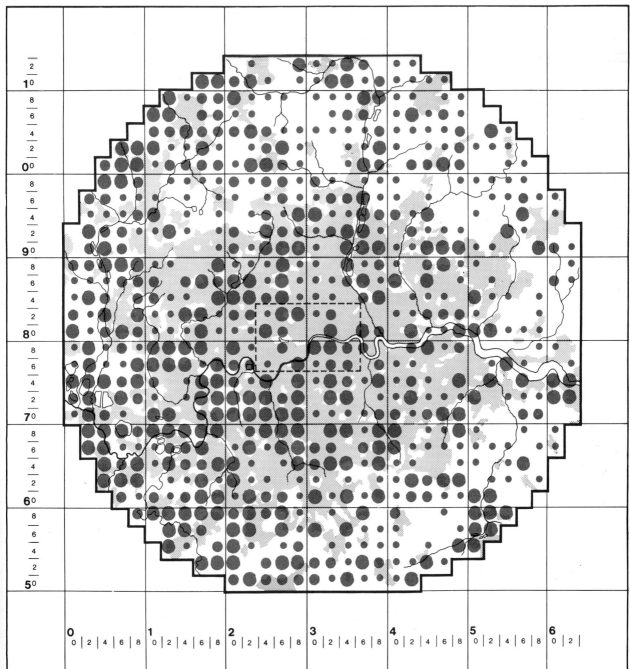

RED-LEGGED PARTRIDGE

Alectoris rufa

Within the London Area this species remains the scarcer of the two partridges and except for one or two isolated instances is confined to the periphery, though records extend much nearer the centre north of the Thames than in the south. One record of breeding away from this outer band was reported in 1971 when a pair nested for the first time in Inner London.

The historical distribution of the Red-legged Partridge is difficult to judge, but there appears to have been relatively little change in the status of this species since at least the 1950s. Earlier references to increases in range or abundance have not continued, except locally, and the species seems to have disappeared from the middle stretches of the Darent valley. Though comparative data for recent years are not available, the Red-legged Partridge probably still outnumbers the Grey Partridge in parts of the Area, especially in Essex. Both there and in Herts the Red-legged Partridge is found throughout most of the agricultural regions and the inner limits of breeding correspond fairly well with the edge of the closely built-up area. South of the Thames it is almost entirely absent from the Chalk downland and surprisingly scarce on the lower ground, which suggests a further decline since the reference by Homes to the fact that it had once been quite common on the lower parts of the North Downs, though even by the 1950s it was much less often reported. The only concentration of records in Kent is now along the Thames east of Dartford.

Atlas records of breeding came from 62 tetrads and evidence of probable breeding from 43, with birds present in a further 86 tetrads. In total this amounts to 22% of the Area compared with 41% for the Grey Partridge. Looking at records from north and south of the Thames separately, the map shows most of the reports of Red-legged Partridges were from the north, with birds present in 30% of tetrads, whereas they occurred in only 11% of tetrads south of the River.

In view of the supposed sedentary habits of this species, its successful colonisation in 1971 of the disused and overgrown Surrey Docks, surrounded by the dense urban development of south-east London, is rather surprising. A pair was seen there in August of that year with eight small young. No doubt the parent birds came originally from some of the remaining marshland breeding areas further east along the Thames.

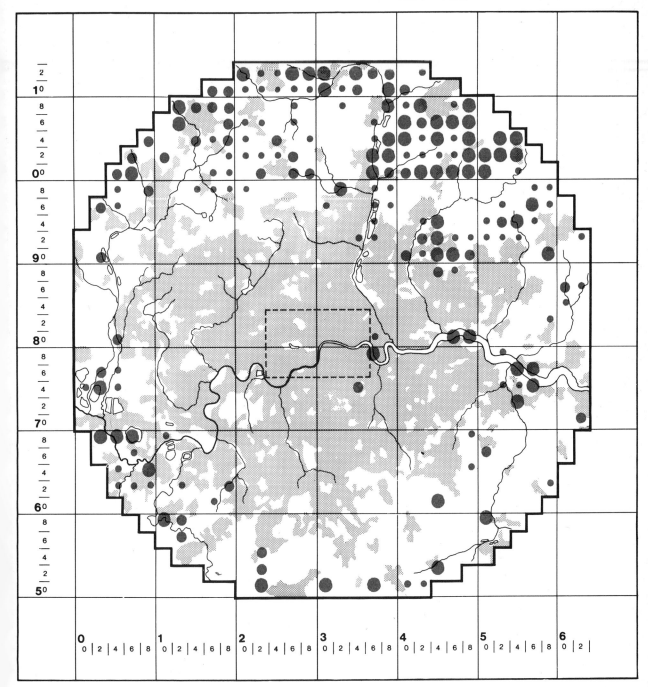

PARTRIDGE

Perdix perdix

More widespread than the last species, the Partridge, conveniently known as the Grey Partridge, is found throughout most of the open country in the London Area and is totally absent only from the heavily built-up localities.

In the late 1940s the Grey Partridge bred regularly as near central London as Chingford, Enfield, Mill Hill, Chiswick, Kew, Beckenham, Woolwich Common and Shooters Hill. Since then it seems to have lost ground in the suburbs where building development has reduced the amount of suitable habitat. Atlas records of inner breeding limits were from Richmond and Roehampton in the west and Chigwell and Plumstead in the east. In Middlesex it bred near Kingsbury and north of Enfield. Apart from the Thames marshes and Foots Cray, few breeding records came from Kent or east Surrey where the birds appear to be restricted to areas south of the North Downs and along the Darent valley.

Distribution shown on the map is perhaps more patchy than expected. Breeding reports during the Atlas survey were obtained from 142 tetrads, probable breeding from 81 and birds were present in a further 126 tetrads. In many cases, especially in the southeast, the latter probably represent breeding pairs in view of the sedentary nature of this species. Thus altogether there were reports from 41% of tetrads in the London Area, compared with 22% for the Red-legged Partridge. Further comparison of the maps shows that the Grey Partridge had a much wider distribution in west Middlesex, Bucks, west Surrey and Kent. Records for this species, however, were more evenly divided between the north and south of the Area with reports from 42% of tetrads north of the Thames and 39% from south of the River, against 30% and 11% respectively for the Red-legged Partridge.

There has been a severe decline in the Grey Partridge population throughout much of north-west Europe, possibly due to changes in farming practice, increased use of herbicides and a consequent reduction in food supply for the chicks (Potts 1970, Parslow). The extent to which the London Area has been affected is unknown, as the Atlas survey was concerned only with distribution and not with numerical status. Except for part of south Herts, where in 1972 the Grey Partridge was said to be possibly increasing, reports for 1967 onwards have referred to declines or scarcity. Little definite evidence, however, has been adduced to explain the desertion of former breeding sites, but loss of habitat through ground clearance was thought to be a contributory factor in at least one instance.

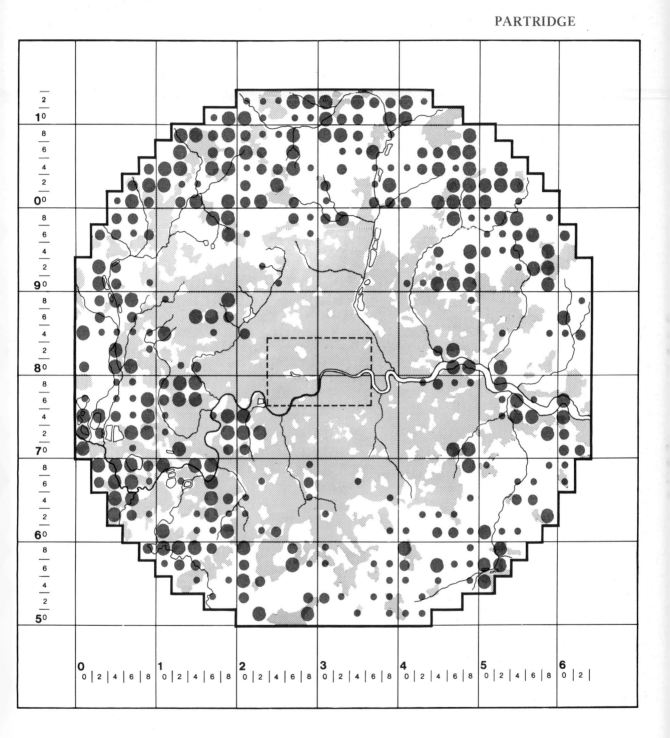

QUAIL
Coturnix coturnix

This summer visitor is extremely erratic in its appearance in the London Area, being much more numerous in some years than others. It may nest annually in the Darent valley, but in other localities it occurs only sporadically.

The Quail is a particularly difficult species for which to obtain positive proof of breeding and most reports are of birds heard calling in the summer. Records shown on the map are fairly typical of the distribution pattern in recent years when the species has been more regularly reported than in the past. Up to 1954 the only two known cases of breeding were from Dartford Marsh about 1900 and near Rickmansworth in 1947, and there were breeding season occurrences that suggested birds were resident in no more than three other localities. Homes, however, considered that the species might in future occur more often as a result of greater emphasis on cultivation of cereals in agricultural areas.

Quails were reported in exceptional numbers from many parts of Britain and Ireland in 1964 (Parslow). This was reflected in the London Area with birds heard calling from at least seven separate localities in the Darent valley between Bean and Shoreham, though summer records elsewhere were restricted to only three scattered sites. Since then the Darent valley has featured in reports almost annually and one farmer claimed to have heard Quail regularly for between ten and twenty years down to 1967. Away from this particular area, records over the twenty years since 1954 have come from two other localities in Kent, about seven in Essex, three in Herts, one in Middlesex and six in Surrey.

Another major influx occurred in Britain and Ireland in 1970 and was considered by Parslow to have been on a similar scale to the 1964 invasion. This hardly appeared to touch the London Area as there were records from only three places in that year, though at one of those, at Thorpe, four birds were heard calling from a cornfield and one was enticed out by a tape-recording of the Quail call notes.

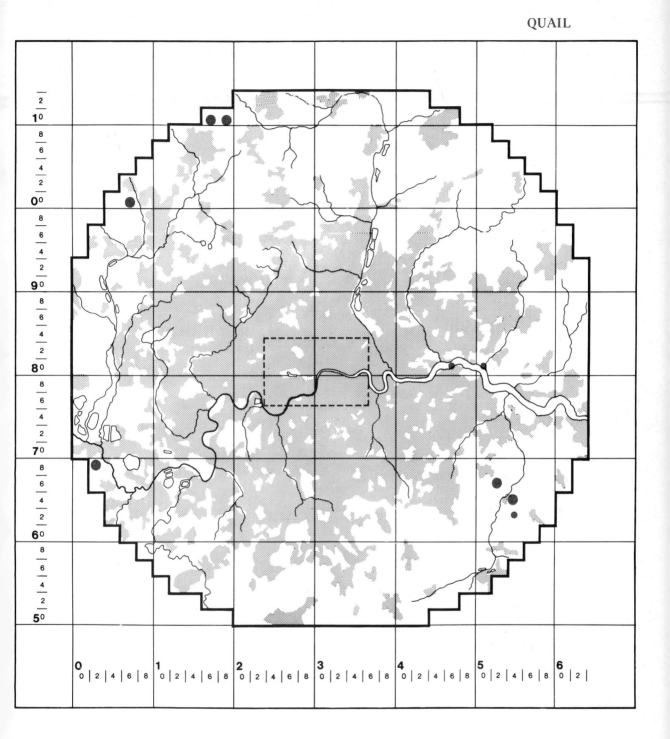

PHEASANT

Phasianus colchicus

Though a widespread resident in the less built-up localities across the northern and southern parts of the London Area, records of the Pheasant are unaccountably scarce from both the extreme east and extreme west.

This species has attracted even less attention than other gamebirds, observers being apparently reluctant to keep records and still more reluctant to submit them. As a result there is little historical information with which to compare the present distribution map. Up to the early 1950s fluctuations tended to be associated with changes in the extent of game preservation and this factor may still account for the puzzling absence of the species in the east and west of the Area.

Large parks and similar open spaces, especially Richmond, Kew and Wimbledon Common, have contained breeding Pheasants for many years and at the time of the Atlas survey the species was still established in these areas. Wimbledon Common and Chiswick were the closest points to central London from which breeding was reported. Away from stretches of open common and parkland, there were a few isolated reports from London suburbs. Breeding occurred at Chislehurst and pairs may have bred near the Brent Reservoir and at Wanstead. There were records from the Thames marshes east of Dartford, but a preference for woodland clearly restricts the Pheasant's distribution to the less densely developed districts.

During 1968-72 the species was reported from 433 tetrads, representing 51% of the London Area. Breeding was recorded in 172 tetrads and birds probably bred in a further 123.

LADY AMHERST'S PHEASANT
Chrysolophus amherstiae

This introduced species was not referred to in *The Birds of the London Area*, but was present during the Atlas survey in one tetrad north-west of Watford. Small feral populations exist in one or two parts of south and east England and this record no doubt derives from the main area of colonisation beyond the boundary of the London Area on the borders of Bedfordshire, Bucks and Herts (BOU 1971).

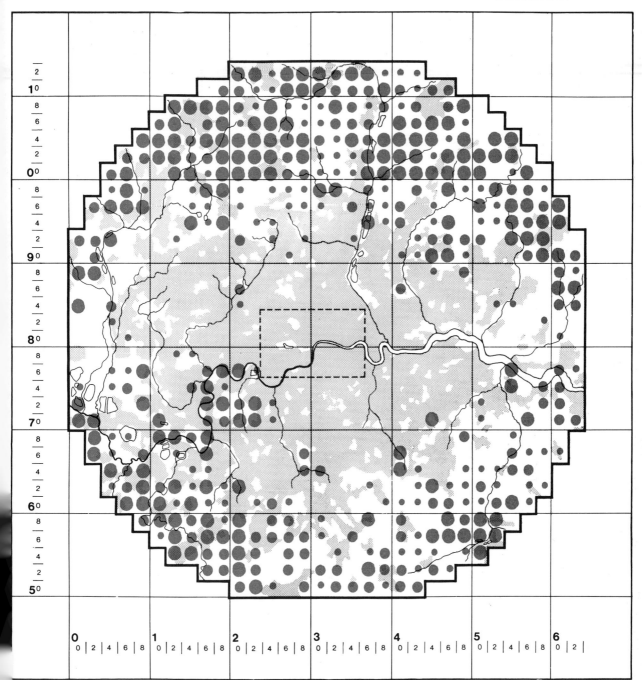

WATER RAIL

Rallus aquaticus

This is a secretive species that can be difficult to locate, but even so it appears to be genuinely scarce in the London Area. It is rarely proved to breed and not recorded at all in some seasons.

Only occasional instances of breeding were reported up to 1954 and there is no subsequent evidence of significant change in the recorded status of the species. Notwithstanding its far-carrying and distinctive call in the breeding season, the Water Rail can be easily overlooked. As a result of the systematic recording methods of the Atlas survey more records became available, but they are unlikely to reflect any real increase in numbers and the map perhaps now indicates the normal summer distribution.

Over the years 1968-72 evidence suggesting definite breeding came from six tetrads, three of which were in the Colne valley and the others from near Welwyn Garden City, Thorndon Park and Ruxley G.P. Breeding probably occurred in an additional 15 tetrads. Distribution closely follows the river valleys, especially along the Colne, where a succession of lakes and gravel pits may add to the attraction of that particular stretch of country.

In the London Area, Water Rails are more frequently seen in the winter months. There is no evidence to show whether birds present during the summer are resident throughout the year, or whether, and if so to what extent, the population is affected by dispersal or migration from elsewhere. From the limited information available there are no firm conclusions that can be drawn relating either to long-term or to seasonal variations, though clearly availability of habitat is likely to be the principal factor limiting any expansion.

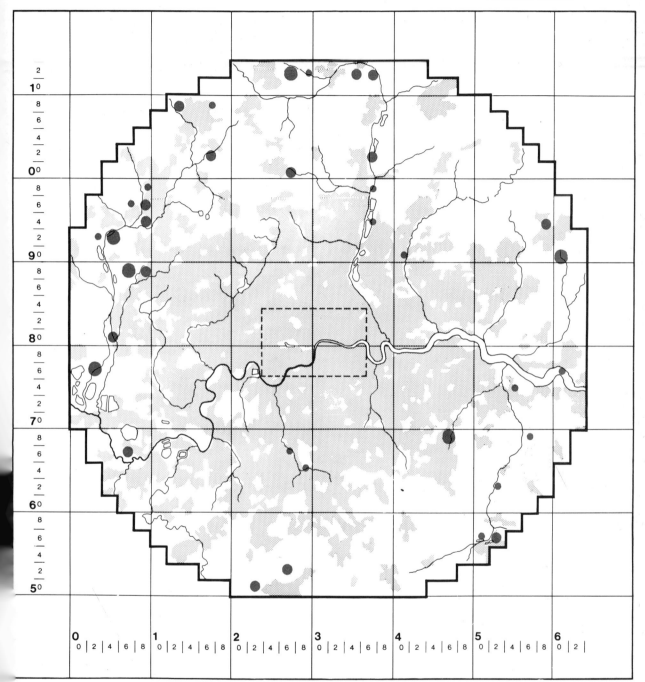

MOORHEN

Gallinula chloropus

A familiar bird in almost all localities where there is water, the Moorhen has a very wide distribution, breeding throughout most of the Area, though it is rather less numerous in the densely built-up parts of London and is apparently absent from much of the downland around Warlingham and Caterham.

Earlier accounts of the Moorhen up to 1954 suggest little change in distribution during the first half of this century and a similar comment is applicable to the present situation. Within the London Area it quickly becomes very tolerant of human disturbance and, as a result, breeds along all the river valleys and at innumerable ponds and gravel pits so long as there is sufficient cover in the form of aquatic vegetation for nesting. It is thus absent from gravel pits when they are newly dug and generally from reservoirs, but breeds annually in most of the central parks as well as many in the suburbs. Its absence from the Warlingham and Caterham areas might be attributed to the lack of suitable waters on the Chalk Downs in these localities and the same reason may explain the few gaps in the extreme north-west where the Chilterns just extend into the Area.

Records from 582 tetrads during the Atlas survey represent 68% of the London Area. Of this total, breeding was proved in 465, the presence of newly hatched birds on the water providing a simple method of establishing that nesting occurred.

Homes listed many localities in Inner London and the suburbs where the species was known to breed, but the distribution revealed by the present survey indicates a more widespread population in these inner areas. This could be a result of better coverage for a species which normally attracts little attention from birdwatchers, though in 1967, the year before the survey began, there were as many as 26 pairs reported from Inner London. Breeding numbers seem to vary widely from year to year with only two pairs in Hyde Park/Kensington Gardens in 1971, but between six and eight in the other survey years. Birds will quickly colonise new habitats and two breeding pairs were reported in the disued Surrey Docks in 1970, increasing to three in 1973.

While there is insufficient evidence from which to conclude that the Moorhen has definitely become more numerous in London, it has clearly held its own during the past seventy years.

76

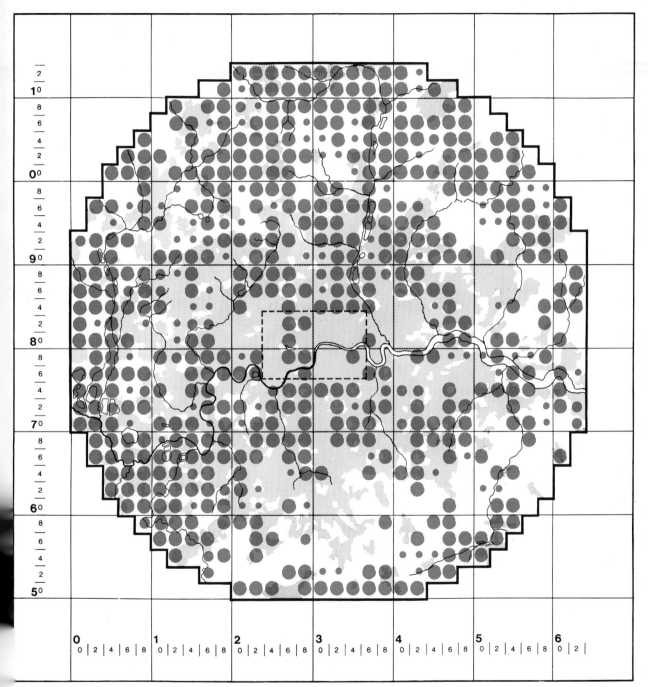

COOT

Fulica atra

The Coot breeds commonly throughout the Area, but is absent from wide stretches of the North Downs and from upland areas of Herts and Essex.

This species always appears to have been less widespread than the Moorhen in the London Area as it tends to require a larger expanse of water. At present the relative status of the two remains much the same, with the Coot absent from many of the small ponds that the Moorhen finds suitable. In a survey of the Coot in 1957 (Homes *et al.* 1960) 80% of breeding records came from lakes, ponds, gravel and clay pits, 15% from reservoirs, 3% from rivers and canals and a few from sewage farms.

Breeding distribution shown on the map can clearly be related to the large number of man-made pits in the west of the Area in Surrey and along the Colne valley, as well as in parts of the Lea and Darent valleys and along the lower reaches of the Thames. Park lakes are occupied by breeding pairs over much of suburban London, particularly those with islands to provide refuges and anchorage for nests. The concentration of records immediately to the south and south-west of central London follows this latter type of habitat from Kew, Richmond and Wimbledon in the west to Peckham, Crystal Palace and Beckenham in the east and extends from Battersea in Inner London south to Mitcham and Morden.

A minimum population of 419 pairs of Coots was shown by the 1957 survey and a maximum of some 160 occupied sites. The latter may be compared with 236 tetrads containing breeding records during the 1968-72 Atlas project. Inevitably this is a somewhat crude comparison as there may be more than one site in a tetrad and also the 1957 survey was known to be incomplete, but the figures suggest there may have been an increase since the earlier count, probably aided by the continued digging of new gravel pits.

Numbers have certainly increased in Inner London this century. The first record of successful breeding was in St James's Park in 1926 when eggs and pinioned birds were introduced. The population grew rapidly there and in other central London parks. In St James's Park numbers have continued to rise since 1954 and as many as 29 pairs bred there in 1956. By 1972 Regent's Park held 15 pairs and Hyde Park/Kensington Gardens 12 pairs, both peak figures in either park.

Reasons for these increases are unknown, but Parslow considered that Coots may have become commoner throughout south-east England as a whole and they may have increased generally in western Europe.

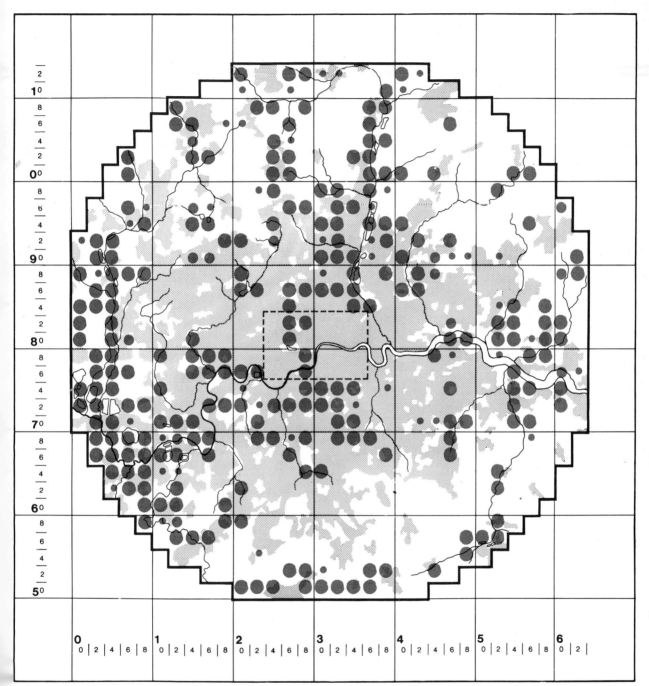

OYSTERCATCHER

Haematopus ostralegus

This is one of London's most recent breeding colonists. Birds were recorded as nesting for the first time in 1971 at both Rainham and Swanscombe Marshes.

At Rainham Marsh the nest was sited on a strip of bare earth beside a channel which had been dug across an area of mud that had dried out and become overgrown. The nest contained two eggs, but they failed to hatch and the pair finally deserted (Noble 1972). At Swanscombe Marsh a pair was seen with two downy young, but their final success was not recorded.

These records came as a climax to a general increase in the occurrence of Oystercatchers in London over recent years, especially along the Thames and its marshes. Improved cleanliness of the River, which is now also attracting large numbers of wintering ducks and waders as described by Harrison & Grant (1976), has undoubtedly been a major factor in this increase and the Rainham pair was regularly seen feeding on the nearby Thames foreshore. There has also been a national increase in the breeding population and range of Oystercatchers (Parslow). Several former breeding sites in southern and eastern England, particularly East Anglia, have been recolonised since about the 1930s along with a tendency to nest in coastal fields rather than on the shore itself, thus following a similar pattern to that found in the Netherlands and Belgium. This suggests that London breeding records form a further extension of the same trend.

Disappointingly the breeding status of the Oystercatcher in London has not been reinforced since 1971. Although birds have been seen regularly along the Thames during the summers of 1972 and 1973, they have nested only once more, again at Rainham, in 1973. Three eggs were laid, but both they and the adults disappeared shortly afterwards. There are several areas, especially along the Thames, suitable for future colonisation, but for the present, Oystercatchers remain one of the rarest breeding species in the London Area.

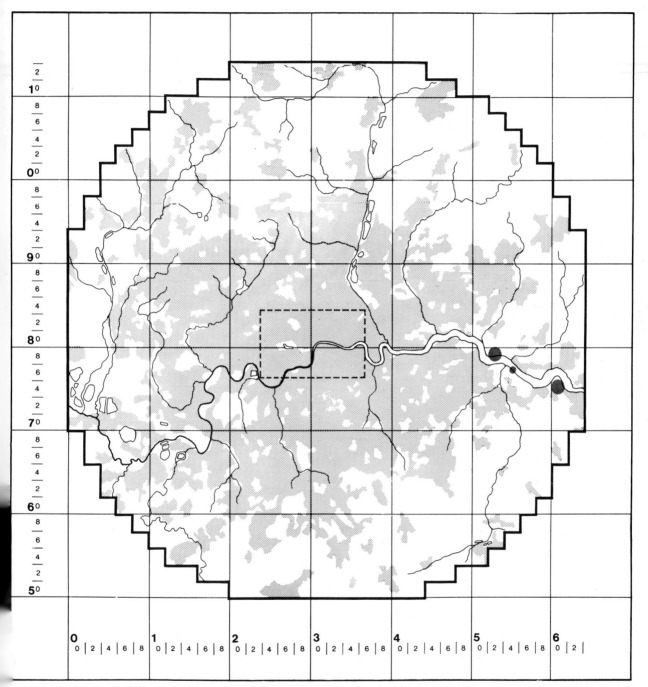

LAPWING

Vanellus vanellus

As the most widespread of the three species of plover nesting in the London Area, the Lapwing is a familiar breeding bird of some outlying parts, but is much scarcer and more local near the built-up zones.

A contraction of its range in the first half of this century was attributed largely to the spread of urban London and the drainage of suitable sites. Data on the size of the breeding population, however, are sparse, but an enquiry in 1957 (Homes *et al.* 1960) indicated a considerable decline within the London Area. At three sites in Herts, for example, the population was halved between 1952 and 1957, falling from 86 to only about 40 pairs. Details of breeding habitats showed that probably over half of the population in the Area was using habitats such as sewage farms, water meadows and damp pasture. The remainder was mainly on arable land, with a few pairs on dry pasture and other sites such as gravel pits, chalk pits and airports.

There can be little doubt that the total population in the London Area has declined further since 1957. Drainage of agricultural land has continued and modernisation of old-style sewage farms has resulted in the loss of flooded fields. Severe winters also have an adverse effect on Lapwings and the species has not fully recovered from the harsh winter of 1962-63; in fact numbers have fallen again in recent years. A contributory cause may be low nesting success through predation by the much increased Carrion Crow (Batten 1972).

On its breeding grounds the Lapwing is a showy bird with spectacular display flights and anxiety behaviour making it difficult to overlook. Thus, where coverage was fairly complete, the map gives a fair idea of its distribution. A clear preference emerges for low-lying ground and river valleys, whereas in upland farming areas the range is more fragmented. This is probably a reflection of the greater breeding success in relatively undisturbed wetland habitats compared with agricultural land which is prone to periodic disturbance from farming activities.

Inner limits of the Lapwing's range demonstrate a tolerance of suburban habitats where suitable and secluded nesting grounds remain. There were Atlas records from such areas as Beddington S.F., the southern part of Walthamstow Reservoirs and Barking Creek. Its readiness to adopt newly available habitat in urban localities was shown at the now derelict Surrey Docks, where a pair was present in 1972 for most of the summer and two chicks were hatched by a pair that nested there in 1973.

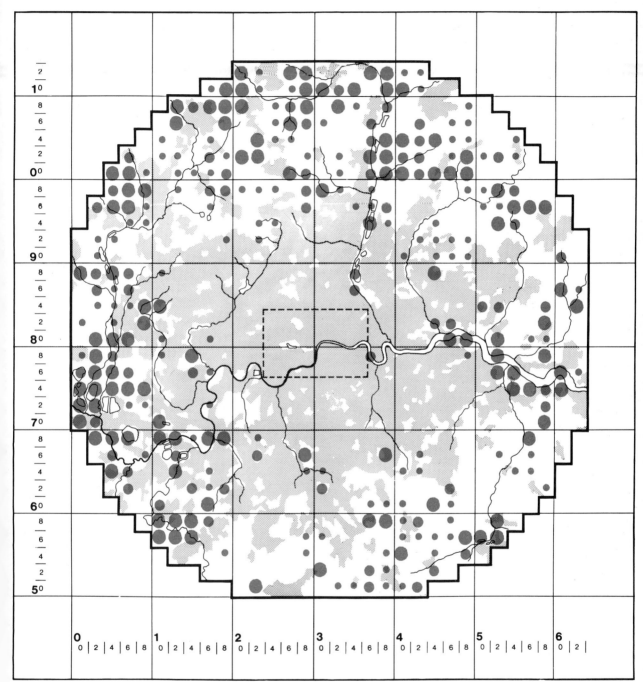

RINGED PLOVER

Charadrius hiaticula

This species now breeds regularly in the London Area, albeit in very small numbers. As the only published nesting record before the 1950s was in 1901, the present situation represents a remarkable change.

First re-established in 1957 when breeding was proved at both Rye Meads and Stone Marsh, the Ringed Plover has since bred in all but four subsequent years up to 1973, involving at least 48 proved breeding pairs. A maximum of seven pairs was reached in 1971 and possibly in 1962 and 1972. The stronghold of the species is along the Thames where 37 of the 48 pairs have nested either at Rainham on the north shore or from Woolwich to Swanscombe on the south. Thames-dredged mud often provided favourable nesting habitat before becoming overgrown. At Swanscombe a total of at least 22 pairs bred between 1959 and 1972, 15 of these in the years 1959 to 1962 when conditions were ideal. In similar habitat at Rainham a minimum of eight pairs bred, all but one from 1969 onwards. Four pairs at Thamesmead between 1969 and 1972 were mainly attracted by habitat changes during construction of the new town, especially the lake where gravelly islands were used as nest sites. Elsewhere along the Thames single pairs have bred at Stone Marsh, Belvedere and Northfleet.

In addition to Rye Meads, reports away from the lower Thames have come from the Walton and Walthamstow Reservoirs, and Nazeing, Stanwellmoor, Bedfont and Kingsmead gravel pits. Temporary habitat created during excavation of the new reservoir at Wraysbury attracted a pair in 1970 and nearby at Wraysbury G.P. in 1971, but this is the only inland locality known to have been occupied for more than one season. A remarkable extension into Inner London occurred in 1973 when a pair raised one young at the disused Surrey Docks.

Gravel pits and reservoir sites have been available throughout this century, so there must be factors other than new habitat to account for the recolonisation of the London Area. Coastal populations in Britain are suffering a widespread decline thought to be due to increasing human disturbance. At the same time in some counties, including Kent, pairs have recently been found nesting in fields (Parslow). Any explanation of these trends is speculation, but there could possibly be a connection between greater disturbance on beaches and the appearance of breeding pairs inland.

In London there is no reason why its position should not be held in the future as suitable habitats are likely to be available for many years, though it would be unfortunate if success was at the expense of its smaller relative the Little Ringed Plover.

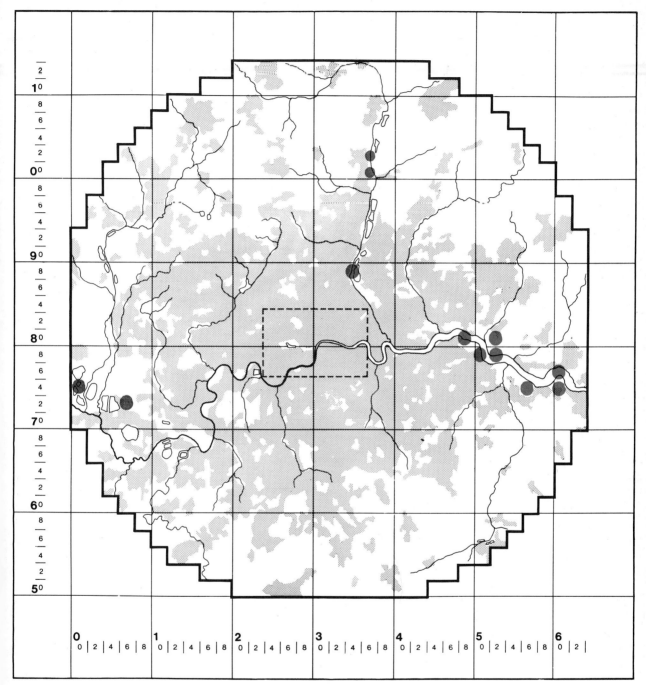

LITTLE RINGED PLOVER

Charadrius dubius

Now an established breeding bird in the London Area, the Little Ringed Plover may be found wherever its specialised nesting habitat exists.

A pair with three young at a gravel pit near Ashford, Middlesex, in 1944 provided not only the first breeding record for the London Area, but also the first recorded occurrence of the species since 1864. By 1954 eighteen pairs were present during the summer, nine of which were proved to be nesting. Thus the London Area became one of the strongholds of Britain's new colonist that was only discovered breeding in this country as recently as 1938 at Tring, Herts. It has since consolidated its position in London as shown in Table 5, which covers the period 1955-74.

A BTO national census in 1973 focused attention on this species and better coverage produced records from 43 sites in the London Area compared with only 22 the previous year. From the late 1950s, however, the population has probably been fairly static, though there is a regular shift of breeding localities as old sites become unsuitable and new ones are colonised. The ability to seek out new nesting sites, even within Inner London, was apparent at the now derelict Surrey Docks. In 1971 and 1972 birds were seen displaying and anxiety behaviour was observed. Breeding was finally proved in 1973 when a pair hatched one young.

Table 5 is not directly comparable with the map as there may be more than one pair at a site and more than one site in a tetrad. Nevertheless the map reflects the habitat requirements of the species, with the main concentrations to the west in the Colne and upper Thames valleys, in the Lea valley and also in the east on the Thames marshes, where, in addition to gravel pits and quarries, the species is also found on sites where dredged mud is dumped. Expansion in the London Area is limited by the amount of available habitat and possibly by losses of eggs or chicks through flooding or industrial activities such as mineral extraction. The future of the Little Ringed Plover, however, seems reasonably assured, provided it is not dispossessed by the more aggressive Ringed Plover, which, as indicated by Parrinder (1975), is colonising the same sites and takes up territory earlier in the season.

Table 5.   Minimum numbers of pairs of Little Ringed Plovers recorded as proved breeding or summering in the London Area, 1955-74 (Note high numbers recorded in special survey in 1973)

	55	56	57	58	59	60	61	62	63	64	65	66	67	68	69	70	71	72	73	74
Breeding pairs	18	15	23	25	19	26	26	20	15	20	33	26	19	26	22	22	17	16	39	15
Additional summering pairs	7	10	4	7	8	11	10	8	15	3	3	13	24	5	16	9	7	18	33	14
Total	25	25	27	32	27	37	36	28	30	23	36	39	43	31	38	31	24	34	72	29
Occupied sites	13	12+	9+	17	16+	21	18	14	22	17	26	22	24	22	24	18	16	22	43	20

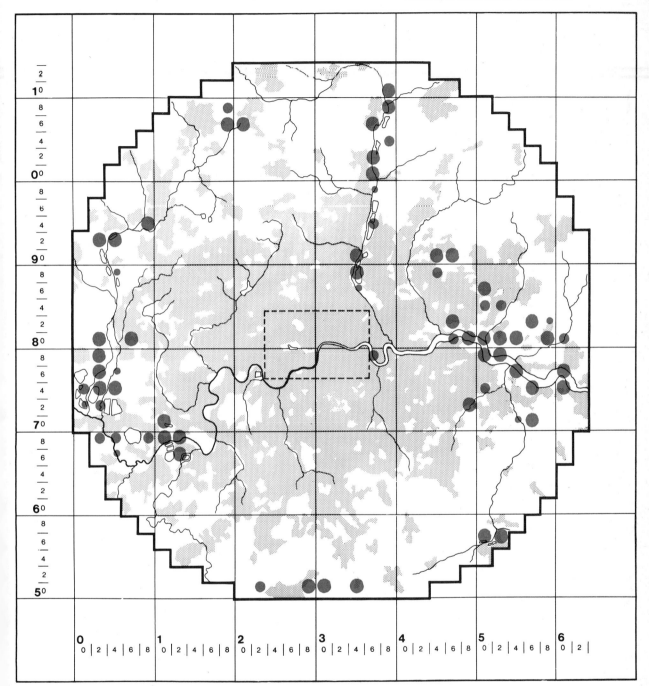

SNIPE

Gallinago gallinago

Although a familiar bird in the London Area, the Snipe is a rare breeding species, with less than two confirmed records annually since 1970.

There would appear to have been little significant change in status compared with that recorded for the years up to 1954. At the beginning of the century nesting was far from annual and occurred at only a few favoured localities. In the later part of the period records became more regular, but were more likely the result of better observer coverage than a real improvement. From 1954 the apparent increase continued, however, and between 1955 and 1962 an average of seven to eight pairs was proved to nest annually. Numbers were severely affected by the hard winter of 1962-63, as were other species that also depend on moist ground for feeding (Dobinson & Richards 1964). In London the breeding population never recovered and over the years 1963-73 dropped to an average of less than two pairs. Snipe also suffer badly from the loss of habitat and this has been suggested as the likely cause of a general decline in many parts of the Midlands and south-east England over the last fifteen to twenty years (Parslow).

During the five-year Atlas period Snipe were recorded from 50 tetrads, but reported as breeding in only seven. This emphasises the difficulty of finding nests or young birds and no doubt the data underestimate the true size of the population. In the remaining 43 tetrads where birds were recorded as present or probably breeding, nesting may have gone undetected. Snipe, however, frequently carry out their showy 'drumming' display flight early in the season over areas which they later desert as they evidently prove unsuitable and some of the records may relate to birds holding territory only temporarily.

Ideal breeding habitat for this species consists of very wet, boggy ground with little disturbance and a lush growth of grass and sedges. The rarity of breeding in the London Area reflects the scarcity of this type of habitat which nowadays is confined to a few old-style sewage farms with flooded water meadows, remnants of low-lying riverside marsh and a few gravel pits which have been left with a fairly extensive marshy area. Continued modernisation of sewage works and drainage of agricultural land are restricting possible nesting localities even further and there is every likelihood that London's breeding Snipe population, already at danger level, will continue to dwindle unless some suitable natural habitat is preserved.

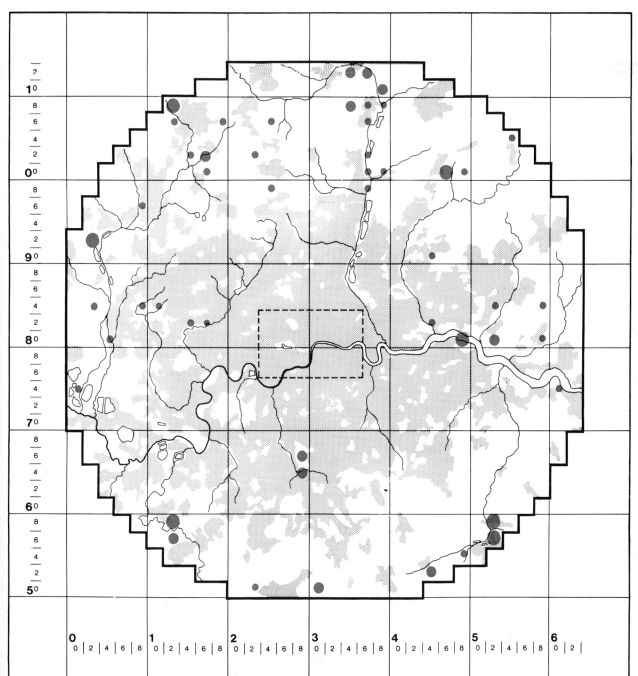

WOODCOCK

Scolopax rusticola

This species breeds in small numbers in those parts of the London Area where it is able to find its rather specialised breeding habitat, which is primarily woodland with patches of damp ground. Most of its usual haunts are well known, but it may be overlooked in other localities.

Its pattern of distribution appears to have shown little change throughout this century. Homes referred to few breeding records up to 1954, but listed a number of probable breeding localities, mainly round the fringe of the Area and principally in Surrey. Since then reports have been more frequent, though much of this apparent increase is likely to have been due to more extensive coverage by observers.

Concentration of effort during the Atlas survey of 1968-72 produced a reasonable picture of distribution, showing the Woodcock to be more widespread than might have been expected from an analysis of past data. Except during its roding flights at dusk, the Woodcock is a difficult bird to locate in the breeding season and, while it is recorded regularly in its traditional sites, a closer check on other areas with stretches of woodland, such as on the North Downs or in parts of Herts, might have permitted a more accurate assessment in earlier years. Definite evidence of breeding is particularly difficult to establish, as is shown by the fact that over the five-year survey nesting was reported from only ten tetrads out of 80 in which the species was found.

In Kent the Woodcock has a fragmented range away from its usual haunts in woodland on the Lower Greensand along the southern boundary of the Area. It is an extremely rare breeding bird in Essex with confirmed nesting from only one site south of Brentwood. The main concentration of records remains in Surrey, where there is a cluster in the south-west of the London Area, and also a breeding record for Richmond Park, the closest one to central London. A pair bred there successfully in 1968 and birds were reported to have been present throughout the following summer.

Woodcock prefer extensive mixed woods or young plantations with wet or boggy ground nearby where food can be obtained and will not tolerate the encroachment of built-up areas. While urban spread may have ousted the species from some localities in the past, its present strongholds seem fairly safe and are preserved to some extent in the form of parks or Green Belt land.

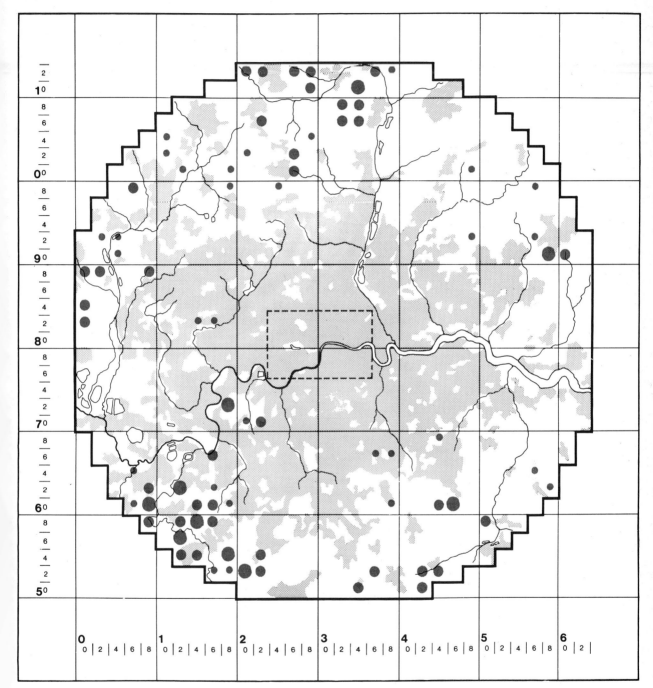

COMMON SANDPIPER

Tringa hypoleucos

The Common Sandpiper is only a very sporadic breeding bird in England south and east of a line from Scarborough, Yorkshire, to the Severn estuary (Parslow), and this status is reflected in the scarcity of records for the London Area.

Homes referred to two records of breeding in the early years of this century, in 1912 and 1913 near Haileybury, but considered the accounts of both occurrences unconvincing. In view of its previous and subsequent history in the London Area, the series of breeding records at Old Parkbury gravel pits between 1950 and 1958 is all the more remarkable. A pair was present in each summer and the birds' behaviour suggested breeding, although proof was obtained in only three of those years. In 1954 adults were seen with fledged young, in 1955 a nest was located from which two young were reared and in 1957 a further two young were reared and a second pair of adults was also present. Since then there have been only two records of proved breeding, both in 1967, when a pair was seen with two young at West Hyde and a nest was found nearby at Maple Cross.

Records of pairs present during the summer behaving as if they might have been breeding have become more frequent in recent years. In addition to the localities already mentioned, there have been reports from Nazeing G.P. and Rye Meads in 1959, Holme-thorpe sand pit in 1962 when courtship display and mating were observed, and Horn-church Chase where two pairs were present in 1965. During the Atlas survey one or two birds were reported throughout the summer at Hamper Mill in 1968 and there were records from Addlestone in 1969 and Thorpe gravel pits in both 1969 and 1970. At Addlestone a pair was present from May until August. Display, song-flight and distraction display were all seen on several occasions and the birds were believed to have bred. Territorial activities were also observed from the pair at Thorpe in 1969 and 1970. They were not thought to have nested in the first year, but in 1970 they were seen to dive at a Canada Goose and drive away a pair of Jackdaws. Again there was no confirmation that birds bred successfully. Under the Atlas coding system, however, distraction display qualified as a breeding record on the map.

Common Sandpipers, usually singly, but sometimes more, may of course remain in some localities well into the summer, but the majority are normally migrant stragglers. Some records on the map indicating no more than presence during the breeding season may therefore refer to such birds.

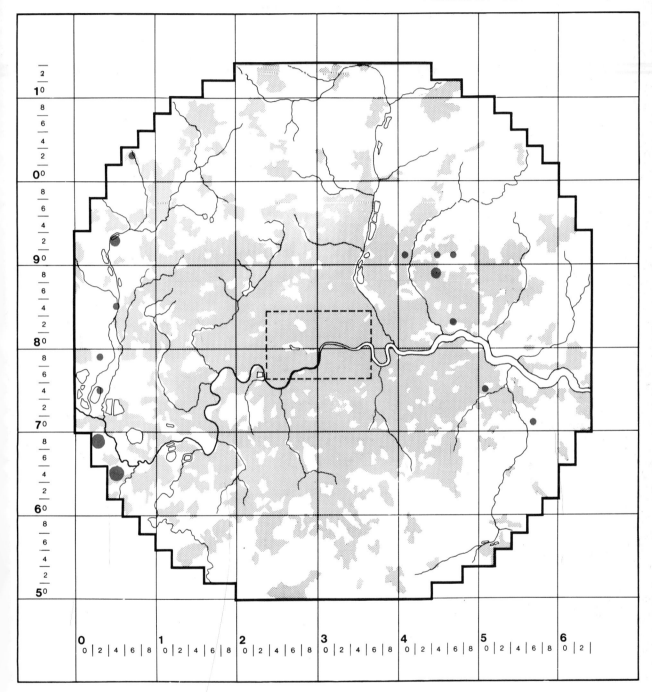

REDSHANK

Tringa totanus

Following a marked decline over recent years, the Redshank is now a scarce breeding species in the London Area.

It extended its range in southern England, including the river valleys of the London Area, during the second half of the nineteenth and beginning of the twentieth centuries (Parslow). By 1939, however, there was already a downward trend as drainage of water meadows affected inland sites, though along the Thames marshes east of Woolwich numbers remained quite high, with an estimated minimum of 80 pairs still present annually in the early 1950s.

Since then the decline elsewhere has continued and the Thames population is now much less. Between 1955 and 1963 the annual average number of pairs present in summer throughout the London Area was about 28, dropping to an average of about 18 over the ten years up to 1973. Counts in both periods were incomplete, but demonstrate the trend. Field drainage may still be partly to blame, though since 1955 the only recorded losses from this cause were at Shepperton where up to two pairs bred until 1970, and part of the Darent valley near Otford and Sevenoaks which has only recently become unsuitable (Harrison 1974). A more direct and measurable cause of the fall in breeding numbers has been the modernisation of sewage farms. At Beddington S.F., for example, up to a dozen pairs used to breed in the 1950s and nesting apparently ceased after 1966; at Rye Meads eight pairs have been reduced to only one; and small sewage farms where birds bred occasionally, such as Elmers End and Epsom, have closed down. In addition to these losses which may be wholly or partly attributable to habitat changes, Parslow shows that there is also some evidence of contraction in the Redshank's European range.

Along the Thames, breeding continues in favoured sites at Swanscombe, Dartford and Rainham, for example, and even into built-up areas where suitable habitat exists, such as Barking Creek and Thamesmead. In 1972 the number of reported pairs from Thames localities, excluding Swanscombe, totalled 18, but as records are incomplete the true population may be nearer 30 pairs. This drop from the early 1950s can be attributed to a combination of factors, principally drainage, ploughing and building. Other remaining strongholds of the Redshank are in the Lea and upper Thames valleys where breeding occurs mainly around gravel pits and reservoirs, as well as in the Mole valley around Stoke D'Abernon where a few pairs breed in water meadows that so far have escaped drainage.

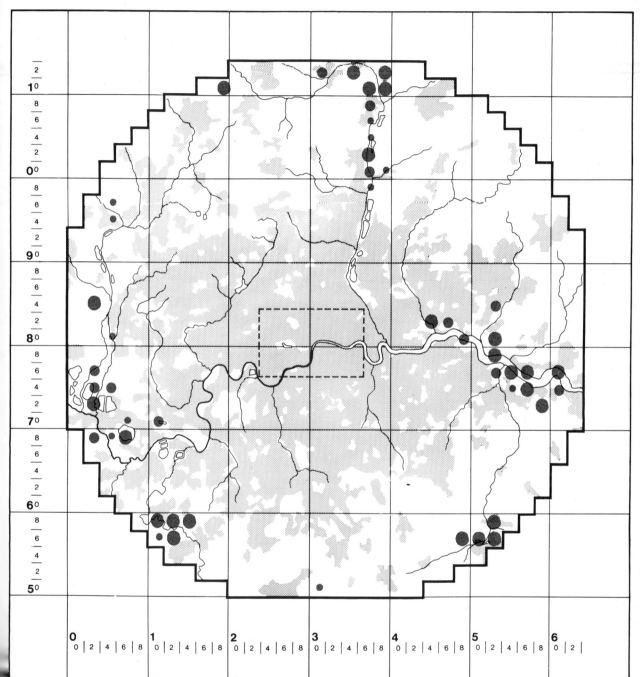

LESSER BLACK-BACKED GULL

Larus fuscus

Although the Lesser Black-backed Gull has not yet been proved to nest in the London Area, there have been a few recent records of pairs taking up residence during the early summer in some of the Inner London parks. It may well breed successfully in the near future.

There has been a massive increase in numbers of this species, both as a migrant and winter visitor, since the late 1920s and in recent years there has also been a trend towards more regular and numerous records during the summer. Although the winter population consists almost exclusively of the Scandinavian breeding race *L.f. fuscus* rather than the British *L.f. graellsii,* and the bulk of the summering birds are immatures, the records clearly show an increasing acceptance of habitats available in London. Recent breeding attempts appear to be a continuation of this trend.

The first pair to show signs of attempting to breed took up residence in St James's Park in 1966. They were present from 26 March until 19 May and although their behaviour and displaying suggested that they might have stayed to nest, nothing materialised. In 1968 and 1969 a pair took up territory during the summer in Regent's Park, acting as if they, too, might nest, but disturbance from building work at the Zoo may have discouraged them in the earlier year. Then in 1970 a pair gave every sign of breeding in Hyde Park, but apparently lost interest when the Lido was opened to the public.

There are no records of any further breeding attempts, though the present status of the Lesser Black-backed Gull in the London Area is similar to that of the Herring Gull in the early years of that species' breeding colonisation and the Lesser Black-backed Gull shows a similar preference for Inner London parks. While it has not shown an increase in its British breeding population comparable with the enormous expansion of the Herring Gull, there is a temptation to suggest that the Lesser Black-backed Gull may also be found breeding in the London Area before long. Any pairs making a serious attempt to do so in Inner London, however, might well face a good deal of territorial competition from the already established Herring Gulls.

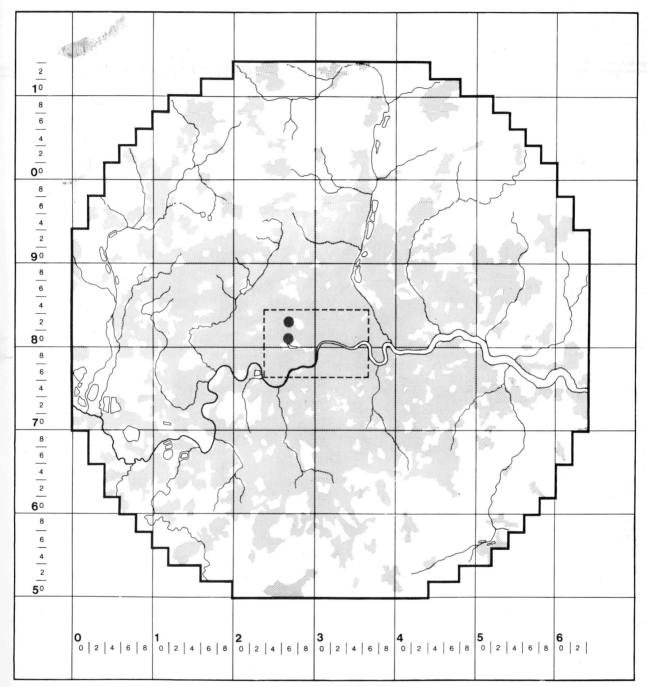

HERRING GULL

Larus argentatus

Since 1963 a small breeding population has become established in Inner London where a pair or two now nest in most years.

This century has seen a massive increase in the wintering and migrant populations of the five species of gulls found regularly in the London Area. In the early years the Herring Gull was rather scarce until numbers began to rise in the 1930s when its breeding population was increasing nationally. Nesting on buildings began to develop widely in the 1940s and roof-top colonies became established in a number of coastal towns (Cramp 1971). Inland sites were colonised from about the same time and the central London records are further evidence of this expansion.

Nesting in London was first recorded in Regent's Park (Wallace 1964). In 1961 and 1962 eggs failed to hatch, but in 1963 three young fledged successfully. Each year the nest site was a mound of artificial rock in the Zoo near the sea-lions and a seabird aviary. A captive flock of several gull species including Herring Gulls, food scraps uneaten nearby and a natural-looking nest site were no doubt major factors in the establishment of this new breeding species in the London Area. Since then birds have nested annually and reared young in at least seven of the thirteen years up to 1973. Four pairs were present in 1968 and the summer flock numbered at least 22 birds in 1973. Birds have nested on buildings within the Zoo as well as on the rock mound and in 1969 a pair bred on the roof of a house in Prince Albert Road just outside the Park. St James's Park has also attracted Herring Gulls. In 1964 courtship, coition and the building of a nest took place, but no eggs or young were seen. At least one pair has taken up territory each year since and nested successfully in six of the ten years up to 1974. These birds have used the pelican rock island, which is again an artificial site with a special food supply.

Birds possibly prospecting for sites were seen in Hyde Park/Kensington Gardens in 1972 and a pair attempted to breed there in 1974, while in 1973 a pair bred successfully on the old War Office building in Whitehall. The only signs of possible breeding recorded outside Inner London have been at the Sevenoaks G.P. reserve where adults have remained until mid-May from 1971 to 1974, though there has not been any evidence of nesting.

In many new roof-top colonies in coastal towns in south-east England numbers have increased to pest proportions (Cramp 1971), but an abundance of food in fishing ports is an attraction which London does not offer. Yet it is surprising that London's population of breeding Herring Gulls has not increased faster or colonised more of the peripheral gravel pits.

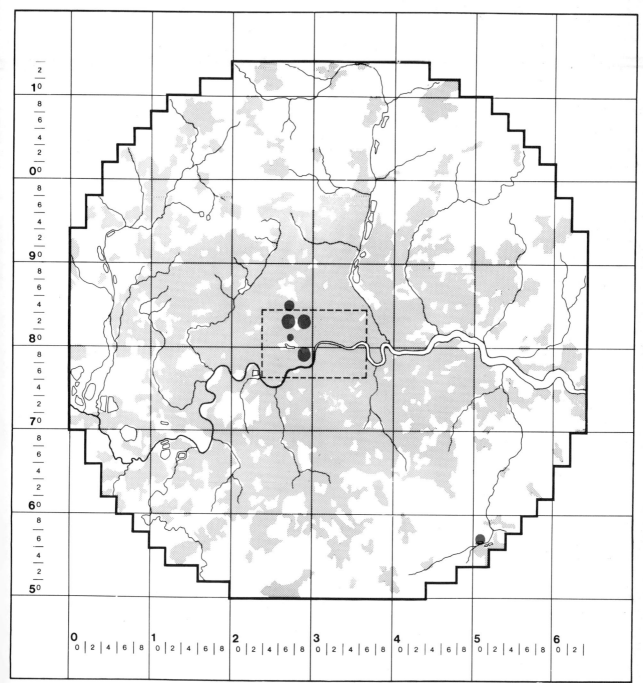

COMMON TERN

Sterna hirundo

Common Terns were first recorded breeding in the London Area in 1958 and since 1963 have nested regularly. Although they are still scarce, the provision of artificial nest sites at Rye Meads from 1972 has resulted in a welcome increase in the number of breeding pairs.

From 1945, and particularly since about 1957, there has been a growing tendency for small numbers to nest inland in eastern England, especially at gravel pits (Parslow). Colonisation of the London Area therefore fits in with this national pattern.

London's first breeding pair in 1958 used the causeway at Queen Mary Reservoir, but the two eggs were destroyed, probably by Grey Herons or Carrion Crows. In the same year a pair was present at Nazeing G.P. though without showing any evidence of nesting. After a gap of three years pairs were present in the summer of 1962 at three localities, the Lea valley, South Weald and South Ockendon, but again no proof of breeding was obtained. Successful nesting was first recorded in 1963 at Cheshunt and, except for 1965, has since continued annually. The total number of breeding pairs and additional pairs known to be present during the summer are shown in Table 6. Nests have generally been built on low islands in gravel pits where changing water levels frequently result in losses through flooding. This was particularly so at Broxbourne gravel pits and led to the scheme for floating rafts covered with shingle to create small artificial islands on water at Rye Meads nearby. A pair of Common Terns quickly took advantage of the first raft in 1972 and successfully reared three young. By 1974 four rafts were in use and a total of 15 pairs of Common Terns fledged 29 young (LVPG).

Apart from South Weald and South Ockendon, all the sites already mentioned are in the Lea valley which is clearly the main breeding area. During the Atlas survey there were also records from the southern part of the Colne valley around Staines, from Swanscombe Marsh and from gravel and sand pit sites at Thorpe, Sevenoaks and again at South Ockendon.

Table 6.   Minimum numbers of pairs of Common Terns recorded breeding or summering in the London Area, 1963-74.

	63	64	65	66	67	68	69	70	71	72	73	74
Breeding pairs	1	1	—	2	4	7	4	11	5	8	17	22
Additional summering pairs	—	1	5	—	1	1	5	1	3	1	—	1
Total	1	2	5	2	5	8	9	12	8	9	17	23
Occupied sites	1	1	3	1	2	3	5	5	4	6	7	7

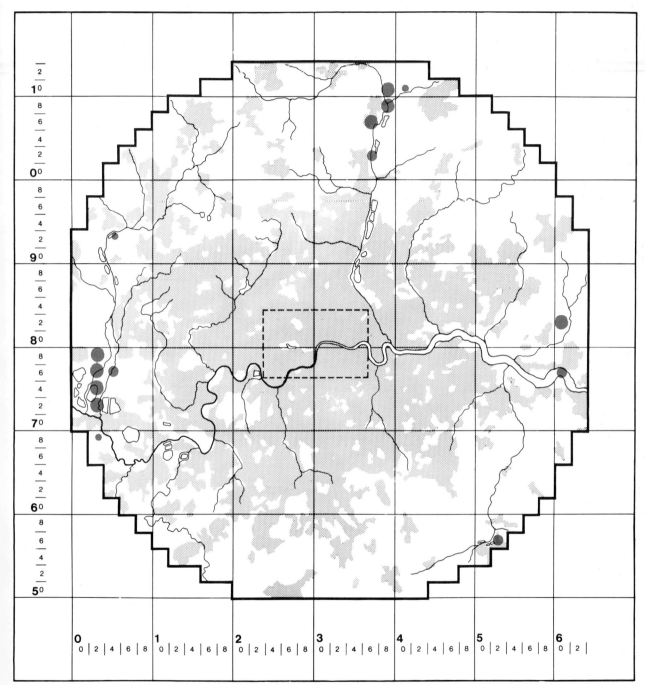

101

STOCK DOVE

Columba oenas

Mainly a bird of rural habitats, the Stock Dove has a wide though discontinuous distribution on the periphery of the London Area having partially recovered from a serious decline in the early 1960s. There are scattered records from the suburbs and it breeds in some central parks.

In the 1950s the Stock Dove was considered a rather local resident, but numerous in some localities such as the Thames marshes between Woolwich and Northfleet where there was a report of 100-150 birds present at Dartford in May 1951. Within ten years, however, numbers slumped and it disappeared from many haunts. The decline started about 1957 and even after some recovery the species does not everywhere appear to have regained its former status, particularly along the Thames where there was a marked absence of records during the Atlas survey.

A similar decline occurred nationally, except in the extreme west and in parts of Scotland, at about the same time (Parslow). Farming practices appear to have greatly affected distribution of the Stock Dove. Firstly the growth of arable farming helped its spread (Murton 1965) and then in recent years intensive use of toxic chemicals probably caused the decline. Evidence of an improvement within the last decade is provided by the BTO Common Birds Census, which shows that numbers on census plots in 1974 were some four times the level of 1964 (B & M 1976).

In Inner London before 1950, Stock Doves nested in Hyde Park/Kensington Gardens and Holland Park and had spread to other parks by 1961, when the population suddenly dropped and there were no reports that year of birds even attempting to breed. Again toxic chemicals were suggested as the cause. Birds from the centre probably obtained their food from open country and were therefore as badly affected as rural birds (Cramp & Tomlins 1966). By the time of the Atlas survey, however, the Stock Dove had returned to Inner London with breeding reports from Hyde Park/Kensington Gardens and Regent's Park.

As the woodland counterpart of the Rock Dove *Columba livia,* the Stock Dove nests mainly in holes in trees, though sometimes on crevices and ledges, in old nests of other birds or the sides of overgrown quarries. Unfortunately many of its primary nesting sites may well disappear with the felling of elm trees affected by Dutch elm disease (Mitchell 1973). Other tree species tend to have fewer holes and large scale destruction of elms could result in increased competition from other hole-nesting birds.

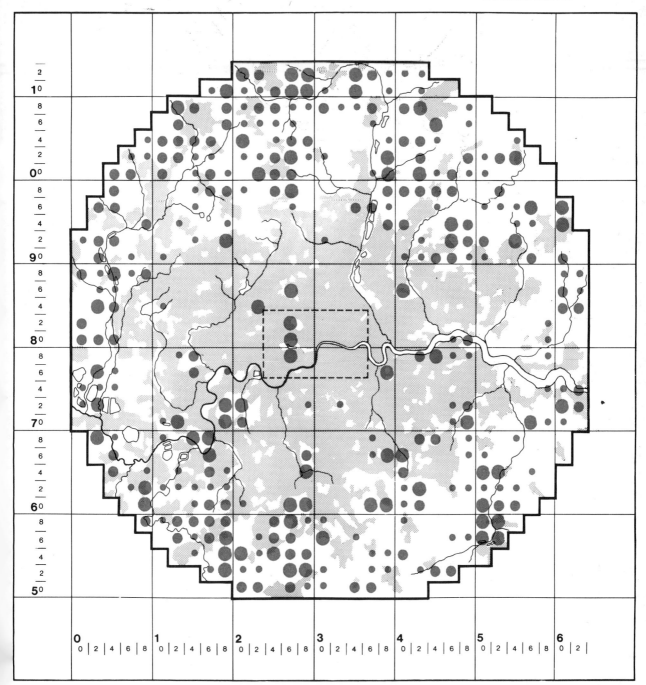

FERAL PIGEON

Columba livia

Familiar to city dwellers, the Feral Pigeon is common in central London and much of the suburbs, breeding in built-up rather than rural areas. It attracts little attention from birdwatchers and while some attempt was made to map distribution during the Atlas survey, the species was clearly under-recorded. Though largely dependent on man for food, it is nevertheless a wild bird and ecologically cannot be ignored.

Even in the last century Hudson (1898) considered Feral Pigeons a nuisance in some parks. As they were bred privately for the table, he was surprised the authorities fed them at public expense. Grain supplied directly or scavenged from feeding horses was probably their staple diet. The disappearance of horse-drawn vehicles, however, had little effect on the Feral Pigeon population, but persecution and lack of food caused a decline during the second world war. Numbers built up again rapidly afterwards and many birds now exist mainly on bread and household scraps, which sometimes cause polyneuritis due to a deficiency of vitamin B (Goodwin 1957). Birds congregate wherever grain is handled commercially, such as near docks and warehouses, and also where it is supplied by sympathetic members of the public, as in Trafalgar Square.

In Inner London numbers may have increased between 1951 and 1965 according to counts in a Bloomsbury square, where more than a threefold increase showed Feral Pigeons some 50% commoner than House Sparrows by 1965, whereas in '1951 they had been outnumbered six to one (Cramp & Tomlins 1966). Counts of feeding birds seemed to give a reliable estimate of local populations as birds were not thought to travel far. A colour ringing study in Hampstead indicated regular feeding stations within half a mile of the nest or roost (Gompertz 1957). No major change in population seems to have occurred recently and attempts at control probably only reduce competition for food, thus giving the remainder a better chance of survival.

Like their ancestor, the Rock Dove, Feral Pigeons are colonial nesters generally occupying dark recesses. The sounds of young in the nest may be heard in any month of the year. Nowhere in London, however, was the species fully reported during the Atlas survey and in Herts it was not plotted by tetrads, resulting in a very incomplete distribution map. Full coverage might well show breeding in every tetrad in Inner London and the built-up suburbs, thinning out through the outer suburbs and becoming scarce in rural areas.

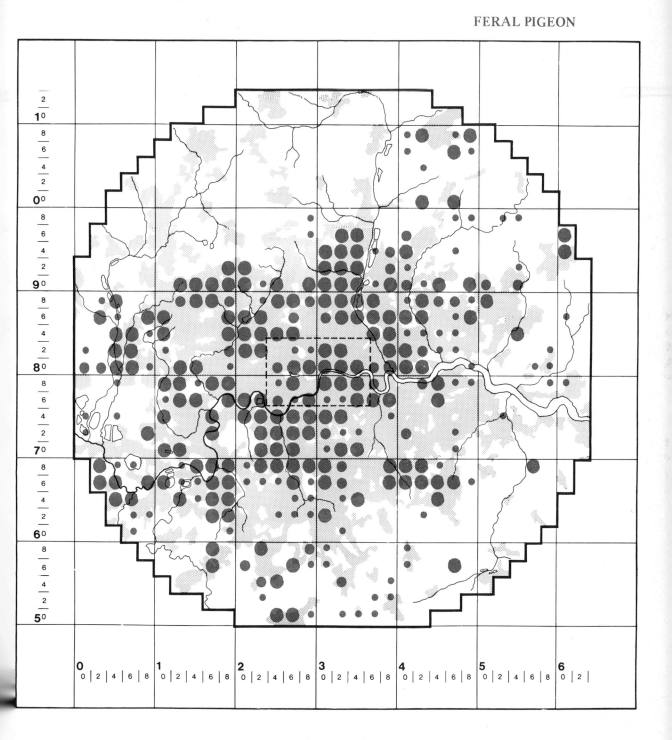

WOODPIGEON
Columba palumbus

This species, which tends to excite comment only by the size of its winter flocks or migratory hard weather movements, is a familiar breeding bird of the London scene. Urban birds are tolerant of man and forage alongside Feral Pigeons, even to the extent reported recently of feeding within King's Cross and Victoria Stations on the tracks and platforms.

In colonising central London in the late nineteenth century, the Woodpigeon has spread from its original woodland habitat, no doubt aided by the existence of parks, gardens and tree-lined roads. Once established, it prospered, except during the second world war when it was controlled by shooting. Numbers have now probably passed pre-war estimates, even allowing for local fluctuations. A decline recorded in Bloomsbury squares between 1962 and 1965 (Cramp & Tomlins 1966) was not reported elsewhere, but in Regent's Park, after an estimate of 100 pairs in 1961 rising to 150 by 1965, a 30%-50% drop occurred by 1968 (Wallace 1974).

Cramp (1972) found that in Inner London the Woodpigeons' diet was mainly bread supplemented by green vegetable matter. This ample food supply throughout the year enables the central population to maintain a longer breeding season and an earlier peak egg-laying period than rural Woodpigeons and may explain why numbers were not reduced by the severe 1962-63 winter. The species in Inner London does not apparently need to fly further out in search of food, except for local movements to areas such as Hampstead Heath for acorns in autumn. It was thus unaffected by toxic chemicals, unlike the Stock Dove and rural Woodpigeon, though the latter soon recovered following a ban on the use of certain chemicals from the beginning of 1962 (Murton 1971).

Usually a tree nester, the Woodpigeon in London often nests on buildings, occupying ledges on facades like those of the Imperial War Museum, Leicester Square Cinema, and also the Natural History Museum where a pair nested at a height of 24m and Imperial College at 58m, both in 1956. In an area in Belsize Park containing 62 similar semi-detached houses, 11 nests were built on drain-pipes in 1962 and 15 in 1963 (Peal 1965). At another unusual site a pair bred successfully in 1965 and 1966 in an underground car park, reaching the nest by way of the ramp used by cars.

During 1968-72 the Woodpigeon showed the expected wide distribution. Breeding was reported from most of the London Area and blank tetrads, most noticeable in the east, were almost certainly due to incomplete coverage. Definite breeding records were fewer in some peripheral areas where nests in the tree canopy are harder to detect. The bird itself is also much warier and more difficult to observe away from towns, where it has less to fear and much to gain from its proximity to man.

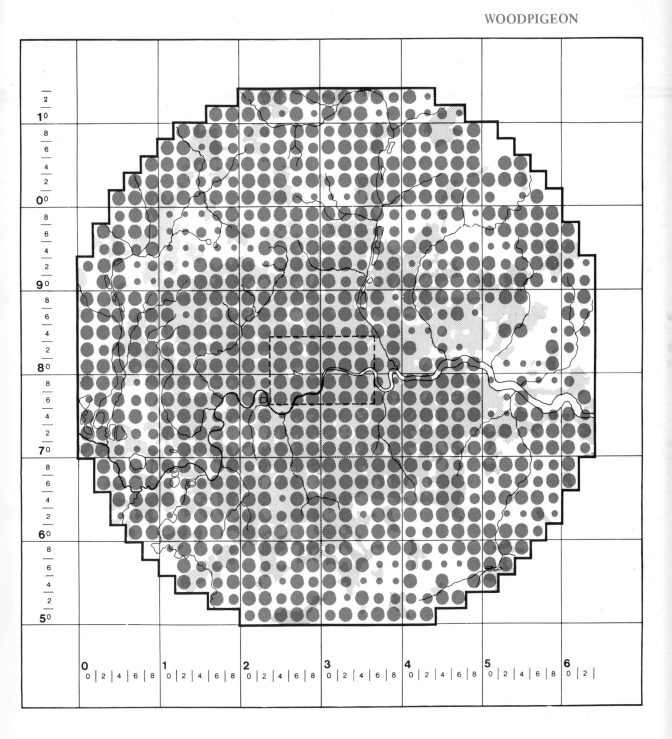

TURTLE DOVE

Streptopelia turtur

Widely recorded in the outer zone, the Turtle Dove is essentially a rural species, but absent from densely built-up areas and probably from south Essex.

Little change in its distribution has been recorded in the present century, except that continued development of suburbia has driven it further from the centre. As with many familiar species it is under-recorded, but it appears to be fairly numerous outside the built-up area, though with local variations. Fewer breeding records were noted in Herts in 1964, for example, and in the same county in 1972 numbers were described as very thin. Yet in that year breeding pairs reached the highest level in nine years at Sevenoaks G.P. reserve and also in scrub and grassland at Bookham where there was a density of 12 pairs in 39ha. Favourite nesting habitat for the Turtle Dove is in bushes or high hedges. At Bookham two unusual nests were found in 1967. One containing two young consisted almost entirely of plastic-covered copper wire and an empty nest nearby was similar except for the addition of some hawthorn twigs.

For the years 1968-72 no breeding records were reported within about 16km of St Paul's Cathedral. The nearest records were from the Bromley Common and Park Langley areas and from Radlett, Waltham Abbey, Hainault and Havering. One or two birds were present in the breeding season in Richmond Park, but nesting was not proved and the inner limit in Surrey was thought to be generally about 24km from the centre at Chessington (Parr 1972).

Surprisingly, Atlas records of the shyer Turtle Dove slightly outnumbered those of the Collared Dove which has become such a familiar sight in recent years. Whereas the Turtle Dove was reported from 455 tetrads, the Collared Dove was recorded in a total of only 392, though relative densities are unknown. The Turtle Dove therefore appears to be more than holding its own in rural areas, but maintenance of its present status will depend largely on preservation of the Green Belt.

Other factors are perhaps also relevant and in Britain the status of the Turtle Dove may be influenced by the distribution of Fumitory, one of its preferred foods, as well as by the loss of nest sites as tall hedgerows disappear (Parslow). Fluctuations could also reflect conditions in its African wintering grounds, though Turtle Doves are thought to winter mainly between $10°$ and $14°$N (Moreau 1972) and appear to have avoided the severe drought conditions that affected the Sahel zone from 1968 to at least 1973 (Winstanley *et al.* 1974).

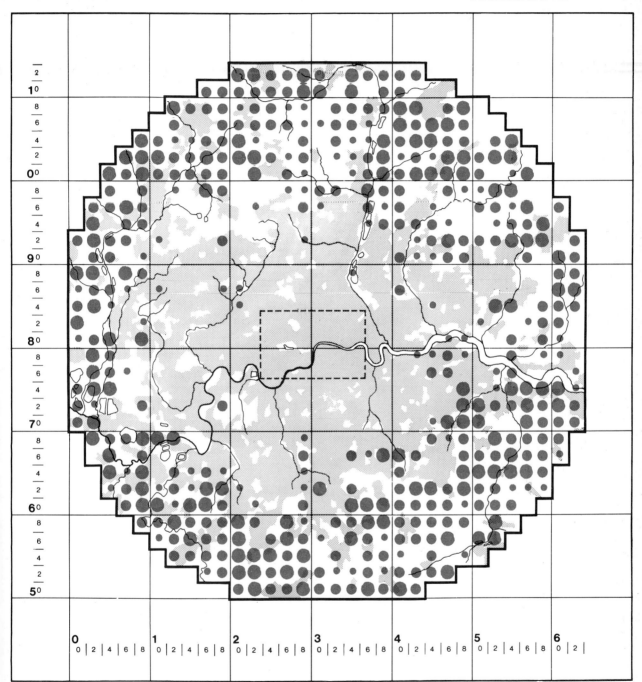

COLLARED DOVE
Streptopelia decaocto

Since first recorded in the London Area in 1957, the Collared Dove has become a familiar breeding bird in the outer suburbs, though it is thinly distributed in rural districts and still absent from the built-up central areas.

Colonisation of London followed a remarkably rapid expansion north-west across Europe from Turkey and the Balkans beginning about 1930. Since the first British sighting in Lincolnshire in 1952 and nesting in Norfolk in 1955, the Collared Dove has spread to most parts of England and much of Scotland, Wales and Ireland (Hudson 1965, Parslow).

An adult at Rye Meads on 23 July 1957 was joined by a second bird in early August and one was seen until September. These constituted the first records for the London Area. The next report was of a flock at Carshalton in late 1961, when birds may also have been present in south-west Middlesex. Breeding occurred in Middlesex in 1962 and in Essex in 1963, when the species was also first reported in Inner London with a single bird in Regent's Park on 2 September. Nesting was confirmed in Surrey in 1964, though it had bred in that county outside the London Area as early as 1960 (Parr 1972), and in Herts and Kent in 1966.

As it became commoner in the London Area interest waned and therefore information about its status diminished, but the rate of expansion appears to have slackened. The Atlas survey thus provides a chance for reappraisal after the initial surge. Breeding records came from 157 tetrads and altogether birds were reported in 392 tetrads. This represents 46% of the London Area and surprisingly is 7% lower than the total for the more rural Turtle Dove. Collared Doves are closely associated with man and quickly take available food such as seeds provided by householders. The main area of distribution is thus in outer suburbs where gardens and tree-lined roads provide nest sites. Most records during 1968-72 were from Kent, Surrey apart from the heaths, and west Middlesex, but were more scattered in Herts and Essex. Records north of the Thames were generally fewer than in the south, but birds bred closer to central London with reports from Barking, Wanstead, Walthamstow and Dollis Hill.

Despite observations in most months, breeding has not been proved in Inner London. In 1975, however, a few wild birds were reported to have been released in one of the Inner London parks. Such introductions are unnecessary for a dynamic species like the Collared Dove though fortunately none appears to have stayed. Had they done so there would then be no way of tracing the species' natural spread in urban London.

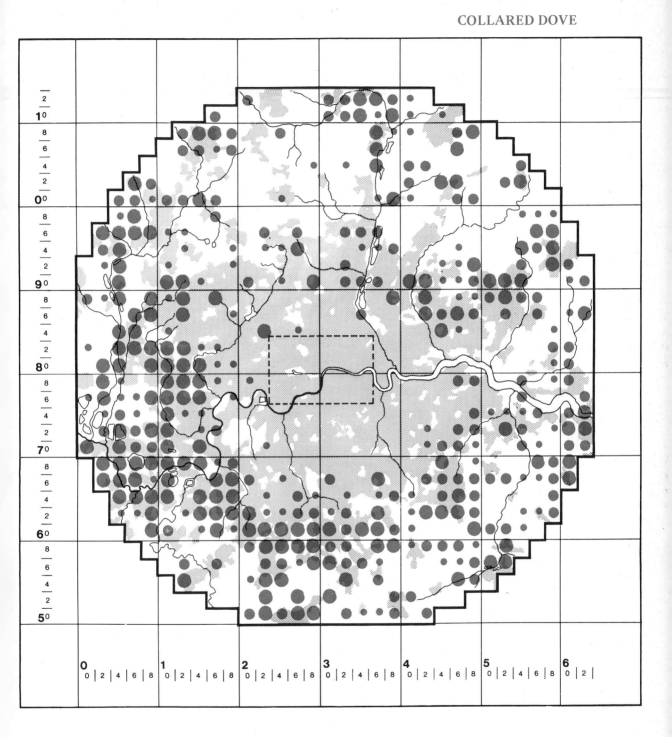

CUCKOO

Cuculus canorus

Although the Cuckoo is a widespread summer visitor to the outer suburbs and rural parts of the Area, its precise status is uncertain. There is no evidence of any major change in the pattern of distribution throughout this century, except that the occasional breeding records from nearer central London now seem to have ceased.

While there have been more frequent references to decreases than increases, comments on population changes for this species remain somewhat contradictory. Numbers at Weybridge, for example, were considered unchanged from 1958 to 1961, but a big decrease was reported in 1964. Yet that was described as a good year in Epping Forest, with nine birds heard in one small area and in Herts 20 were heard calling in Broxbourne Woods. Birds were reported to be numerous in Essex in 1970, a view not reflected elsewhere, and in 1972 some reports referred to the species as rather scarce and others as exceptionally numerous. Inevitably there are variations in observer coverage and such comments can only relate to local areas. Additionally, in a long-distance migrant like the Cuckoo, normal annual fluctuations tend to mask any long-term trends, although Parslow refers to decreases in several areas in England and Wales dating from the 1950s.

There were records from 457 tetrads during the Atlas survey; breeding was reported in only 64 and probable breeding in 265. Many of the latter were based on the presence of singing males, which is an uncertain indication of breeding as females of course may not always be present. Furthermore, in some localities the same bird may have been recorded in more than one tetrad as the far-carrying song could be difficult to plot accurately on a map. Thus a total of 457 occupied tetrads may be high, though on the other hand evidence of breeding from only 64 over a period of five years is surprisingly low.

There is no recent evidence of the Cuckoo's choice of hosts in the Area, but of the records referred to by Homes, 38% related to Dunnocks and 13% to Robins, with the balance accounted for by Reed Warblers, Pied Wagtails and Whitethroats in that order, and a small number of records covering a further 20 species. No decline is apparent in either the Dunnock or Robin, though since about 1968 Whitethroats have been considerably reduced. Foster parents are therefore still readily available and any decline in numbers of Cuckoos seems likely to be attributable to other as yet unidentified causes, including perhaps climatic changes.

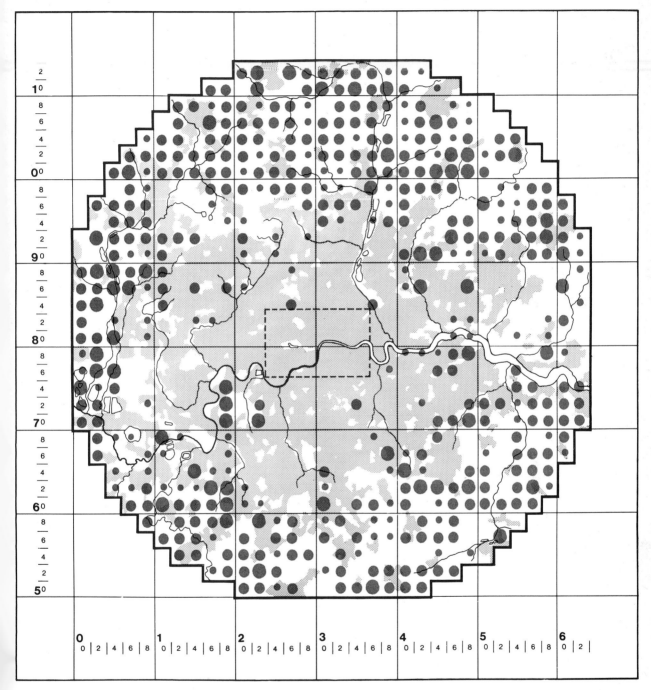

BARN OWL

Tyto alba

The Barn Owl has a somewhat local distribution confined mainly to the outer zone of the London Area, but is apparently absent from much of Kent and Middlesex.

In the early years of this century the Barn Owl was evenly distributed in the rural areas around London, but a marked decline was recorded in the second and third decades. Although still holding its own, at least in Kent, in the 1950s, another even more severe decline followed and there was only one definite breeding record for the whole of the London Area in both 1962 and 1963. Recovery was slow with confirmed nesting at only two sites in each of the next two years, increasing to three in 1966. A survey in 1967 revealed seven breeding pairs and a further 15 tetrads in which birds were present without proof of nesting (Montier 1968). This related just to one year and was thus not wholly comparable with the Atlas project which extended over five seasons. There is little doubt, however, that records during 1968-72 showing breeding in 28 tetrads and probable breeding in a further 20 represent a genuine increase, even if the extent of that increase is somewhat uncertain.

Of the breeding records shown, the nearest to central London was at Richmond Park. Other reports from suburban areas included Osterley Park and near Waltham Abbey, Chigwell and Romford, but generally the Barn Owl favours rural areas, though this does not explain the absence of records from Kent.

Much of eastern England was affected by the fall in numbers in the early 1960s (Prestt 1965). Parslow concluded that loss of habitat was the most likely cause of the long-term decline, though the recovery after 1963 suggests that other factors were involved. Mortality during severe winters like 1947 (Parslow) and 1962-63 (Dobinson & Richards 1964) seriously affected the Barn Owl population and poisoning by agricultural chemicals was considered to be at least a contributory cause.

Unlike the Tawny Owl, the Barn Owl has not adopted city life and therefore has a very restricted distribution in the London Area. It also occasionally suffers from interference in the breeding season from egg collectors and vandals, such as at Collier Row, Romford, in 1971 when a pair's traditional nesting tree was burnt down. Where breeding birds are undisturbed they are now nesting successfully and given adequate protection and mild winters the population may gradually increase, at least in the outer parts of the Area.

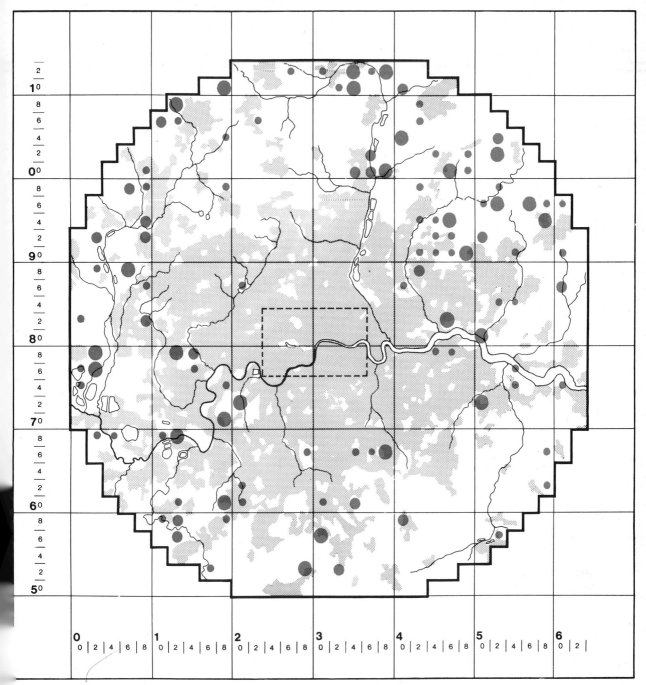

LITTLE OWL

Athene noctua

This resident species is widely distributed over much of the London Area, though it is absent from the more densely built-up habitats.

After its introduction into England at the end of the nineteenth century, the Little Owl appeared to reach its maximum density in the London Area in the 1930s. There followed a decline, attributed to the depredations of gamekeepers, but the species showed evidence of a recovery before the end of the next decade. Later comment is scanty, but in 1961 the species was described as very rare at Ruislip and in 1962 there were only two records in the whole of the London Area. Another noticeable recovery followed and by 1967 breeding records came from 49 localities.

Its decrease in the early 1960s matched the national pattern for this species and Parslow referred to suggestions that the Little Owl may have suffered from the effects of persistent insecticides, though there was no proof of this in the London Area. In some parts of the country numbers have also been reduced during prolonged severe winters, notably that of 1962-63. In London, however, there was an improvement in the number of breeding records following the harsh conditions of that particular winter, but of course observers may have searched more diligently the following season to check the after-effects on local populations.

During the Atlas survey birds were reported as breeding or probably breeding in 161 tetrads. This doubtless exaggerates the extent of any increase in view of the intensive coverage over five seasons. The number of records received in 1973 fell sharply once the impetus of the Atlas project ended, thus emphasising the difficulty of assessing changes on the basis of casual observations. Whatever the magnitude of intervening fluctuations, however, the distribution revealed by the map may not be much different from that of the early 1950s. At that time the nearest breeding locality to central London was Dulwich Woods. Twenty years later the species was still present there, though breeding was not then confirmed. Nearest breeding records to the centre came from Thamesmead, Crossness and Richmond Park. Areas of greatest density were in Herts and Essex, in the latter particularly in the northern part and along the Lea valley. Little Owls appeared to be scarce in south Essex and along the Thames marshes, though lack of records may be due in part to incomplete coverage at a suitable time of day. There was a wide distribution over south-west Surrey, but the gap in the east of that county and the patchy distribution in Kent are both surprising and unexplained.

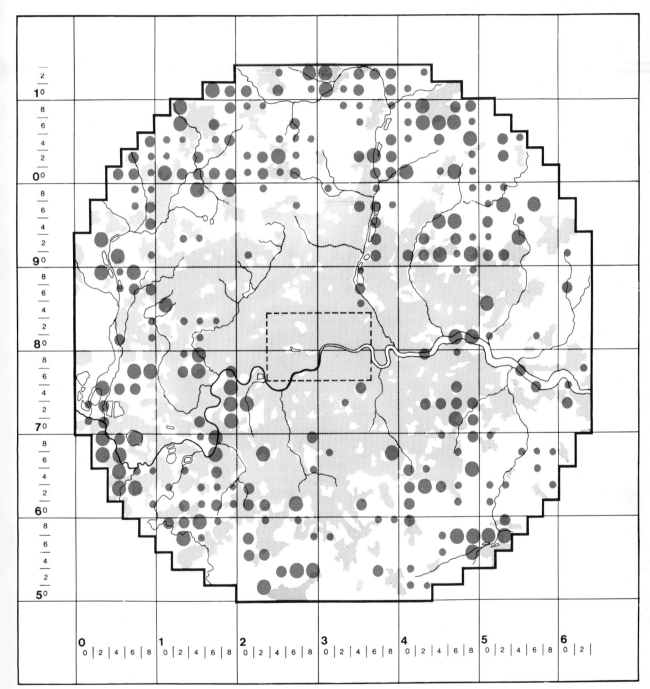

TAWNY OWL

Strix aluco

This is the commonest owl nesting in the London Area and is found in almost all localities except along the lower Thames and the southern slopes of the North Downs.

In 1900 the Tawny Owl was scarcer than the Barn Owl in the London Area, but by the 1930s it was well established. Nationally, numbers increased up to about 1950 (Parslow) and an inquiry by Prestt (1965) showed the Tawny Owl as the most numerous breeding bird of prey in 1963. In rural areas toxic chemicals may have affected it, but this would apply less in suburbs and towns, although a survey of the London Area in 1967 produced only 48 definite breeding records (Montier 1968). This was far fewer than shown by the Atlas survey, but the two studies were not strictly comparable. In view of the owl's sedentary habits and the difficulty of locating nests on private property, records of probable breeding, generally based on birds heard calling, are likely to be good evidence of nesting. On this basis the 1968-72 map shows 374 occupied tetrads, covering 44% of the London Area. There is little recent indication of density, but Richmond Park in 1967 held six definite and a further 13 possible breeding pairs (Parr 1972).

As the only owl to have adopted city life, the Tawny Owl was reported from 14 Inner London localities in 1959 and during 1968-72 records came from 12 of the 16 Inner London tetrads west of St Paul's. Nesting has occurred in most central parks as well as some Bloomsbury and South Kensington squares (Cramp & Tomlins 1966). The species is mostly absent from the eastern central area where open spaces are fewer. Gaps elsewhere may be due to inadequate coverage, as nocturnal species in residential areas are more likely to be recorded than those in less populous spots which may not be visited when owls are active.

While the Tawny Owl prefers to feed on rodents, birds are readily taken and at Holland Park formed over 90% of their diet, with House Sparrows 27%, Feral Pigeons 17% and thrushes and Starlings 37%. At Bookham Common, however, mammals accounted for 90% of their prey (Beven 1965). Pellets collected in Hyde Park/Kensington Gardens and Regent's Park contained mainly House Sparrows, but a Wood Mouse and a Noctule Bat were also found, while at a site in Esher pellets contained a high proportion of frog remains. This ability to exploit available sources of prey and a tolerance of man have no doubt helped the Tawny Owl to succeed in a densely populated environment.

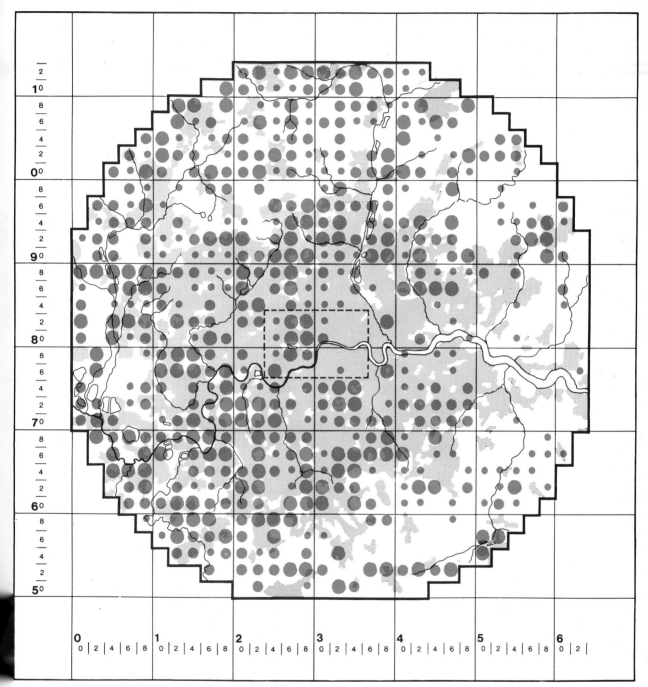

LONG-EARED OWL

Asio otus

Though clearly a very scarce bird in the London Area, the precise status of the Long-eared Owl is uncertain. It is a particularly retiring species, perhaps more so than the other owls, and without a specially thorough search it can easily be overlooked. Yet in spite of the much greater interest in birdwatching in recent years there are still very few reported.

The present distribution of this species appears to be little different from that given by Homes. Having been described as not uncommon in Surrey and west Kent at the beginning of the century, numbers subsequently fell and have remained at a very low level since 1945. There were only occasional records of birds seen in the London Area between 1959 and 1967 and no indication throughout that period that any breeding pairs were present.

During the succeeding five-year Atlas survey breeding was reported from two tetrads and probable breeding occurred in six more, all in the northern part of the Area, though even here there was no certainty that breeding occurred annually. These figures are in contrast to earlier reports which were able to list only three nesting attempts north of the Thames up to 1954. South of the River, the reverse applies and there was only one record during the survey period. Birds have been recorded from Orpington on a number of occasions since the mid-1950s, though without any definite suggestion of breeding. In 1973, after the end of the Atlas survey, a pair bred at Dartford Marsh. This attempt was unsuccessful, however, as the young were taken by boys. One or two birds were seen occasionally in the same locality in the early and late months of 1974, but they were not known to have bred that year.

Parslow referred to a severe decline in the Long-eared Owl during this century over much of the country and thought this might have been attributable to competition from Tawny Owls. Although the latter have increased considerably in the London Area over this period there is no evidence to suggest that they have had any detrimental effect on the London population of Long-eared Owls. It is a species that has a preference for coniferous woods and yet it has signally failed to take advantage of the large increase in such plantations in many of the outer parts of the Area since the second world war.

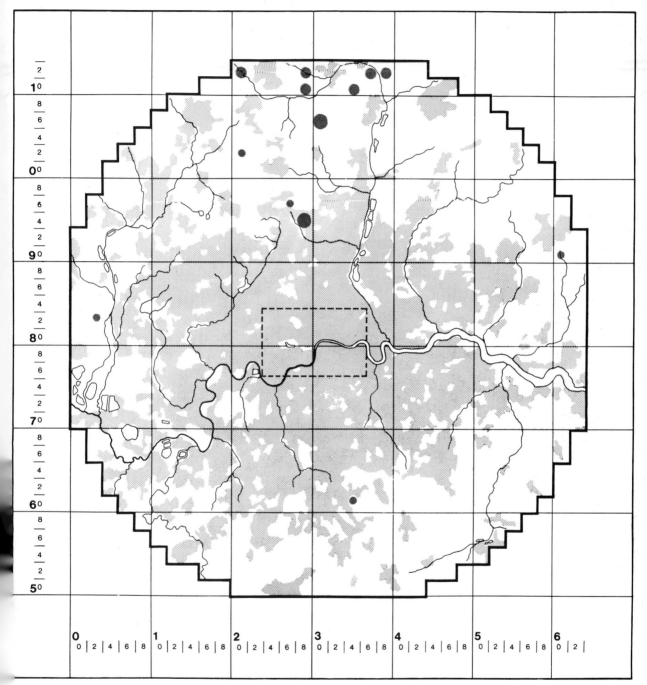

NIGHTJAR

Caprimulgus europaeus

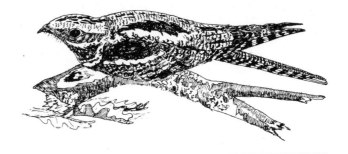

As a scarce summer visitor, the Nightjar has very specific habitat requirements and is thus almost entirely restricted to a handful of commons and young forestry plantations near the periphery of the London Area.

There has probably been a declining population throughout this century and references to an increase after the second world war may simply have reflected a renewal of interest in birdwatching. Since then numbers appear to have been further reduced. For example, in 1963 there were at least 14 pairs in the Broxbourne area, but this was down to five pairs by 1968 and only a single pair was reported in 1972. Similarly there were up to four pairs at Esher Common in the late 1950s, but only one pair a decade later. On the other hand, at Limpsfield up to eight birds were churring in 1972 against two in 1958. Perhaps all such records simply indicate unexplained annual fluctuations rather than an overall trend and one year's figures may not be particularly meaningful. A Nightjar census was carried out in 1958, however, and resulted in reports of about 28 pairs or singing males in some 14 localities. This compares with records during 1968-72 of birds breeding or probably breeding in 23 tetrads, but here again the apparent increase probably does not represent anything more than better coverage during those years.

In the past the Nightjar could be found much nearer the centre of London and as late as 1950 a pair nested, although unsuccessfully, in Richmond Park. It now occurs mainly round the edge of the Area. Broxbourne Woods are still a regular haunt, though the only Atlas record of confirmed breeding north of the Thames was from Coopersale Common in 1969. The species was more widely reported in the south where there were records from the Joyden's Wood area and from Surrey heaths such as Headley, Walton, Banstead and Limpsfield. Birds were also still found at Esher Common and at Prince's Coverts, Oxshott, despite the growth of conifers planted in the late 1940s (Parr 1972).

In reviewing the status of the Nightjar, Parslow noted a general decline in numbers and suggested that climatic changes might be responsible. A trend towards cooler, wetter summers could reduce the supply of moths and other night-flying insects on which it principally feeds. Loss of habitat and human disturbance have also been significant factors (Stafford 1962), particularly in the London Area where the outward spread of suburbia and increasing numbers of visitors trampling over the heaths are a threat to the remaining small Nightjar population.

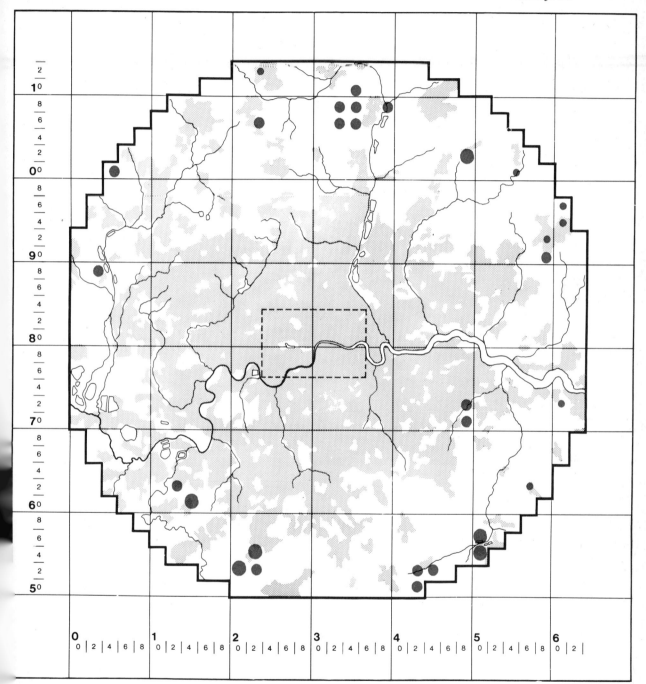

SWIFT

Apus apus

This is a common and widespread summer visitor, absent only from parts of central London and apparently from some of the more rural districts, principally in the east of the Area.

In general the pattern of distribution is not greatly different from that described by Homes, except that there is evidence of an extension of the breeding range into Inner London since the mid-1950s (Gooders 1968). This appears to have continued, with Swifts reported in 1972 and 1973 from three new sites as close to the centre as Bayswater and Islington (Cramp 1975). Apart from these localities, the north and south boundaries of Inner London represent the approximate inner breeding limits and in the west they breed at Hammersmith and Fulham. Few observations are received from the east side of central London and even the five-year Atlas survey produced records from only two tetrads in that urban habitat.

Discussing the breeding habitat requirements of another aerial feeder, the House Martin, Cramp & Gooders (1967) drew attention to the reduction in atmospheric pollution since the introduction of clean air legislation in the 1950s which may have led to an increase in the numbers of flying insects. Gooders (1968) considered this was also relevant for the Swift and showed that both species had penetrated into Inner London along the most noticeable stretch of clean air. He also suggested that, as aerial pollution decreases with altitude, Swifts, which generally feed at higher levels than House Martins, are able to extend their range closer to the centre. In examining distribution by tetrads as in the Atlas survey, small changes in range are not apparent, but the Swifts breeding at Westbourne Grove, Paddington, support this theory.

Apart from food, nest sites are the other obvious requirement for breeding Swifts. Usually, or perhaps invariably in the London Area, they nest in buildings. Victorian and Edwardian houses are often especially suitable, though modern houses are less so. The absence of breeding evidence from the south side of the North Downs and the patchy distribution in Herts and outer Essex can probably be attributed to a lack of suitable buildings for nesting. Blank areas around Rainham and Purfleet are unexplained and may be partly due to inadequate coverage as it seems unlikely that nesting sites there are totally lacking.

Once occupied, nesting sites may continue to be used for many years. One such site in a house in Mill Hill was used for at least forty-three consecutive years up to 1966.

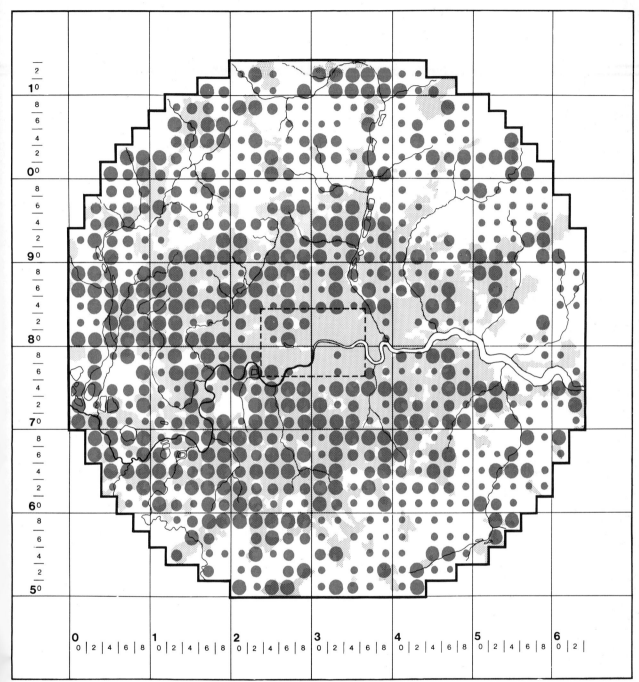

KINGFISHER

Alcedo atthis

Although it has a fairly wide distribution along the rivers and streams of the outer part of the Area, numbers of Kingfishers fluctuate according to the severity of the winters.

In the early decades of this century Kingfishers bred as near the centre of London as Southall, Hampstead, Highgate and the Blackheath, Lee, Lewisham and Bromley districts, but all these localities seem to have been deserted before 1940. Meadows (1972) attributed the absence from inner areas mainly to polluted waters, though building development along some stretches of rivers in suburban areas and occasional culverting to prevent flooding are also likely to have been contributory factors.

As a result of two consecutive severe winters, particularly that of 1962-63, the Kingfisher temporarily disappeared as a breeding species in the Area. A similar collapse occurred widely in Europe, and in England and Wales numbers were reduced to about 5% of previous levels (Dobinson & Richards 1964). With the following series of mild winters recolonisation of former haunts was rapid. Meadows (1972) described the recovery in the London Area and showed that on the Thames and its southern tributaries, principally the Wey, Mole and Darent, numbers appeared to reach a maximum level by about 1968 and on the River Lea about three years later. Table 7 shows that by 1971 there were records of 62 summering Kingfishers in the Area compared with only two birds altogether in 1963.

During the Atlas survey the nearest breeding records to central London were at Edmonton on the River Lea Navigation Canal in 1970 and 1971 and at Walthamstow Reservoirs also in 1971. A pair at Kew Gardens in 1972 excavated a nest-hole, but subsequently deserted. Overall there was evidence of birds breeding or probably breeding from 83 tetrads. Although this was the result of a five-year survey, the total is not too dissimilar from the latest figures shown in the table and probably gives a reasonably accurate indication of distribution, bearing in mind that a continuation of mild winters will have enabled the population to expand further.

Table 7. Numbers of adult Kingfishers recorded in the London Area during April-June (main breeding season), 1963-71 (Meadows 1972)

	63	64	65	66	67	68	69	70	71
River Thames and south of the Thames	2	10	26	17	30	29	16	26	23
North of the Thames	—	10	6	6	7	19	29	24	39
Total	2	20	32	23	37	48	45	50	62

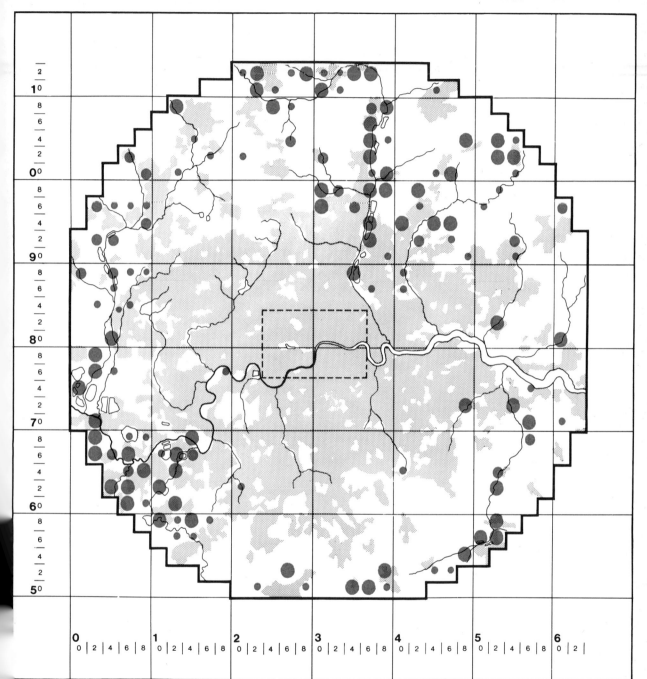

GREEN WOODPECKER

Picus viridis

After a rather slow recovery from the severe winter of 1962-63 when its population plunged to the lowest level for several decades, the Green Woodpecker is now relatively well established in its primary habitats of wooded parkland and deciduous woodlands, but is nowhere abundant, nor has it regained its former status in suburban and marginal habitats.

Apart from temporary fluctuations caused by harsh winters, the Green Woodpecker's distribution has shown little change throughout the century, though the population may have been on a slightly upward trend at least until the mid-1950s when it was probably increasing even in the inner suburbs. In fact a pair bred in Inner London, in Holland Park, between 1952 and 1954. Discussing the increase in London, Fitter (1949) considered a contributory factor had been the ageing of many trees planted in the nineteenth century and which had reached a stage of decay capable of providing insects for food and nesting holes. These changes were also part of a widespread increase in other parts of the country as the species extended its range northwards, possibly aided by reafforestation and an increase in the Wood Ant (Parslow). In the late 1950s the Green Woodpecker was probably affected marginally by toxic agricultural chemicals, but its greatest setback came in the hard winter of 1962-63. For several years afterwards the species was absent from many regular localities in the London Area and some were not recolonised until 1970 or later.

During the Atlas survey there were reports of breeding from 106 tetrads and probable breeding from 153, together amounting to 30% of the London Area. Birds were also reported as present in the breeding season from a further 111 tetrads. As expected, the largest proportion of records was in mainly rural areas, notably in Surrey and particularly in stretches of mixed pasture and woodland. Penetration into the suburbs was most evident in the west, in the parks and commons at Osterley, Kew, Richmond and Wimbledon, all previous strongholds with mature woodlands. Breeding records at Hampstead and Dulwich showed isolated inroads into the inner suburbs, but the species is now absent from the centre and there is no indication that the earlier nesting records from Holland Park will be repeated.

Since 1962-63 there has been a long series of mild winters allowing the population to recover, but the Green Woodpecker's preference for ground feeding, often at the nests of Meadow Ants, and away from woodland clearly makes it vulnerable to severe weather conditions.

128

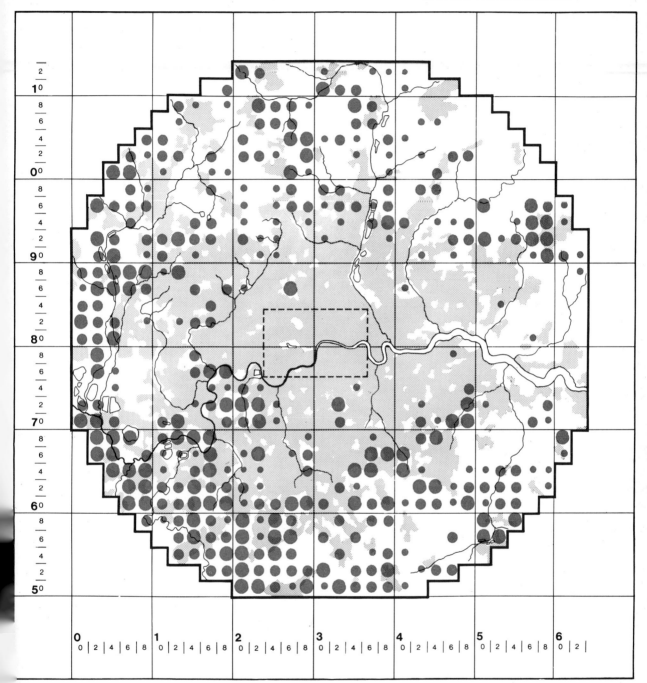

GREAT SPOTTED WOODPECKER

Dendrocopos major

This species is widespread throughout much of the London Area, except in the relatively treeless parts of south Essex and the Thames marshes.

Until the beginning of this century, the Great Spotted Woodpecker was comparatively scarce, but by 1954 it had so increased that it had colonised several London parks and had become as common or commoner than the Green Woodpecker in wooded areas. This was especially so in Surrey, where before 1910 it had been rare (Parr 1972). Though subject to local fluctuations, this period of expansion may be continuing in the outer suburbs and rural parts of the London Area. The national population trend has shown a similar overall increase and expansion of range without any subsequent marked decline (Parslow). As a woodland species finding much of its food on trees, it survived the severe 1962-63 winter better than the Green Woodpecker. It is also less wary of man and thus readier to visit bird tables, which is an advantage to a suburban population in cold weather.

During 1968-72 breeding was recorded in 162 tetrads and probable breeding in 124, totalling 33% of the Area. Thus the Great Spotted has a slightly wider distribution than the Green Woodpecker and is also probably more numerous, though the maps of course give no indication of density. In Surrey and much of Kent the Great Spotted Woodpecker is widespread; north of the Thames distribution is more patchy. Blank tetrads in the east are areas where coverage was less complete, though lowland Essex and land bordering the Thames also hold fewer woods or wooded parks.

In central London, where the species has never been common, breeding numbers in the Inner London parks have dwindled. Last records of breeding in Regent's Park were in 1961 (Wallace 1974) and as early as 1956 in Kensington Gardens, where birds were forced to abandon the site after tree-felling in 1954 (Sanderson 1968). It held on longer in Holland Park where there was one pair breeding or possibly breeding in most years up to 1965. Though birds have been seen regularly since then and hole-making has occurred, no further definite proof of nesting has been obtained. The species could be on the point of recolonising Kensington Gardens, however, as a pair held territory there in 1976 and possibly nested. Juveniles are sometimes seen in the parks, but they may simply represent post-breeding dispersal of birds reared outside the Inner London boundary.

There does not appear to be any cause for concern about the status of the Great Spotted Woodpecker over most of the London Area, but the position in the centre is uncertain. Perhaps its recent reappearance in Kensington Gardens will lead to a further period of regular breeding in the Inner London parks.

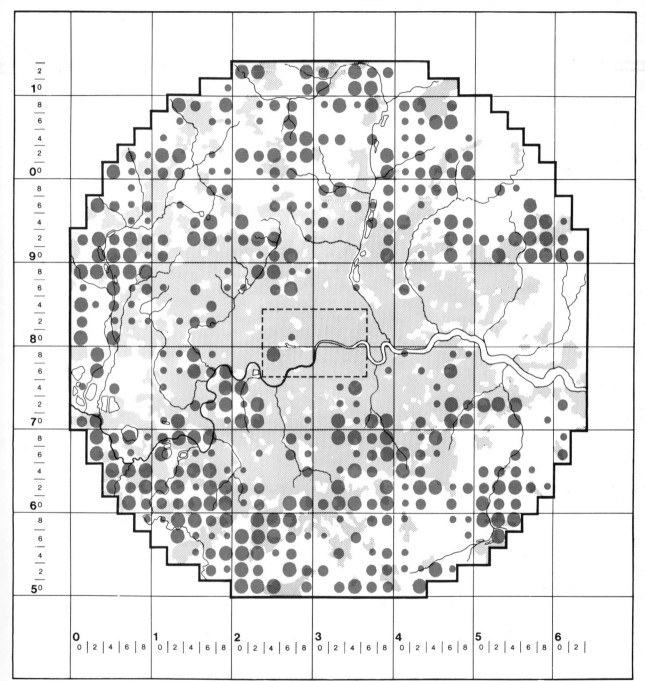

LESSER SPOTTED WOODPECKER

Dendrocopos minor

This elusive species is considered widespread but not numerous in rural parts of the London Area, especially Surrey, and it is also present in wooded parks and gardens in suburbia. In Inner London it is seen occasionally, but only outside the breeding season, as in 1976, when it was recorded in Hyde Park/Kensington Gardens at both ends of the year.

Homes described the relative scarcity of the Lesser Spotted Woodpecker compared with the other two woodpeckers in the London Area, though this centred on the rapid increase of the latter rather than on any decline of the first. The general impression for the Lesser Spotted of an apparently stable population seems to match the national pattern shown by Parslow. Between 1954 and 1960 there were few comments on the status of this species in the London Area, but since 1960 the number of breeding or suspected breeding pairs has risen from six in 1962 to 26 in 1967, when reports came from 15 localities with an inner limit of Brent Park, Hampstead Heath, Hayes Common, Wimbledon Common and also Richmond Park where there was a minimum of seven pairs. There is no indication that the hard winter of 1962-63 greatly affected this species.

Probably because of improved coverage, the increase in reports continued throughout the Atlas survey. Records averaged 34-35 pairs annually, with Surrey still the stronghold. Suburban habitats elsewhere included Petts Wood, Kelsey Park, Dulwich, Osterley Park and Perivale. Atlas records came from 228 tetrads, of which 63 showed evidence of breeding and 76 of probable breeding, together amounting to 16% of the London Area. A comparison of the three woodpecker maps thus confirms the view that the Lesser Spotted is the least common. This species, however, is easily overlooked as it tends to remain hidden in the side branches and canopy of trees, though at Berrylands S.F. in 1964 two birds were seen feeding on dead, insect-covered plants of Mugwort and Hogweed.

The Lesser Spotted's inconspicuous behaviour may explain the gaps in parts of the London Area. Yet a thorough search can produce surprising results. Following a 1967 report from Richmond Park that it may have outnumbered the Great Spotted and possibly the Green Woodpeckers, a careful record was kept for the Epsom, Ashtead and Oxshott areas during 1969 and sightings totalled 31 for the Lesser Spotted, 26 for the Great Spotted and 14 for the Green. Other studies in Surrey, however, still showed the Lesser Spotted as the least numerous on Common Birds Census plots (Parr 1972). Such variations suggest there may be scope for investigation into its true status.

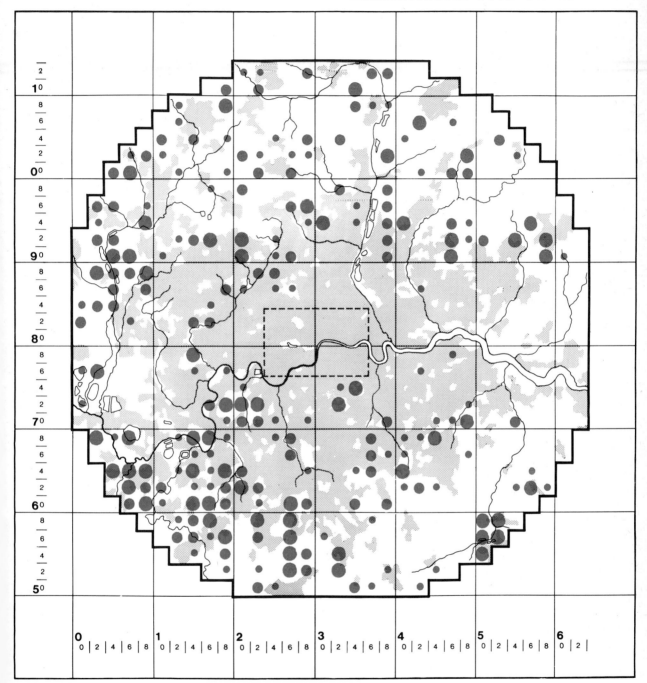

WRYNECK

Jynx torquilla

By 1973 the breeding population of Wrynecks in the London Area was believed to be down to only two pairs, one in Herts and one in Kent. There was no evidence of breeding in 1974 and the Kent site at least may have been deserted. In the absence of any nesting records from other parts of England and Wales, the two London localities may be the last to be occupied in southern Britain, though recent records from Scotland suggest that the species might successfully establish a foothold in the north.

Yet the Wryneck has not always been a rarity. Less than a hundred years ago it was relatively common, breeding in most English and Welsh counties. Since then its range has contracted and its numbers have decreased drastically (Monk 1963, Parslow). A similar decline is also occurring in many countries of western Europe (Peal 1968).

In the London Area, at the turn of the century, it was still a fairly numerous breeding species in the outer suburbs and surrounding country. It frequently nested in large suburban gardens and bred at Hampstead regularly until 1908. Elsewhere it persisted in some suburbs until 1915 and later, holding on much longer in rural areas where regular breeding localities were occupied well into the 1940s. By the mid-1950s it was becoming rare with breeding limited to a handful of scattered pairs.

During the 1960s the number of pairs reported in the London Area during the breeding season reached 17 in 1964 and 15 in 1965, but proof of nesting was scarce and in most years the records were far fewer. Tracing the subsequent decline is made more difficult by the reluctance of observers to publicise breeding sites and by the secretive nature of the species itself. The Atlas survey, however, confirmed the scarcity and showed that the main stronghold at that time was centred on the gravel terrace heathland and orchards of north-west Kent where birds probably bred annually until 1973. A Herts locality was occupied, again probably annually, up to 1973, but the breeding record from Surrey, from Warlingham in 1968 (Parr 1972), appears to have been the last for that county.

No biological or climatic evidence has been found to explain the Wryneck's decline in Britain. Neither its dependence upon insectivorous food, mainly ants, nor its preference for nesting in orchards seems related to such a long-term trend. Competition with other hole-nesting species could be a factor or perhaps there could be some, so far, unknown evolutionary change that requires a closer study of the ecology of the Wryneck, in both its breeding range and wintering quarters.

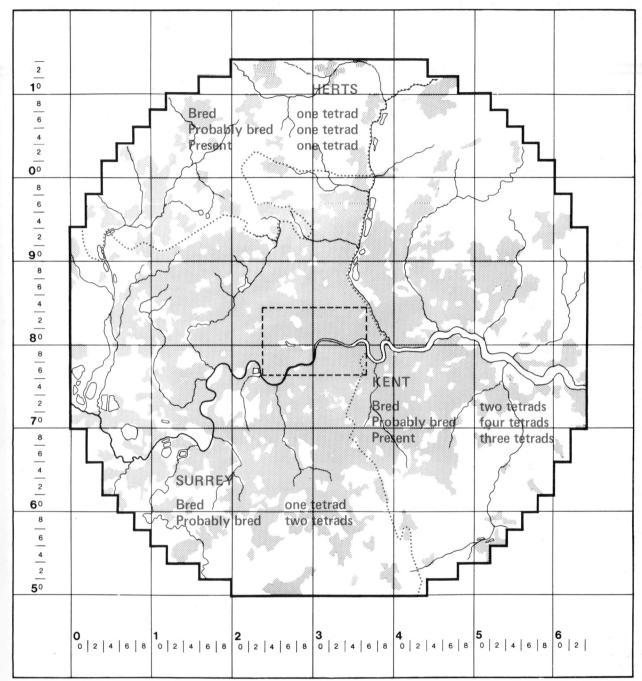

HERTS

Bred   one tetrad
Probably bred   one tetrad
Present   one tetrad

KENT

Bred   two tetrads
Probably bred   four tetrads
Present   three tetrads

SURREY

Bred   one tetrad
Probably bred   two tetrads

135

WOODLARK

Lullula arborea

As a gradually disappearing species in the London Area, the Woodlark is now very little recorded and breeding was reported from only three tetrads during the five years of the Atlas survey.

There were few reliable breeding records in the early years of this century, though small colonies existed in the south-east of the Area and a pair nested in Herts in 1915. Recolonisation began in the 1920s and the pattern of fluctuations between 1924 and 1957 has been described by Harrison (1961). Over the fifteen years up to 1938 annual records of pairs or single birds, mainly singing males, reached a maximum of about nine, but numbers dropped again at a time of several severe winters and the next breeding record was not until 1944. This marked the beginning of a dramatic increase to a peak by 1950 of about 47 breeding season records. Such success, however, was disappointingly short-lived. After 1952 a decline commenced from which the species has never recovered and by 1954 reports of occupied territories did not exceed 25. Subsequent data are summarised in Table 8, which shows that even the Atlas survey failed to produce more than a scattering of Woodlark records.

Climatic conditions may have a marked effect when numbers are already low and the Table suggests that the winter of 1962-63 struck the final blow to London's already greatly diminished population. Nonetheless the Woodlark's decline between 1952 and 1962 and failure to recover after 1963, both periods of mild winters, imply that other factors are operating. Fluctuations in London correspond with the national pattern, particularly in the south of England (Parslow). Viewed in this wider context, the decline may be connected with a contraction of the Woodlark's European breeding range, of which Britain is on the north-western edge.

Ideal Woodlark habitat in England has consisted of sandy heaths with heather and scattered trees, but Chalk downland and even rough grassland in clay areas have been occupied. Such habitats, often protected as Green Belt land, are still available for the species in the London Area should the Woodlark ever show signs of re-establishing its former range.

Table 8.　Minimum numbers of Woodlarks known to be present in the London Area during May-July (main breeding season), 1955-74

	55	56	57	58	59	60	61	62	63	64	65	66	67	68	69	70	71	72	73	74
Breeding pairs	9	1	7	8	—	—	1	5	—	—	1	—	—	—	1	—	2	—	—	—
Additional pairs or singing males	12	12	8	9	9	10	6	3	3	—	1	1	3	2	—	—	—	1	—	—
Total	21	13	15	17	9	10	7	8	3	—	2	1	3	2	1	—	2	1	—	—
Occupied sites	12	6	10	9	6	?	6	5	1	—	1	1	2	2	1	—	2	1	—	—

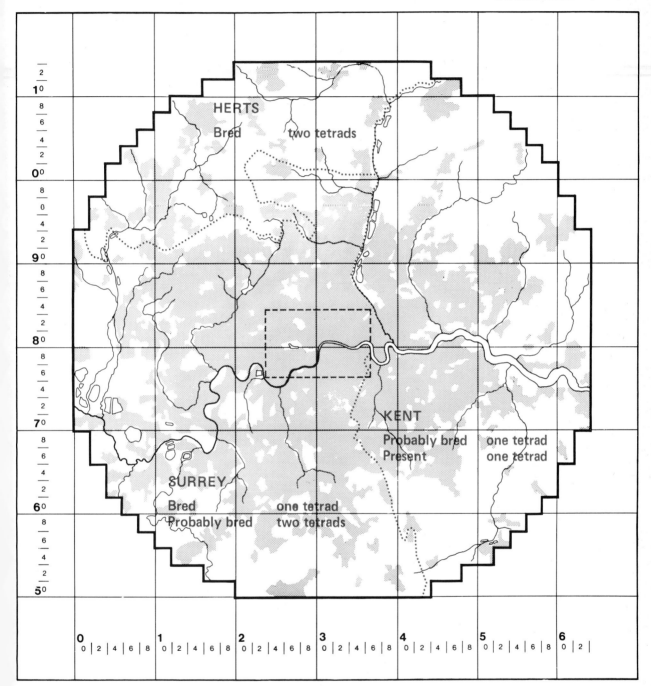

HERTS
Bred   two tetrads

SURREY
Bred   one tetrad
Probably bred   two tetrads

KENT
Probably bred   one tetrad
Present   one tetrad

SKYLARK

Alauda arvensis

Take almost any arable field or uncut grassland and there the Skylark is likely to find a nesting site. As such areas become scarcer, the species, though still widespread, is retreating towards the outskirts of the London Area.

It is frequently seen in central London outside the breeding season, but the main interest for this survey lies in its inner breeding limits. Sites occupied in the 1950s included Wimbledon Common, Wormwood Scrubs and Hampstead Heath, while Simms (1962) recorded breeding on Dollis Hill during the same period. Since then the position has been poorly documented until the Atlas survey. Beddington S.F. held 14-15 pairs in 1954-55 (Milne 1956) and Rye Meads nine pairs in 1961 (Gladwin 1963), but otherwise breeding was considered hardly worth comment. An exception was in 1960 when two pairs, one of which bred and reared young, were present at Old Ford, near Bethnal Green, in a site only 1.2km from the Inner London boundary and surrounded by factories and goods yards.

Although Skylarks feed among growing crops, there was no evidence that the species suffered any serious losses from pesticides in the London Area. Potts (1970) found the main food of the Skylark in west Sussex was coleoptera, especially *Feronia melanaria,* a predator of the soil fauna, so that the species was unaffected by herbicides. A temporary setback, however, was caused by the hard winter of 1962-63 with reports in the London Area of decreases in Surrey and on the North Downs.

Parslow found that distribution of the Skylark has remained largely unchanged over the country as a whole and in the London Area, when the Atlas survey obliged observers to take stock of the species, it was shown to be still nesting widely outside the built-up zone. Breeding records nearest the centre of London were from the Brent Reservoir and Willesden area, the Lea valley as far south as Hackney, Richmond Park, Wimbledon and Surrey Docks. The blank tetrads away from the centre, largely in Essex and Kent, were probably due to lack of coverage rather than other factors. As with most species, fluctuations from unknown causes sometimes occur, but observations indicate that because of man's activities nesting has diminished over the years at such sites as Cassiobury Park where excessive mowing of the grass has reduced the amount of suitable habitat (Magee 1972). On the other hand, the closing of Surrey Docks provided a new site where, in 1971, the presence of three breeding pairs and a recently fledged juvenile provided the first record of nesting in Inner London.

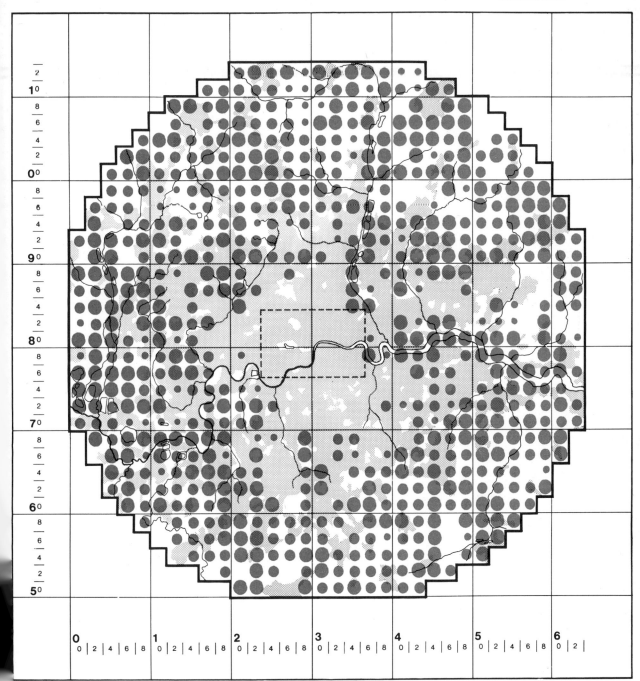

SWALLOW

Hirundo rustica

This summer visitor has a wide distribution throughout suitable areas of open countryside around London. In the suburbs its range is more fragmented, but it is likely to be found wherever sufficient open ground exists, with buildings to provide nest sites, and particularly where there is water and an expanse of natural vegetation to provide an abundant supply of insect food.

The inner breeding limits of the Swallow have been steadily pushed outwards by the spread of London. At the beginning of the century it was nesting in inner suburbs such as Neasden, Wembley, Hornsey, Wood Green, Stratford, Dulwich, Streatham, Barnes, Chiswick and Acton, while it was described as common in Willesden, Finchley and Enfield. There is insufficient present information to judge whether its numerical status has suffered to any marked extent, but while it still nests in Finchley and Enfield, for example, it could now hardly be described as common in those localities and elsewhere the inner limits have moved slightly further out. The Atlas map, however, suggests that there have not been any particularly far-reaching changes in distribution.

Less widespread than the House Martin in the London Area, the Swallow nests on ledges, usually inside buildings such as barns and sheds, and it is unlikely to find sites as readily as the House Martin which builds on the outside walls. Over the five-year survey period, Swallows bred in 454 tetrads, probably bred in 71 and were recorded in the breeding season in a further 146 tetrads. This total of 671 represents 78% of the London Area.

In recent years there have been indications of a small but significant return to some inner suburbs. During the Atlas survey nesting records came from areas such as Walthamstow Reservoirs and Wimbledon, and also Hampstead Heath in 1969 for the first time since 1952. The most notable record, however, was of a pair which nested successfully and reared at least two young in Regent's Park in 1968, the first in Inner London for exactly sixty years.

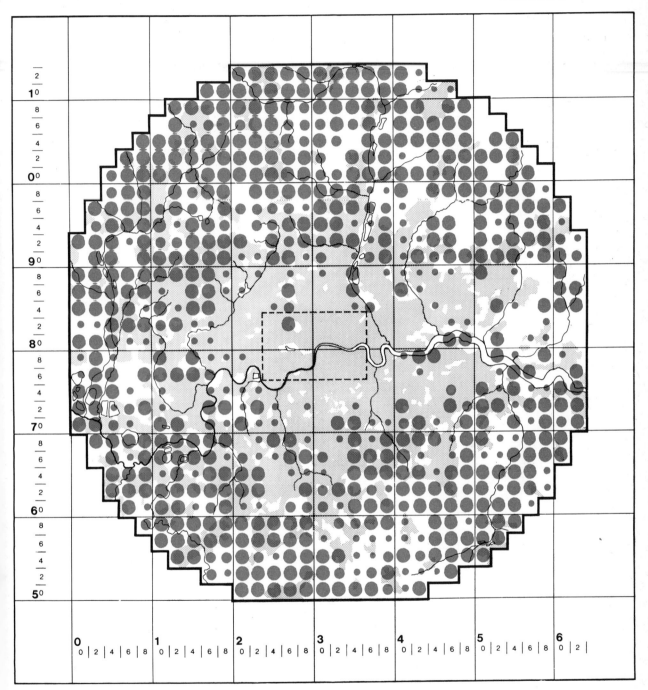

HOUSE MARTIN

Delichon urbica

The House Martin is widespread and quite common in the outlying parts of the London Area, specially in some rural towns and villages. It occurs more widely in the suburbs than the Swallow, and in and around Inner London an encouraging come-back in recent years is still continuing.

Earlier this century the House Martin was declining in London and its inner breeding limits gradually receding. By the early 1950s, however, there were signs of a recovery. Breeding was reported from Highgate in 1952 after an absence of fifteen years and from Tooting in 1953 where nesting had not been reported since the 1930s. These records appear to have been the beginning of a general expansion in the Area. Numerical data to confirm this are lacking, but the distribution shown on the map suggests a consolidation of range compared with the earlier position.

Details of colonies in the inner suburbs and Inner London are more complete than for elsewhere and show clearly a remarkable recolonisation, including a return to Inner London where breeding in 1966 was the first to be recorded since 1889. The pattern of spread based on Cramp & Gooders (1967) and Atlas data for 1968-72 is shown in Table 9.

House Martins also appear to have increased in numbers, at least in central London. The original colony in St John's Wood rose from six nests in 1966 to 25 in 1972, and in Fulham birds have moved into at least two more roads since 1969. In the east of Inner London breeding was reported in 1969, 1970, 1972 and 1973, the number of nests increasing from one to four, and in 1973 nesting was also recorded in Islington.

Parslow found no significant increase or expansion nationally, which suggests that local factors have applied in central London. One reason put forward by Cramp & Gooders (1967) was that reduced smoke concentrations resulting from the smokeless zone legislation had possibly led to an increase in the number of flying insects available as food. Mud for nest-building is also important for House Martins and the extensive rebuilding in many parts of London, which often left open ground exposed for many months, may have provided accessible sources of material.

Table 9.   Increase in House Martin distribution in part of central London shown by total number of tetrads (4km^2) in which breeding recorded in 1945-49, 1960-66, 1968-72

10-km sq/(total number of tetrads covered by earlier surveys)	TQ28/ (25)	TQ38/ (25)	TQ48/ (10)	TQ27/ (25)	TQ37/ (25)	TQ47/ (10)	Total
1945-49 (Cramp & Gooders 1967)	–	–	–	6	–	–	6
1960-66 (Cramp & Gooders 1967)	6	2	–	10	4	3	25
1968-72 (Atlas data)	14	9	3	18	7	8	59

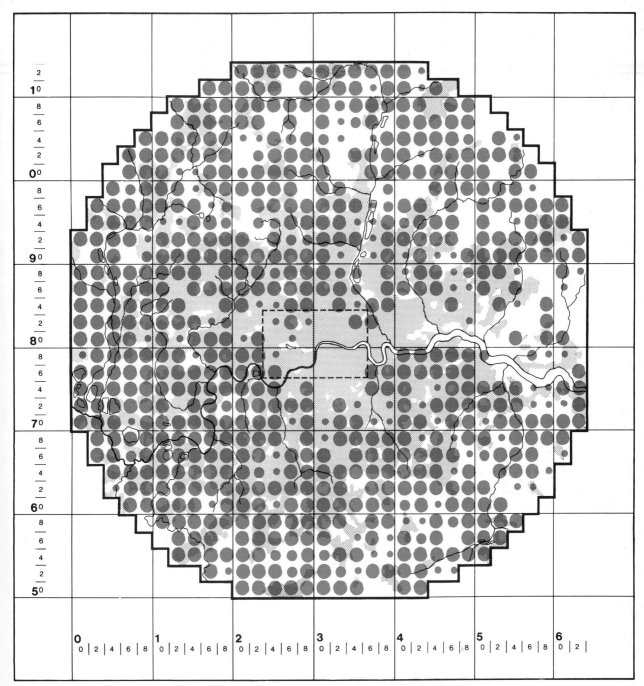

SAND MARTIN

Riparia riparia

Although the least numerous of the hirundines in the London Area, the Sand Martin is relatively common in localities where its specialised nest site requirements can be met.

Nau (1961) listed breeding colonies in 39 tetrads in the London Area in 1960. For the Atlas survey breeding was reported from 106 tetrads. Some of the apparent increase could be due to better coverage obtained during 1968-72, but at the same time the Sand Martin might have been expected to benefit from the growth of mineral extraction which provides additional nesting sites in the resulting cliff-faces. Other reports, however, suggest that the Sand Martin has seriously declined in this country, possibly through climatic changes south of the Sahara (Mead & Pepler 1975). Certainly peak counts of migrants over Staines Reservoir have indicated a drop in numbers. Annual coverage may not have been consistent, but records of 3,000-5,000 birds in 1968 and 1969 fell to 700 in 1971 and in 1972 no large numbers were reported in either spring or autumn. There are no current breeding figures to show the extent of any decrease in the London Area and a repeat of the 1960 survey might be advisable, provided the effects of habitat changes could be assessed.

Human activity is of prime importance in the ecology of Sand Martins in the London Area. This century the only known natural nesting site was in a sandy bank of the Thames near Shepperton. Man-made sites have included drainage pipes in walls or banks near water. One at King George V Reservoir and another in the banks of the Grand Union Canal at Harefield, both still occupied in 1960, had been in use probably since 1918 and 1919 (Nau 1961). Sand, gravel and chalk pits, however, are by far the commonest habitats, especially when near or containing water. In working pits, excavation often renders sites unsuitable and pit banks crumble through natural erosion, resulting in a regular changeover of breeding areas. Nau (1961) put the rate of turnover of colonies at 6.5% per annum.

Atlas reports came from only 178 tetrads, 21% of the London Area, and the map reflects the restricted habitat preferences of the species. Obvious concentrations are in the valleys of the Lea and Colne and in low-lying areas where there is quarrying. Along the southern edge of the Area sand pits of the Lower Greensand provide suitable habitat. The Sand Martin's tolerance of industrialised areas is illustrated in such localities as the lower Lea valley where colonies lie just outside Inner London, and at Bow Creek a little to the east.

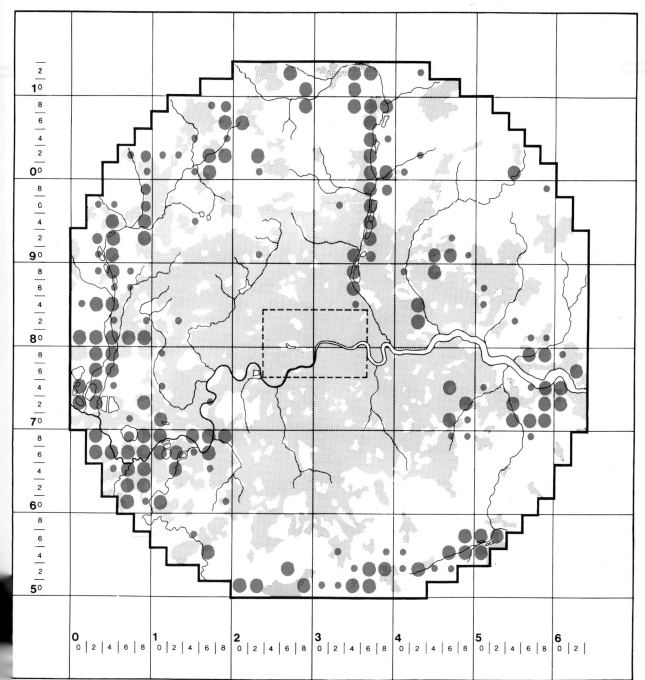

CARRION CROW

Corvus corone

This is one of the most widespread species, breeding throughout the London Area, even in the centre, wherever there are trees for nesting and open grass areas to provide feeding grounds.

There has been a general expansion in the Carrion Crow population during this century, largely as a result of a reduction in persecution. In the early 1950s the species was common in all parts of the Area except where open spaces were few, as in some built-up localities. Since then there may have been further growth in the population in outlying areas like Surrey, which produced three reports of increases in 1970, and, in addition, numbers in Inner London have risen significantly. Thus the situation in London conforms to the national picture, which also showed a marked increase over the whole of the species' British range during the fifty years up to the early 1960s and especially during the last thirty years (Parslow).

Evidence of the adaptability of the Carrion Crow and its success in man-made habitats is shown on the map·by its almost continuous distribution across the London Area. Many of the gaps appear to be mainly due to incomplete coverage, except in Inner London where its absence from some tetrads is the result of a lack of suitable areas for feeding and nesting. Summarising its status in Inner London for the period 1951-65, Cramp & Tomlins (1966) found it to be thriving, with pairs nesting in parks as well as some of the squares and other open spaces. There were signs of a slow increase during the period and by 1965 there were probably between 30 and 50 pairs in the 103.6km^2 of central London. During the Atlas survey, the Carrion Crow was reported as breeding in 15 of the 24 tetrads wholly or mainly within the Inner London boundary and in only three of the remaining central tetrads was it not recorded during the summer. Not surprisingly its strongholds in such an urban habitat are in the parks, and during the Atlas years up to ten pairs nested in Regent's Park and between 11 and 15 each year in Hyde Park/Kensington Gardens.

As the population has increased in more rural parts birds may have been forced to move into suburban and urban habitats previously unoccupied, so that pressure of numbers could be contributing to the growth within the built-up areas where persecution could never have been a material factor. Nevertheless Carrion Crows clearly require little in the way of specialised habitat and the height at which they nest provides them with a considerable degree of protection from disturbance.

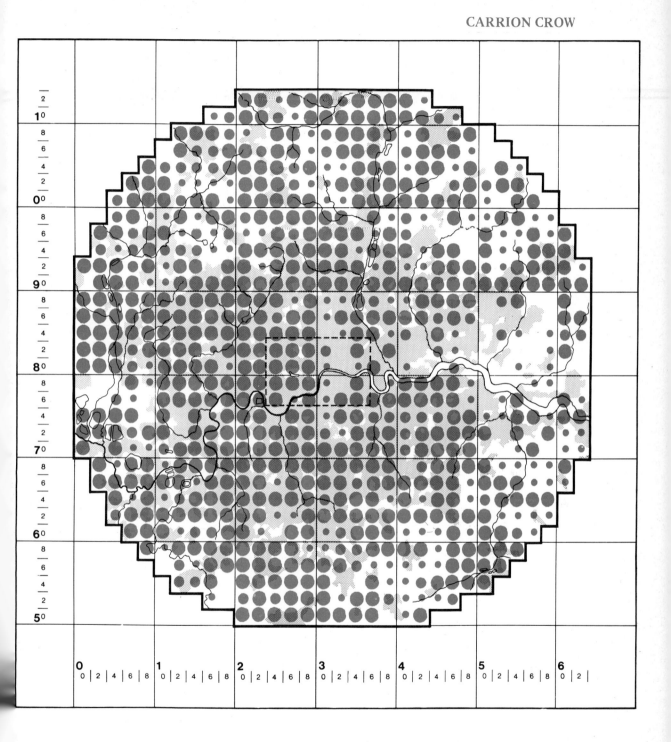

ROOK

Corvus frugilegus

In contrast to the Carrion Crow, the Rook seems to be declining, though it still occurs widely in the open countryside around London. Within the suburbs its range is more fragmented and few rookeries remain inside a radius of 18km from the centre.

With the growth of London's human population and expansion of the built-up area, the inner breeding limits of the Rook have been pushed steadily outwards. At the beginning of the century it still bred in Inner London, the last record being in 1916 when four pairs nested in a plane tree in the Temple. Felling of trees hastened its extinction in the centre, but the ultimate reason, as London grew bigger, was the lengthening of the daily journey in search of food. Rookeries in the inner suburbs continued to be occupied for much longer, such as the one at Lee Green, used until 1947, but urban sprawl gradually eliminated the large feeding areas that seem to be an important requirement of this colonial species, in contrast to the solitary nesting Carrion Crow which can manage with a smaller area of open ground.

A census in the London Area in 1945 and 1946, with almost complete coverage, produced a total of 355 rookeries containing 9,971 nests. Atlas data are not directly comparable, though breeding records from only 160 tetrads seem to indicate a drastic reduction within the London Area. There have been few specific comments, but a rookery at Wrotham Park with 54 nests in 1972 was showing a drop of 28% and in 10-km square TQ25 in Surrey numbers in 1973 were only one third of those in 1970. Parker (1970), discussing rookeries near Hainault, referred to nine losses between 1948 and 1968 that could be only partly explained by tree-felling.

A similar pattern of decline since the early 1950s has been noted in other parts of Britain. Dobbs (1964) found a sharp drop in Nottinghamshire between 1958 and 1962 and Sage (1972) recorded a fall of 23% in the number of rookeries over the whole of Herts between 1961 and 1971. Reasons for all these changes are hard to deduce. Toxic seed-dressings may have had an effect in the early 1960s, as grain can form a large part of the bird's diet at certain seasons, but numbers have not recovered despite a ban on the more persistent organochlorines. Continued use of chemicals on the soil, however, may reduce the quantity of soil invertebrates, resulting in less food for the Rook. Recently Dutch elm disease has killed many elms and though this is scarcely a factor in the decline, the loss of nesting trees could adversely affect any recovery.

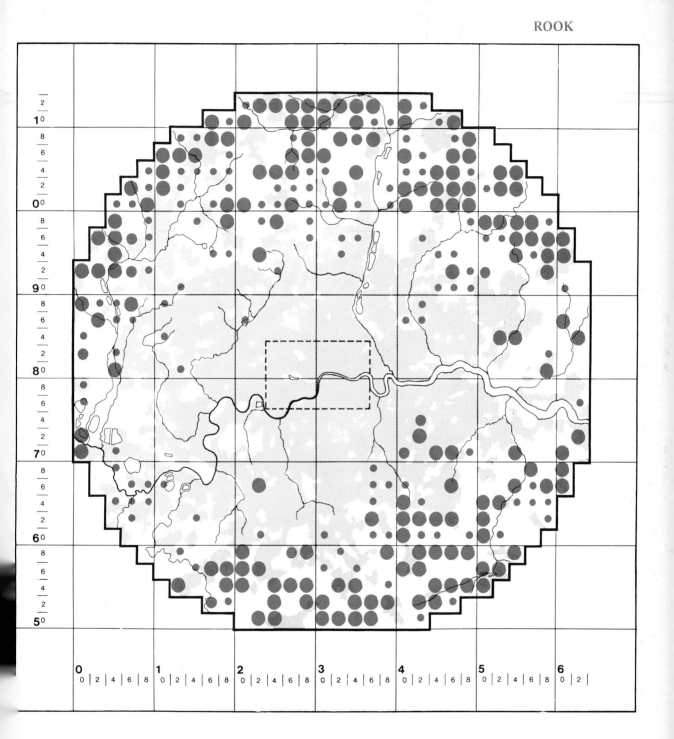

JACKDAW

Corvus monedula

The Jackdaw is mainly confined to the rural areas, parkland and the outer London suburbs, in all of which it is a fairly common resident.

There was a considerable increase in the species in rural parts of the Area up to the early 1950s. Numbers varied in the more built-up habitats, but in some districts the Jackdaw was regarded as abundant, though the break-up of estates, felling of old timber and eviction from buildings accounted for local decreases. Except in Inner London, where its history has been followed more closely, there has been little evidence of changes either in distribution or numbers over the succeeding twenty years.

As the map shows, there were few records in the central built-up area during 1968-72. A pair nesting in Kensington Gardens in 1969 provided the last record of the Inner London colony that had been present on and off for at least seventy-five years. Numbers had been low for some time and successful breeding may not have occurred every year in spite of the provision of nest-boxes. Other sparsely populated areas were Middlesex in the west and south Essex and the Thames marshes in the east. There may be fewer trees to provide nest sites bordering the Thames, but some of the numerous quarries might have been expected to attract the Jackdaw. Elsewhere the distribution is somewhat patchy with breeding records during the Atlas survey from 198 tetrads out of 461 in which the species was found. In the inner suburbs there were breeding records close to central London from six tetrads that include parts of Richmond Park, and also from Greenwich Park and around Wanstead and Hornchurch. Breeding may since have ceased in these last two localities as a report in 1973 stated that the nearest nesting site to the City was then at South Weald Park.

Parslow found that most reports from England and Wales indicated an expanding population at least until the 1950s with no signs of any subsequent reverse. The BTO Common Birds Census population index for farmland census plots has also shown little change since records started in 1963, except for a temporary drop in 1970 (B & M 1976). The onset of Dutch elm disease and the consequent loss of old trees could possibly rob the Jackdaw of many potential nesting sites, but this may not be such an important factor for suburban populations.

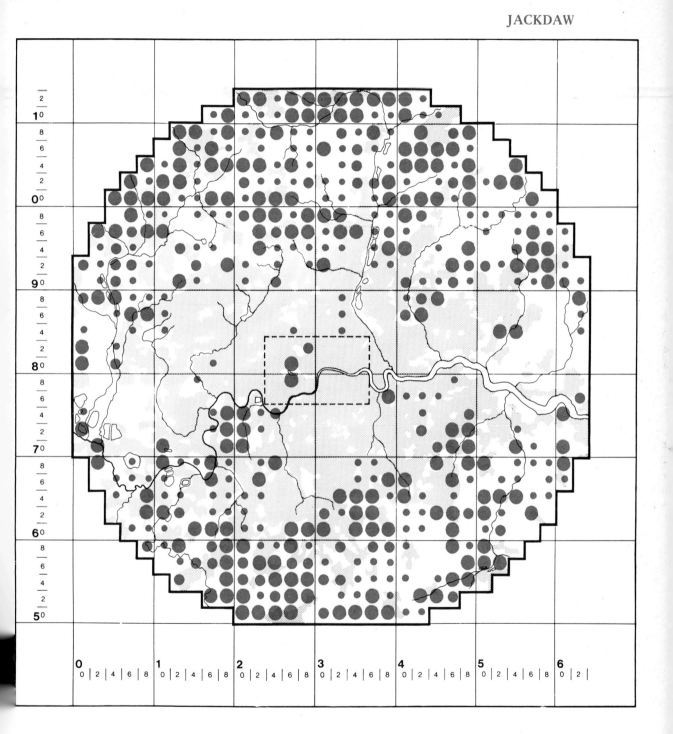

THAMES POLYTECHNIC LIBRARY

151

MAGPIE

Pica pica

A familiar resident species in the London Area, the Magpie is common in rural habitats and in suburban localities with parks and large gardens. A gradual spread towards the centre resulted in the first Inner London breeding record in 1971.

Its present wide distribution is very different from the position at the beginning of this century when the Magpie was extremely scarce in the London Area. A reduction in gamekeeping during the first world war allowed it to spread into new habitats and since then the population has continued to expand. By the 1950s the species was spreading inwards through the suburbs and during the following decade there were comments that it was becoming bolder and visiting bird tables in some localities.

Expansion into suburban areas has also occurred in other parts of the country, though in recent years there may have been a decline in some rural populations (Parslow). There is no evidence of this in the outer parts of the London Area. Breeding records during the Atlas survey came from 418 tetrads, almost half the total in the Area. Reports showed that the Magpie was widespread, especially south of the Thames where it was established well into the inner suburbs as far as Woolwich, Dulwich, Wimbledon, Richmond and Kew. Breeding at Kew Gardens was suspected for the first time in 1969 (Parr 1972). North of the Thames the species appears to be absent from much of east London and the built-up suburbs of south Essex. It is a fairly adaptable species and, although it usually builds huge domed nests, it seems to be as much at home in hedgerows as in the tops of large trees. In these eastern localities, however, there are fewer large expanses of parks and gardens resulting in less suitable habitat both for nesting and feeding.

Early this century a few pairs of Magpies bred in the central parks, but there seems to be no doubt that the birds originally came from captivity. This is not likely to apply to the present increasing number of Inner London breeding records. In Hyde Park/Kensington Gardens a pair built a nest in 1969, but deserted after being harassed by Carrion Crows which stole sticks from the nest. Another nest was built in 1970 and again in 1971 when at last two young were reared. Regent's Park was occupied during the same period and in 1971 a well fledged juvenile was seen. More recently there were up to five pairs in Regent's Park in 1975 and four occupied territories in Hyde Park/Kensington Gardens in 1976. Nesting has also been reported from Buckingham Palace Gardens and birds have been seen in the breeding season in St James's Park and Victoria Park.

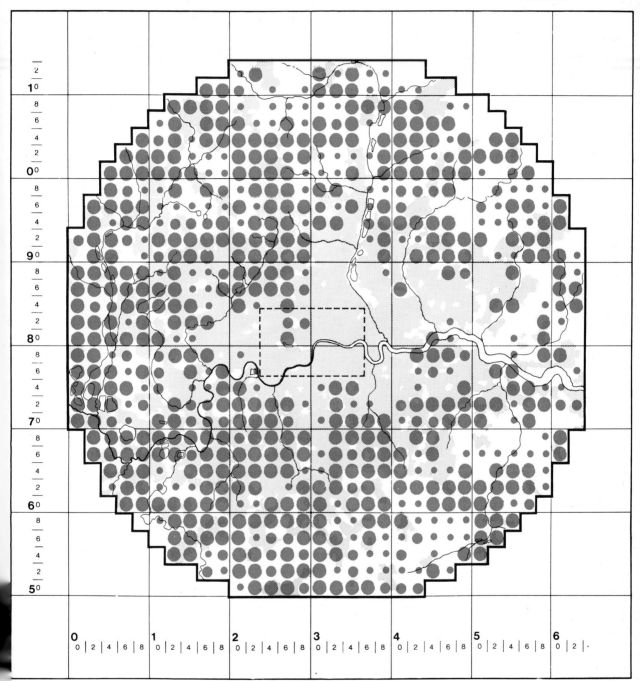

JAY

Garrulus glandarius

Like the Magpie, this species has also benefited from a reduction in persecution from gamekeepers and it now shows a very similar pattern of distribution in the London Area, though occurring more widely than the Magpie in the inner suburbs and in Inner London.

In the early years of this century the Jay was already well established in the Area. Since then it has become more numerous and spread into parks and other open spaces in otherwise urban localities, so that by the 1950s it was breeding annually in most of the Royal Parks of Inner London. Some further expansion into new areas may have continued in recent years and the population has probably continued to grow. A report of 70 being shot at Badger's Mount on one day in 1971 gives an indication of the high numbers that may occur.

Described by Voous (1960) as a typical palearctic wood bird, the Jay in London now nests in a variety of habitats, but the patchy distribution shown on parts of the map reflects the need for areas with trees, perhaps especially oaks, as acorns form an important part of the Jay's diet. Of the inner zone, that to the west offers ample attractive breeding localities, while immediately to the east and across south Essex, where these features are scarce, the Jay is correspondingly less common.

Records during the Atlas survey came from 637 tetrads, which is comparable with the 660 for the Magpie. Definite evidence of breeding, however, came from only 289 tetrads, 45% of the records against 63% in the case of the Magpie. There are difficulties in obtaining confirmation of actual nesting in many suburban areas where birds may be out of sight in private gardens, but with the Jay the low figure also reflects the species' shy and retiring nature during the breeding season and the fact, as recognised by Campbell & Ferguson-Lees (1972), that its nest is one of the hardest to find of all the corvids.

Nesting in Inner London was first recorded in 1930, about forty years ahead of the Magpie. By 1965 Cramp & Tomlins (1966) put the population at 15-25 pairs, breeding in many of the parks, in some of the squares and occasionally on buildings. During the survey years there were up to six pairs in Hyde Park/Kensington Gardens, five in Regent's Park and records of nesting in other localities such as Holland Park, St James's Park, Brompton cemetery and Ladbroke Grove.

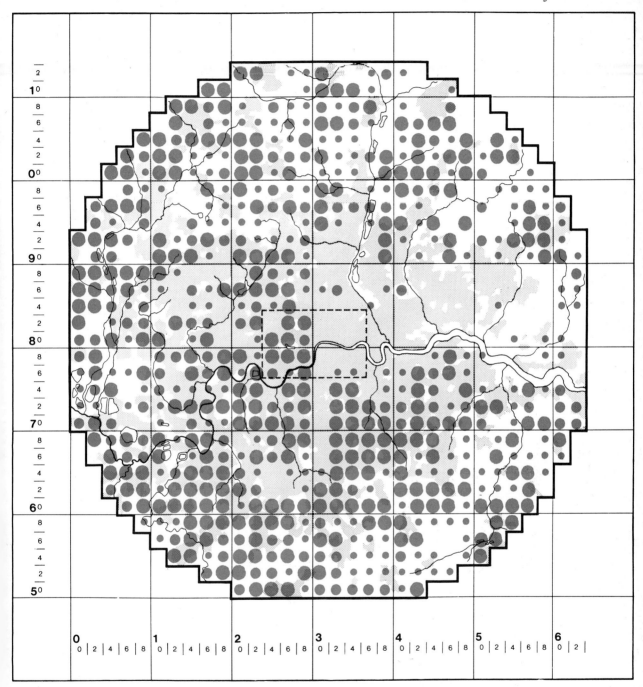

GREAT TIT

Parus major

This is a widely distributed species breeding throughout the London Area and probably absent from only the most densely built-up central zone and stretches of the Thames marshes.

While the status of the Great Tit showed little change in the first half of this century, numbers increased slightly, at least in some localities, after 1950, perhaps levelling off in the late 1960s (Cramp & Tomlins 1966, Beven 1976). In oakwood at Bookham Common, where there were no nest-boxes and nesting was confined to natural sites, an average of 9.3 territories per year was recorded during 1949-56, increasing to 10.4 in 1958-63 and 15.8 over the years 1964-69, then falling slightly to 15.0 in 1970-74. Regular counts from Inner London parks have shown a similar pattern. In Regent's Park there was an average of just over six pairs in the years 1959-63 increasing to over 13 pairs in 1964-68 (Wallace 1974), while in Hyde Park/Kensington Gardens the average number of territories in 1966-69 was 20 and in 1971-74 rose to 23, with a low of 12 in 1966 and a peak of 29 in 1972.

Data from the BTO Common Birds Census (B & M 1976), which show a more rapid rise in the population index for farmland than for woodland since 1970, suggest that woodland populations may be at about their maximum density, thus forcing an expansion into sub-optimum habitats. If this is the case in the London Area there may have been a comparable movement from localities such as Bookham and the large parks into less favourable situations, though there is no available evidence to indicate whether this is so.

Distribution of the Great Tit, as shown by the Atlas survey, was very similar to that of the Blue Tit. In common with maps for several other species the only extensive blank area was from the densely built-up urban centre eastwards into south Essex. As the Great Tit is adept at using artificial nest-holes where natural holes or crevices are unavailable, a scarcity of trees there in which to search for food during the breeding season may be a limiting factor. Coverage in that area, however, was less complete than elsewhere and birds may have been overlooked.

Although the Atlas survey gave no indication of numbers, all reports for the London Area agree that the Blue Tit is the more numerous of the two species. Comparison of populations at Bookham Common, for example, for the years 1966-74 showed that the ratio of Great Tit to Blue Tit was about 8:10, while at Hyde Park/Kensington Gardens the figures were approximately 5:10 over the same period.

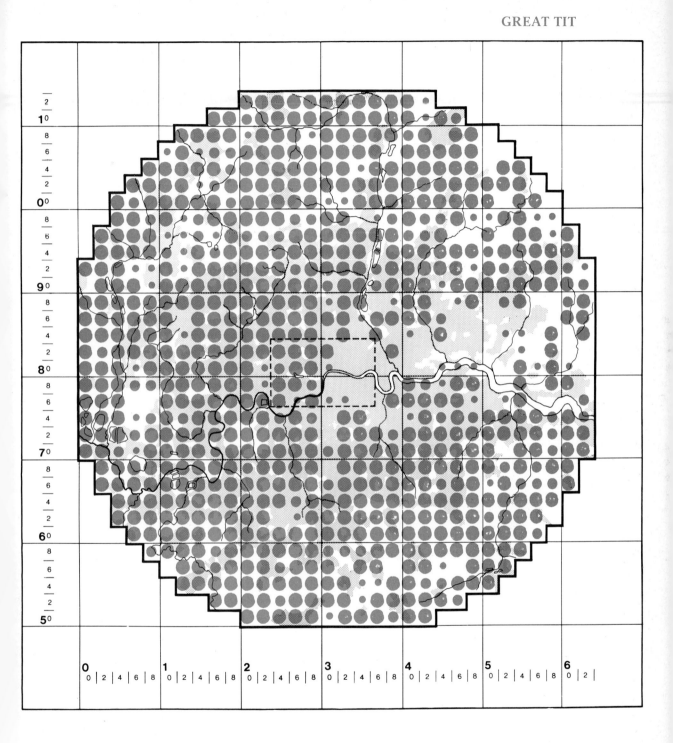

BLUE TIT

Parus caeruleus

The Blue Tit is the most numerous tit species in the London Area, probably absent from heavily built-up localities, but found most commonly in larger parks and mature woodlands where nesting holes are abundant.

Although there was no evidence of significant population fluctuations in the Area up to 1950, numbers appear to have increased during subsequent years. In Regent's Park an average of 13.8 pairs in the years 1959-63 increased to 19.8 over the next five years up to 1968 (Wallace 1974). Similarly in oak woodland at Bookham Common territories increased from an average of 11.8 in 1950-56 to 15.5 in 1958-63, thereafter averaging 19.0 up to 1974 (Beven 1976). Figures provided by regular censuses in Hyde Park/ Kensington Gardens since 1966 show a rising trend, reaching a peak of 70 territories in 1972 but down to 42 in 1974. A comparison of the numbers at these last two London Area sites with the BTO Common Birds Census population index for woodland and farmland is given in Table 10.

National BTO figures in the Table show a significant expansion on farmland, while in London, on the evidence from two Inner London parks, there has been considerable growth in numbers in parkland. At the same time woodland populations are growing, if at all, at a much slower pace.

Records during the Atlas survey came from 793 tetrads. Gaps shown on the map north of the Thames eastwards from central London indicate an area where observer coverage was less complete than elsewhere and there are unlikely to be many tetrads where a pair or two of Blue Tits could not be found with diligent searching. It is well known as an opportunist nester, making considerable use of nest-boxes and other artificial sites such as lamp-posts and bus-stop signs when natural holes are in short supply. In fact out of 41 territories in Hyde Park/Kensington Gardens in 1967, eight nests were found in lamp-posts.

Table 10. Occupied territories of Blue Tits at Bookham Common and Hyde Park/ Kensington Gardens compared with BTO Common Birds Census population index, 1964-74

	64	65	66	67	68	69	70	71	72	73	74
Bookham — oakwood	19	22	17	16	20	19	20	15	16	19	26
Hyde Park/Kensington Gardens — parkland	?	?	22	41	27	57	58	52	70	53	42
CBC index (1966 = 100)											
Woodland	100	103	100	104	108	105	106	109	114	113	121
Farmland	97	107	100	103	109	108	113	127	127	132	139

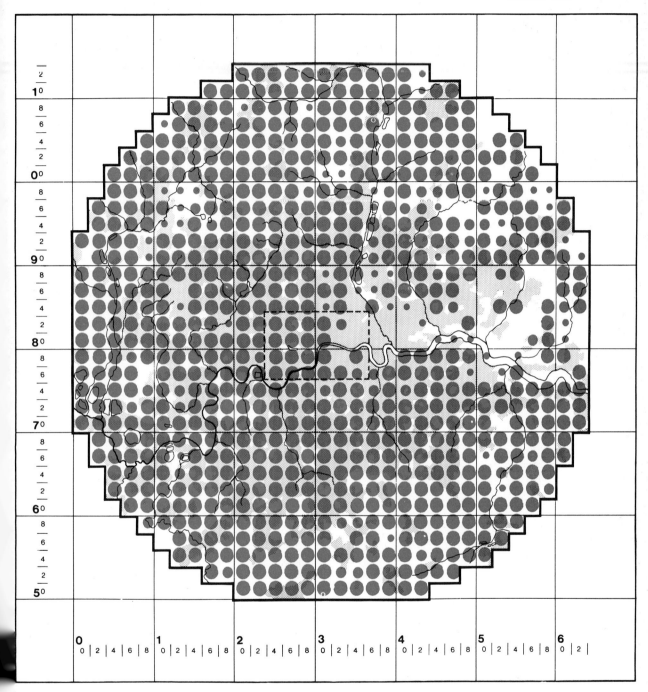

COAL TIT

Parus ater

Numerically the Coal Tit is in third place among the tit species after the Blue and Great Tits. It is mainly resident, with breeding records for the Atlas survey from most parts of the London Area, though its distribution is patchier than for the two previous species and it appears to be absent from predominantly built-up habitats.

Numbers close to London showed a decrease in the first half of this century. Since then the trend has been reversed and the Coal Tit, generally regarded as having a preference for conifers, has expanded into new areas, notably Inner London where previously it had nested only sporadically. In 1965 it was still considered as an irregular nesting species in central London (Cramp & Tomlins 1966). Apart from an isolated record of adults with young in Marlborough Place, NW8, in 1953, definite breeding records had been confined to Kensington Gardens in 1947, Regent's Park in 1951 and possibly 1953, 1955 and 1965, and Holland Park in 1958, 1959 and regularly from 1962. From the mid-1960s nesting occurred annually in Regent's Park where a minimum of four pairs was present in 1968 (Wallace 1974). The greatest expansion, however, has been in Hyde Park/Kensington Gardens and as many as 16 pairs held territory there in the years 1972-74. Outside these parks, Inner London breeding reports during the Atlas survey came from Buckingham Palace Gardens in 1970 and Battersea Park in 1971, both based on the presence of fledged juveniles. By 1973 birds had spread into St James's Park where adults were seen in the breeding season collecting and carrying food.

As with other resident species, the Coal Tit has undoubtedly benefited from the recent series of mild winters, resulting in increases in many areas. Figures from the BTO Common Birds Census, which show the population index for the Coal Tit in all habitats at 264 in 1974 compared with a base of 100 in 1966 (B & M 1976), clearly suggest that numbers are still growing. If this is so in the London Area there has probably been further infilling since 1972, when the Atlas survey ended with records from 543 tetrads, amounting to 63% of the whole Area. The scattering of blank spaces on the map, especially in the outer, more rural parts, is difficult to explain, though the species can be easily overlooked where it is only thinly distributed. It may not yet have colonised many inner localities, however, and land in south Essex and along the Thames marshes, where there are few patches of woodland, may also remain unattractive.

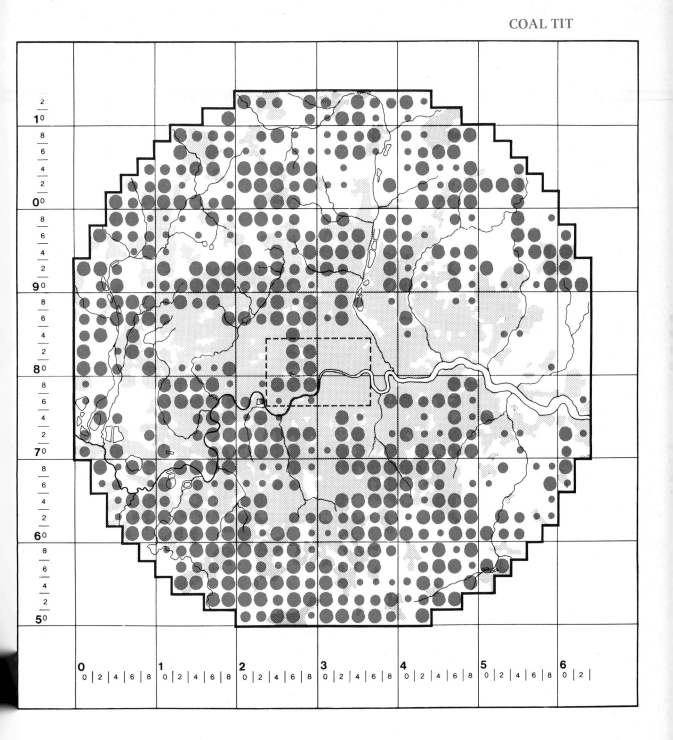

MARSH TIT

Parus palustris

Distribution of the Marsh Tit in the London Area is limited to rural districts and woodland habitats in the more open suburbs.

There appears to have been a general pattern of retreat by the Marsh Tit as a breeding species this century as parts of London became more densely built-up. Dixon (1909) described it as a possible breeding bird in Battersea Park, Regent's Park and in the vicinity of Kilburn in the early years, but since then the sole record for Inner London is of probable breeding in Holland Park in 1937. By the mid-1950s the inner limits for the species north of the Thames were considered to be Ruislip, the northern part of Middlesex and wooded areas in Essex. South of the River, birds occurred at Dulwich, but Wimbledon Common, Richmond Park and Kew appeared to have been deserted. In south-west Middlesex and south Essex it was described as scarce.

Reports for the Atlas survey show a very similar pattern. There were only isolated breeding records across the centre of the London Area, but the northern limits were much the same with records still coming from Ruislip and the areas around Stanmore and Mill Hill. Beyond these localities and south of the Thames, Atlas records were widely scattered. Overall there were breeding records from 114 tetrads, probable breeding from 63 and reports of Marsh Tits being present in a further 100 tetrads. In total these numbers are slightly in excess of those for the Willow Tit, and yet there were only 152 tetrads in which both species were recorded. Disregarding the possibility of confusion between the two species, which perhaps cannot be entirely ruled out, the Atlas results suggest that there are differences in habitat preferences. Some work has been done on this question in oak woodland at Bookham Common. This showed that over a period of twenty-six years about 47% of Marsh Tit territories were in the damper and more low-lying habitat, against 69% of those of the Willow Tit (Beven 1976). Numbers involved were small and a much wider study would be required to test such a hypothesis more thoroughly.

Little information is available on numbers of pairs in any London localities. At the national level the BTO Common Birds Census population index (B & M 1976) has shown a decrease of about one-third between 1965 and 1974, though this trend has not been followed at Bookham Common where the population in the 16ha sample of oak woodland varied from one to four pairs, with an annual average of 2.6, the highest number being reached in 1973 (Beven 1976).

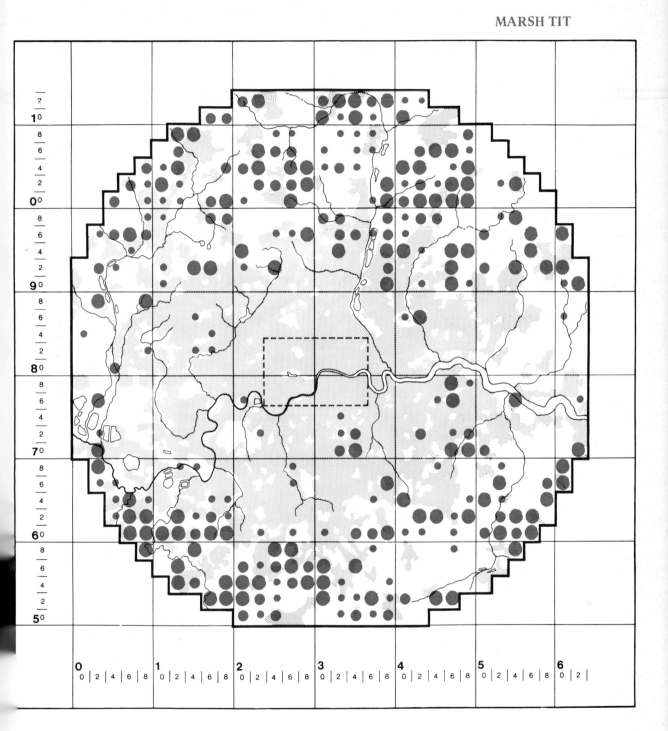

WILLOW TIT

Parus montanus

This is possibly the least widely distributed of the tit species breeding in the London Area. Evidence of its habitat preferences is not entirely clear, but it may be limited by the extent of damp woodland and wooded commons containing well-rotted stumps in which it can excavate a nest-hole. Thus with few exceptions it occurs beyond the main suburban limits.

Owing to the difficulty of distinguishing between Marsh and Willow Tits, the status of the Willow Tit has not been satisfactorily established. Little is known of its distribution before the 1940s and in fact specimens obtained at Hampstead and identified in 1897 were the first definite British records. By the 1950s Surrey was considered the main centre of the London Area population and it was also well established in Herts and north Essex. Breeding records during the Atlas survey from Hampstead Heath and the Brent Reservoir indicated the inner limits north of the Thames, but to the south, apart from Wimbledon Common, the species tended to be further from the centre. Not too much significance should be attached to recent reports of increased breeding numbers as this may only reflect improving identification abilities or more observers.

Two reports in the 1930s from localities where both Willow and Marsh Tits occurred indicated that the former was the less numerous. In the Sevenoaks district the ratio was 1:10 and in the Brentwood/Romford area the ratio was put at 1:3 or 4. Since then the position has varied. At Ongar in 1971 the Willow Tit was thought to exceed the Marsh 2.5 times, but at Hainault the following year these figures were almost exactly reversed. In the west of the Area at Cassiobury Park, Black Park and Rush Green the Willow Tit was again reported to be in the majority. While no firm conclusions can be drawn from these conflicting accounts, they suggest an increase in the Willow Tit in relation to the Marsh Tit.

At Bookham Common, Beven (1973) found that the mean ratio of Willow and Marsh Tit territories in 39ha of scrub during 1964-72 was 1.6:1.0 and in 16ha of oakwood during 1949-72 was 2.5:7.0. Absence of overlap in 14 out of 22 woodland territories suggests an ecological separation perhaps related to differing feeding and nest site requirements as discussed by Lack (1971). The Marsh Tit, for example, has a stronger beak allowing it to feed on harder seeds, yet the weaker billed Willow Tit excavates its own nest-hole. Such distinctions may explain the differences in distribution shown on the maps where the Willow Tit appears in 262 tetrads, in 110 of which there was no record of the Marsh Tit.

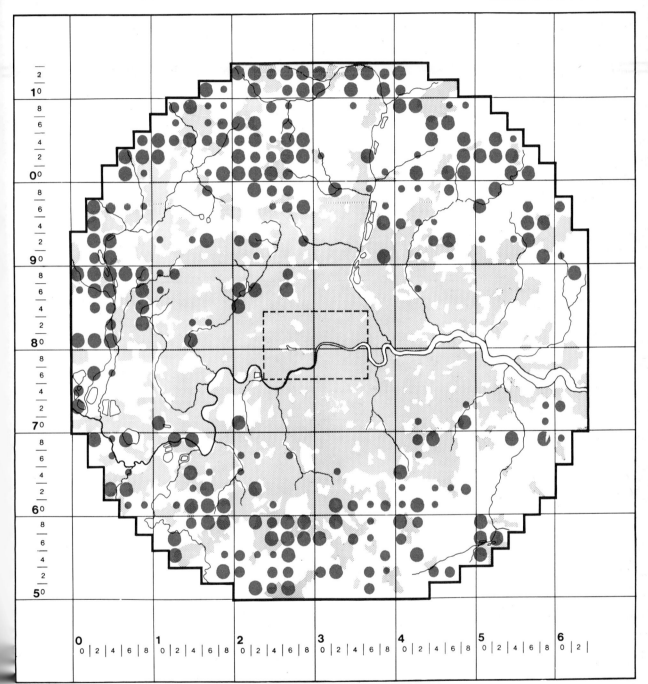

LONG-TAILED TIT

Aegithalos caudatus

This is a widely distributed species in rural areas and in outer suburbs where large gardens, patches of scrubland and hedgerows provide suitable nest sites, and recently it has also expanded into Inner London.

Homes found that the Long-tailed Tit had disappeared from a number of formerly occupied habitats. Breeding had not been recorded from Kew since 1938 and Hampstead Heath since 1951 and suburban spread seemed to be driving the species further out. It also suffers badly in severe winters and following that of 1962-63 its breeding strength was greatly diminished over the whole country (Dobinson & Richards 1964). In parts of the London Area the population was entirely or almost entirely wiped out, as in census plots at Bookham Common where, after nine or ten pairs in 1962, there was none in 1963 (Beven 1964). Since then a series of mild winters has led to a dramatic increase in breeding numbers and by the time the Atlas survey started the population was back to the 1962 level.

Numbers continued to grow during the survey years of 1968-72 and there were more frequent reports of birds in winter in the Inner London parks. This increased activity culminated in a record of a bird carrying nesting material in Holland Park in 1971 though there was no proof that breeding actually occurred that year. Nesting was evidently successful in 1972, however, as young birds were seen in the Park in May and June and two pairs also bred in Hyde Park/Kensington Gardens.

The population has expanded throughout the country and the BTO Common Birds Census population indices in 1974 were standing at almost two and a half times the 1966 level on farmland and nearly three times the 1965 level in woodland, both earlier years being the first for which figures are available (B & M 1976). For the London Area, the map shows a mainly rural pattern of distribution, particularly in Surrey, Herts and north Essex. Nearer the centre, both Kew and Hampstead Heath have been recolonised and there were also reports of breeding up to an inner limit of approximately Joyden's Wood, Chislehurst, Bromley, Beckenham, Dulwich, Wimbledon, Richmond Park, Chiswick and Osterley Park, though further north, apart from an isolated report from Wanstead, there were few records closer than Chingford or Enfield.

After the end of the survey there were several comments that 1973 and 1974 were good breeding seasons, especially south of the Thames. There were no reports in 1973 of nesting in Inner London, but a considerable upturn in 1974 resulted in three pairs breeding out of four present in Hyde Park/Kensington Gardens and up to five pairs present in Regent's Park.

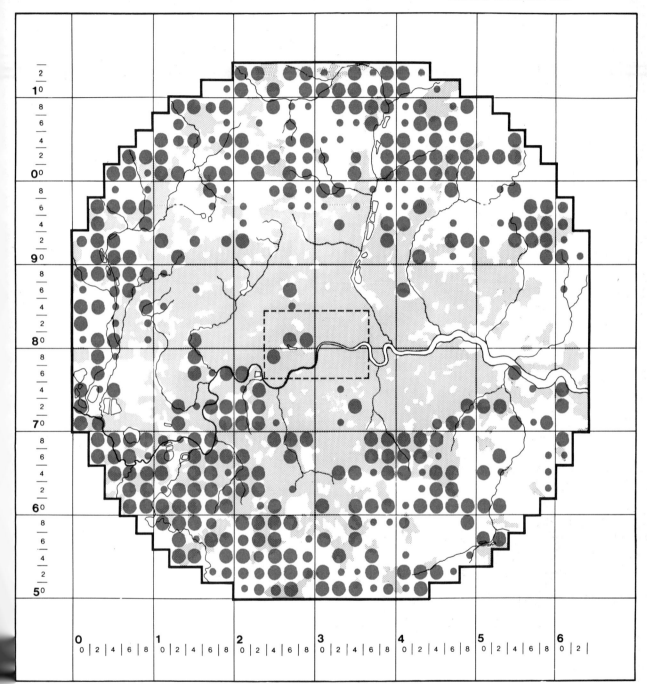

NUTHATCH

Sitta europaea

The Nuthatch is a fairly common resident of wooded and parkland areas. It is most widespread in the south and south-west of the London Area, where it extends inwards from the countryside through the suburbs of Surrey and west Kent. North of the Thames it is found widely in Herts, though records are rather few in Middlesex and Essex.

As a woodland bird that has adopted parks and large gardens as acceptable habitat, the Nuthatch has survived in such places well inside the built-up area as suburbia has expanded, though even by the early years of this century it had disappeared from many Middlesex localities. Since the 1950s, however, there seems to have been a slight increase both in range and numbers. It increased noticeably in Northaw Great Wood in the early 1960s (Sage 1966) and its status has improved in Essex in a narrow band eastwards from Walthamstow to Brentwood.

Records for the years 1968-72 came from a total of 401 tetrads, 47% of the London Area, with breeding in 221 tetrads, probable breeding in a further 104, and presence in the breeding season reported from the remaining 76 tetrads. Distribution in suburban areas reflects the existence of wooded parks and garden habitats. Inner limits of nesting now include Wanstead, Hampstead, Osterley Park, the Kew/Richmond/Wimbledon area, Dulwich, Shooters Hill and Abbey Wood.

As an insectivorous species, the Nuthatch may have benefited from clean air legislation introduced in the 1950s, resulting in less accumulation of soot on the trunk and bark of trees where it obtains its food and which Fitter (1945) suggested may originally have been the cause of its desertion of Inner London. At all events, two pairs bred successfully in Inner London in 1958 providing the first records this century. One was found in Holland Park and one in Kensington Gardens. A pair also nested, but unsuccessfully, in Battersea Park. These records followed increased numbers seen with tit flocks the previous autumn (Cramp & Tomlins 1966). Sanderson (1968) considered that as far as Kensington Gardens were concerned there were no reinforcements from outside, although according to Hurcomb (1962) two pairs were said to have been released in the Gardens during 1956. Nesting occurred there in at least six years up to 1964, but the species then decreased and remained only a rare visitor up to 1976 when one pair nested again. In Holland Park a pair nested each year until 1963, with two pairs in 1960, 1961 and 1963; a nest-hole was excavated in 1970, and in 1971 one pair bred successfully.

168

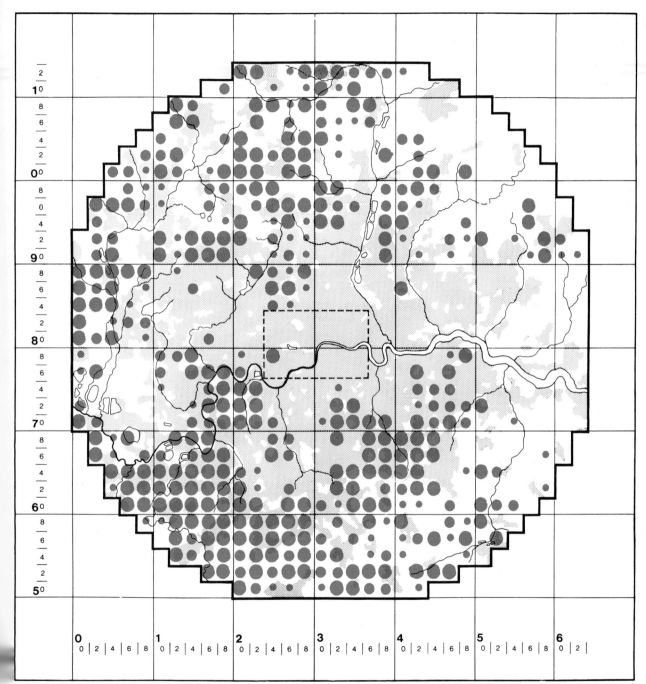

TREECREEPER

Certhia familiaris

Distribution of the Treecreeper in the London Area is broadly similar to that of the Nuthatch and the species is resident in most wooded and parkland habitats.

The information available is insufficient to show whether the status of the Treecreeper has changed during the twenty years since the mid-1950s when it was described as resident in all suitable localities though in small numbers. In fact the present range of this familiar bird, taken for granted by many observers, is probably very similar. During the Atlas survey it was found widely distributed south of the Thames, with more Kent records than for the Nuthatch. North of the River it was well represented in Herts and the northern part of Essex, but rather sparse in Middlesex. Except for records of nesting in Kensington Gardens, the inner limits largely coincide with suburban, well wooded parkland, such as Greenwich Park, Dulwich, Wimbledon, Richmond, Kew, Hampstead and Wanstead Park. The latter is an isolated locality in southern Essex, an area with limited habitat suitable for the Treecreeper.

Numerically the species may have increased, benefiting from the recent series of mild winters after the losses that occurred during the severe winter of 1962-63. The BTO Common Birds Census population index shows that, on farmland habitats, the Treecreeper, by 1974, was over two and a half times more numerous than in 1966 (B & M 1976). More sheltered conditions in woodland are likely to result in higher survival rates during the winter so that populations there may remain nearer capacity, leaving less scope for dramatic increases and the major expansion would thus occur on farmland.

Although unobtrusive with a quiet song compared with the loud call of the Nuthatch, the Treecreeper was recorded during the Atlas years in 434 tetrads, slightly more than the Nuthatch and covering 51% of the London Area. Considering the difficulty of obtaining proof of nesting, however, the lower proportion of breeding or probable breeding records than for the Nuthatch, 66% against 81%, is not surprising.

In Inner London the Treecreeper breeds intermittently in Kensington Gardens. The first record was in 1945, followed by further proof of nesting in 1952 and 1954 (Cramp & Tomlins 1966). After an interval of fifteen years one pair was again proved to breed in 1970. A pair probably did so in the next two years and in 1973 there was a remarkable increase to four occupied territories. Proof of nesting is difficult to obtain in the Park, but the position has evidently been maintained as three pairs definitely bred in 1976.

170

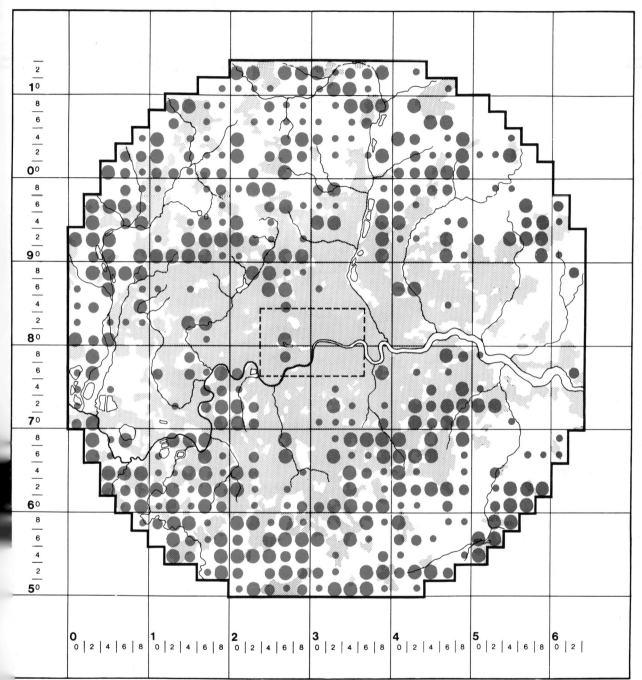

WREN
Troglodytes troglodytes

This is one of the most common and widespread species in the London Area and is resident in all but the most heavily built-up habitats.

Although subject to considerable fluctuations, reflecting survival during the winter months, there has been little overall change in the status of the Wren during the present century. Numbers are reduced during prolonged periods of severe weather, but recover within a few years. Reports after the hard winter of 1962-63 indicated that birds resident in urban and suburban areas of London suffered less than those in rural habitats. There was no evidence of a decrease in the Highgate and Hampstead areas; at East Molesey numbers were only slightly down; and in south-west London birds were recorded as breeding in good numbers.

Mild winters since 1963 have allowed the population to increase and Table 11 gives some idea of the extent of the recovery. This Table shows the BTO Common Birds Census population indices for 1962-74 alongside censuses from sample plots in the London Area. By 1973 the Wren had become the commonest bird on woodland census plots (Batten & Marchant 1975) and on farmland the population showed a tenfold increase over ten years.

London Area Atlas records for the years 1968-72 showed that the Wren was found in all except 75 tetrads. Lack of suitable habitat probably accounted for its absence from some of the most central localities, but elsewhere the gaps are more likely to indicate inadequate coverage.

In Inner London numbers have increased since the 1950s resulting in annual breeding reports from Hyde Park/Kensington Gardens, Regent's Park, Holland Park and Buckingham Palace Gardens. Nesting is also recorded in some years in St James's Park, St John's Wood and Battersea Park (Cramp 1975). Few Wrens are found in central London away from parks and large gardens, but in 1961 and 1962 a pair nested in the City at Cripplegate and a pair was resident there throughout the summer of 1972.

Table 11. Trend of Wren breeding population based on occupied territories, 1962-74, showing recovery after severe winter of 1962-63

	62	63	64	65	66	67	68	69	70	71	72	73	74
Bookham — oakwood	12	1	5	11	17	25	26	24	25	17	26	27	27
Potters Bar — farmland	?	?	1	4	6	15	17	22	18	15	22	22	22
Hyde Park/Kensington Gardens — parkland	?	?	1	1	—	5	8	12	15	10	14	18	23
CBC index (1966 = 100)													
Woodland			57	69	100	144	147	139	118	150	199	239	252
Farmland	140	31	47	73	100	158	173	173	165	194	258	307	328

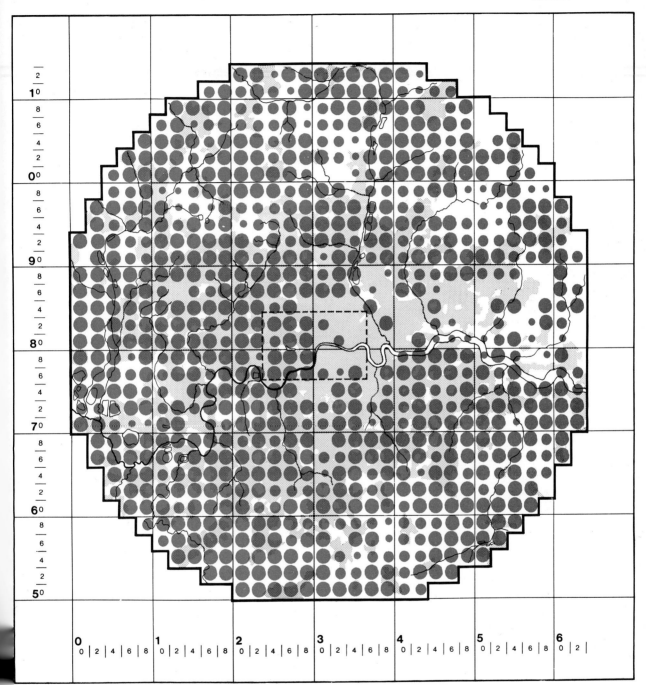

BEARDED TIT

Panurus biarmicus

Since 1959 the Bearded Tit has become a regular autumn and winter visitor to the London Area in small numbers, but it has qualified for inclusion in the Atlas survey through breeding at one locality in Herts.

Following eruptions of the East Anglian breeding population, a male Bearded Tit was seen in the winter of 1959-60 at Northfleet. In the autumn of 1960 there were reports of about 30 birds, including 15 at Walthamstow Reservoirs, six at Stanborough, five at Swanscombe, two at Northfleet and singles at one or two other localities. These were the first records for the London Area. It has since been recorded annually, the main localities being situated along the Essex and Kent Thames-side marshes, and the Lea and Colne valleys, with occasional reports from other sites such as Pen Ponds in Richmond Park and the Brent Reservoir. First arrivals generally appear in October and birds depart in March, some staying until April.

Stanborough Reedmarsh, near Welwyn Garden City, almost on the northern boundary of the London Area, was one of the early sites in the Area visited by Bearded Tits and the first proof of breeding within the Area was obtained there in 1966. The following summary of events is taken from Gladwin (1976).

A pair was seen nest-building in April 1966 and the following month a nest was found containing recently hatched young. Later a second pair was seen, also with young, and a minimum of 13 birds present in July suggested that one or both pairs may have had second broods. Subsequently two pairs nested or attempted to nest in 1968, 1971 and 1972 and one pair in 1973. There was no evidence of fledged young in 1971 and in both 1972 and 1973 the reedmarsh was destroyed by fire. Successful nesting therefore appears to have been confined to 1966 and 1968. In 1970 the site was declared a nature reserve, a move which may gradually ensure more protection and stable conditions for the Bearded Tit.

Gladwin discusses the reasons why the species should choose that particular site in preference to others in Herts that are visited regularly by Bearded Tits in winter and concludes that maintenance of the water level is important. There are probably several localities within the London Area containing reedbeds with permanent standing water throughout the breeding season, so perhaps in time others will be occupied. Breeding colonies already exist in a number of counties outside East Anglia and the Bearded Tit would be a most welcome addition to London reedbeds.

174

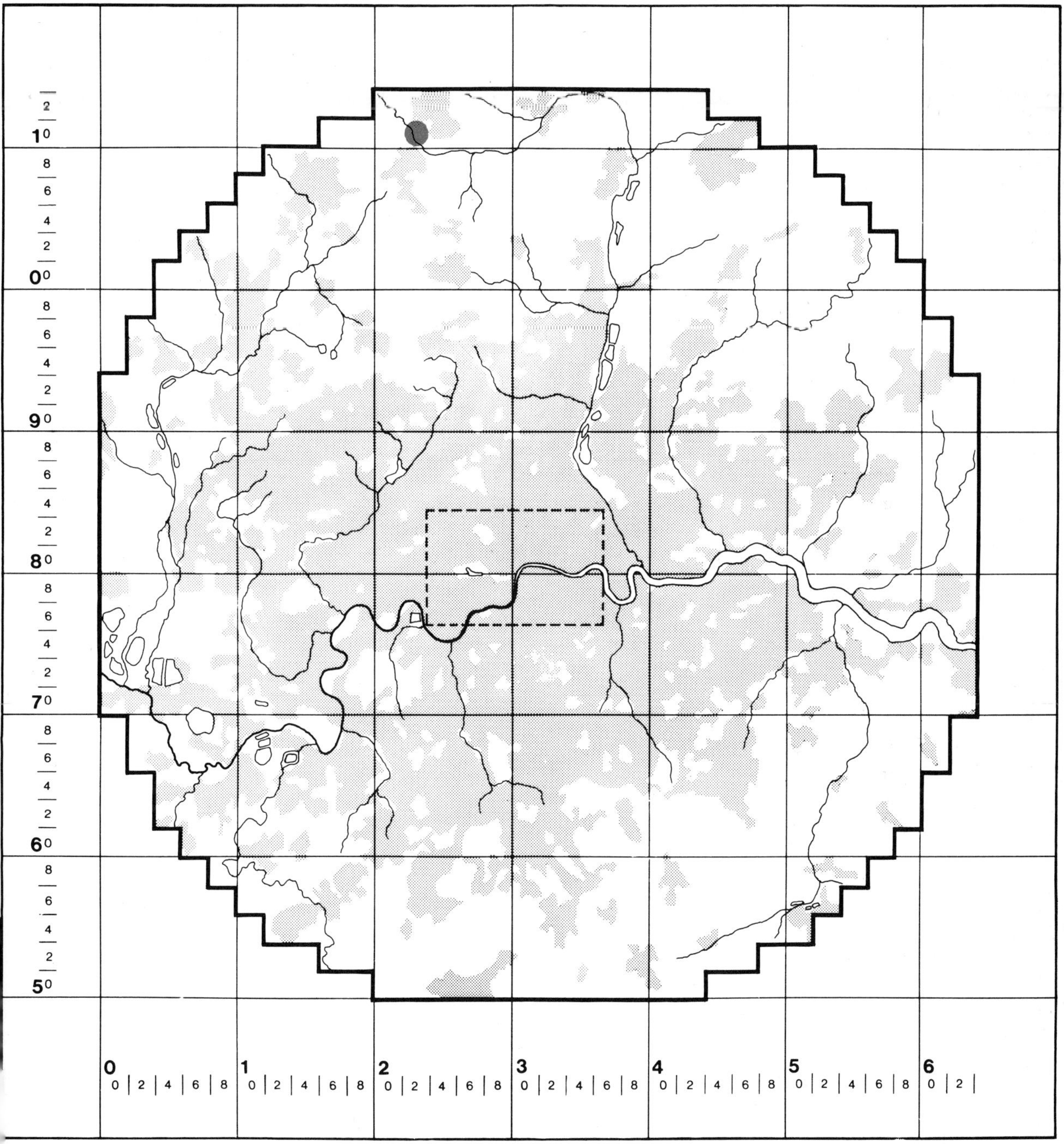
2
10
8
6
4
2
00
8
6
4
2
90
8
6
4
2
80
8
6
4
2
70
8
6
4
2
60
8
6
4
2
50
0 1 2 3 4 5 6
0 2 4 6 8 0 2 4 6 8 0 2 4 6 8 0 2 4 6 8 0 2 4 6 8 0 2 4 6 8 0 2

MISTLE THRUSH

Turdus viscivorus

The distinctive early song of the Mistle Thrush is now much more widely heard in the heart of London than in the early years of this century. Numerous probably only in the rural zone and outer suburbs where more of its original habitat of tall trees near open ground survives, the species is nevertheless well distributed throughout the Area.

During the period of 150 years up to the mid-1950s the Mistle Thrush had extended its range into gardens and parks, not only in this country, but in much of western and central Europe (Voous 1960). In that time it had spread into man-made habitats in London and finally colonised the centre, though as late as 1929 only a few pairs nested in Inner London. Here it increased particularly between 1929 and 1952. Later progress did not occasion much comment and Cramp & Tomlins (1966) summed up the situation with an estimate of 25-30 pairs. Numbers reported subsequently ranged from a total of 25-27 pairs in the central parks including Battersea and a small park at Wapping in 1967, to a mere seven territories listed in 1971 from Hyde Park/Kensington Gardens, Archbishop's Park at Lambeth, Lincoln's Inn and South Kensington. Overall, however, the population has probably remained relatively stable.

Outside Inner London numbers appear to have expanded in recent years, corresponding to the gradual increase throughout the country noted by Parslow. This trend is not readily apparent from a map concerned solely with distribution and showing some surprising gaps in Kent just south of the Thames, in west London and along the west side of the Lea valley. Gaps east of London in south Essex are probably largely the result of inadequate coverage, but in many areas the Mistle Thrush could easily be overlooked nesting in a tree-lined road, as it builds and flies higher than the other thrushes. Individual territories, too, are large and hard to define. Clapham Common in 1965, with one pair per 6.5ha, had the highest density recorded in Surrey suburbs (Parr 1972). Reports of breeding in more enclosed areas during the Atlas survey referred to pairs nesting in plane trees in Ladbroke Grove and Russell Square, at a site in Stepney and on a building in Lincoln's Inn.

Although the Mistle Thrush is considered susceptible to prolonged severe weather (Snow 1969), the winter of 1962-63 did not apparently cause any serious depletion (Dobinson & Richards 1964) and the mild winters since then have allowed the species to prosper. There is still no sign that in London it has exploited its largely urban habitat to the full.

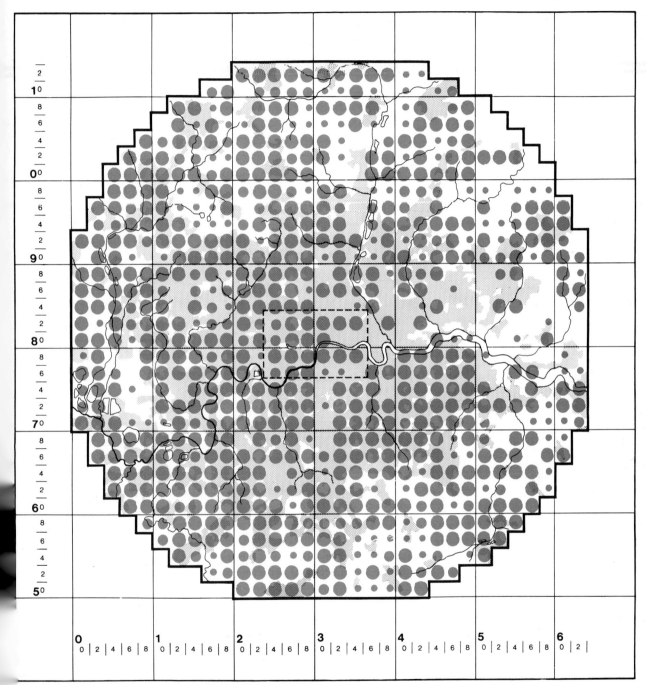

SONG THRUSH

Turdus philomelos

As a widespread species in the London Area the Song Thrush has a very similar distribution to the Blackbird, though numerically its status appears to differ considerably.

After being as common or commoner than the Blackbird before 1914, the Song Thrush had declined markedly by 1954, especially compared with the Blackbird which had made spectacular advances. In some localities the relative abundance of the two species had been reversed as early as the 1920s. While the basic cause in these earlier years is unknown, a period of colder winters in the 1940s probably had an adverse effect on the Song Thrush.

Between 1954 and 1967 available evidence suggests that the rural population, for example at Bookham, was more or less stable with a rapid recovery after the cold winter of 1962-63. In Inner London, however, during the same period, the species showed signs of increasing and Cramp & Tomlins (1966) indicated that the position in 1965 was improving with about 150-175 pairs of Song Thrushes in Inner London against an estimated Blackbird population of 500-750 pairs. A ratio of 1:4 is similar to figures taken from Common Birds Census studies in Surrey (Parr 1972) where overall the proportion was 1:3. For suburban areas, where the habitat is mainly gardens, the difference between these two species may be greater, an impression reinforced by data from Dollis Hill where the Song Thrush was outnumbered 26 or 27 to one by the Blackbird (Simms 1962).

Winter conditions tend to be less severe and minimum temperatures higher in central London than in more open areas. Nevertheless the sheltered Inner London parks still show a varied pattern of increases and decreases. A survey in Regent's Park covering the years 1959-68 had a peak of 80 pairs in 1965, after which numbers fell to 50 for the following three years (Wallace 1974). On the other hand, in Hyde Park/Kensington Gardens 1968 was a peak year with 64 territories which dropped back to 45 in 1969 and at 30 in 1973 had almost returned to the level of 1966.

While the Song Thrush has much more limited habitat preferences than the Blackbird, rarely nesting on buildings and keeping mostly to bushes, creeper or low trees at a height of one to four metres, there can be few localities in the London Area where it cannot find a nest site. Blank tetrads on the map are probably due to lack of adequate coverage, particularly those in the outer zones, though the species may in fact be absent from some of the most densely built-up central area.

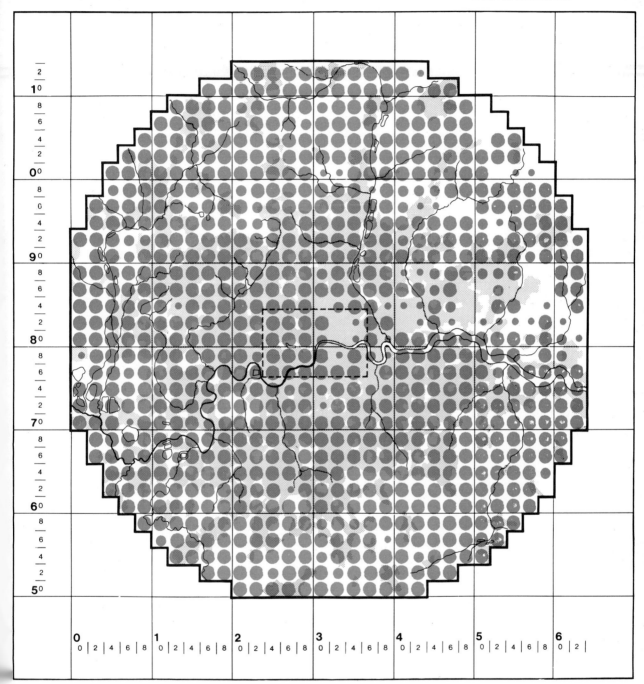

BLACKBIRD

Turdus merula

After a population explosion in the nineteenth and early twentieth centuries, this basically woodland species is another that has successfully adopted a city life. The Blackbird is now very common in the London Area and gaps on the distribution map can only be due to inadequate coverage.

Much of the expansion of this species has been attributed to its more opportunist breeding and feeding habits than the other thrushes. Thus, whereas in established oak-wood at Bookham Common numbers were virtually unchanged from 1954 to 1974 (Beven 1976), at Sevenoaks G.P. reserve, where new habitat was created, Blackbirds increased to fill the niche that became available (Harrison 1974). The severe 1962-63 winter appeared to have little effect and the only locality where any marked change was noted was Dollis Hill where almost the entire population disappeared and only half the number returned to breed in 1963 (Simms 1965).

Later information has been patchy, but indicates a slightly different trend between rural and built-up areas. In suburban and urban London the basic habitat, like the rural Bookham oakwood, has probably changed relatively little, but unlike Bookham, Blackbird numbers seem to have expanded, though with fluctuations, until at least 1974. By 1965 Cramp & Tomlins (1966) estimated that the 103.6km^2 of Inner London held 500-750 pairs, making the Blackbird the fourth commonest breeding species.

According to Parslow and the BTO Common Birds Census indices, the Blackbird increased until at least 1969 throughout Britain. In London numbers in Hyde Park/ Kensington Gardens were at their highest recorded level in 1974 when the number of territories rose to 123 compared with 60 in 1966. Yet in Regent's Park there was a steep drop in 1966 and again in 1968, ascribed by Wallace (1974) to pressure on nesting space despite a tolerance of high densities. Calculations of territory size in Bishop's Park, Fulham, indicated about 0.6ha per pair (Strangeman 1975), less than one-tenth the size of Mistle Thrush territories on Clapham Common (Parr 1972).

This pressure on space has forced the Blackbird into unusual nest sites. Examples were given by Cramp & Tomlins (1966), but more recently nests have been found on a girder about 3.5m up under the roof of Cannon Street Station, at a height of about 10m on County Hall and, at the other extreme, below pavement level on a basement ventilation outlet in Finsbury Circus. In spite of such enterprise there are signs that the Blackbird may have reached saturation point in many areas and its population is stabilising at a level the existing habitat can support.

THAMES POLYTECHNIC LIBRARY

WHEATEAR

Oenanthe oenanthe

Although a regular spring and autumn passage migrant through the London Area, the Wheatear has been no more than an occasional breeding species since the early years of the century.

From north of the Thames there have been only three satisfactory records of breeding, one in 1920 and two in 1930. Nesting occurred more regularly south of the River, particularly in the first decade when birds could be found on open high ground at such localities as Epsom Downs, Reigate, Banstead and Walton and Headley Heaths. Nearer London, nesting was reported from Wimbledon Common and, until 1908, annually in Richmond Park. By 1918, however, breeding had all but ceased except on Park Downs, Banstead, where a pair or two persisted up to 1930 (Parr 1972).

In the London Area the Wheatear used to nest mainly on Chalk downland or heaths, usually occupying holes in the ground, especially rabbit burrows. Other favoured sites such as crevices in stone walls or beneath undisturbed stones were not often available, but in 1946 two pairs nested in a pile of bricks at Blackheath. This marked the start of another period of infrequent breeding attempts. In 1947 two adults seen with three young on Woolwich Common had probably nested nearby; in 1949 a nest was found on a corporation dump at Upper Warlingham; and a pair in Richmond Park in 1955 still constitutes the most recent record of successful breeding. Since then pairs have been present for all or most of the breeding season at a bombed site at Cripplegate in 1959, at the site of a new reservoir at Walton in 1961, at Mill Hill in 1962, and at Littlebrook Power-Station near Dartford in 1965. During the Atlas survey a pair in 1969 again remained on Dartford Marsh and in the following year birds built, but then abandoned, a nest at Holmethorpe. Under the Atlas coding system this last record and a report of juveniles seen near Woolwich are shown as large dots on the map.

The general pattern of decline corresponds closely with evidence from elsewhere in southern England (Parslow). Loss of habitat through ploughing of downland or reafforestation was considered a contributory cause as well as disappearance of the Rabbit, but these factors occurred when the Wheatear was already a rare breeding species in the London Area. With the continuing spread of suburban London and increasing recreational pressures on the remaining open spaces, it is unlikely to return to nest regularly, but while it continues to pass through on migration there is always a chance that once in a while an occasional pair will find a suitable rural or even industrial site and stay to breed.

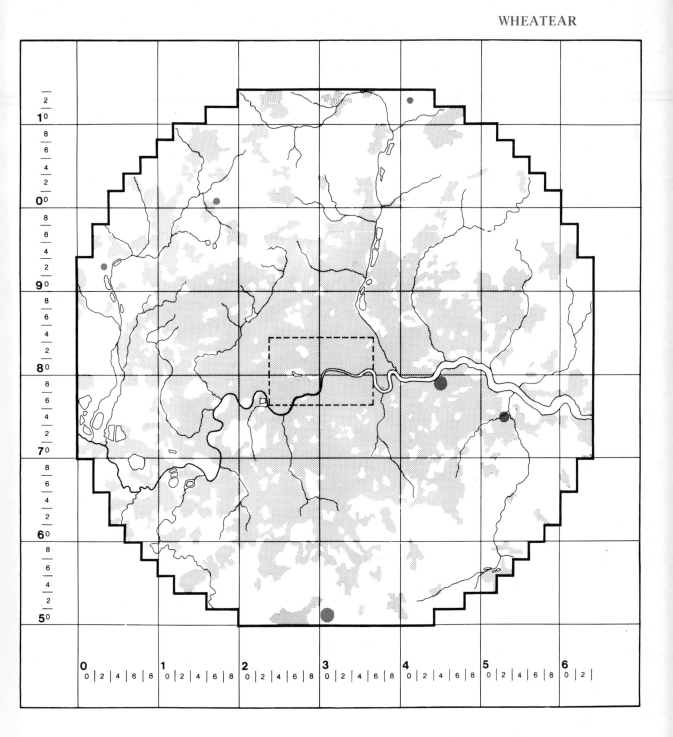

STONECHAT

Saxicola torquata

After being lost as a breeding species following severe winters, the Stonechat now breeds regularly in small numbers, though a remarkable increase was reported in 1974 after the end of the Atlas survey.

While never common, even in its former strongholds on the heaths of Surrey and Kent, the Stonechat has decreased this century and by the mid-1950s it had almost disappeared as a breeding species. A 1933 survey produced records from a total of 17 localities. None was found in either Essex or Kent, though the species may have been missed on the little-watched Thames marshes where a few pairs now breed annually. By 1947 hard winters had reduced the London population to only one pair, which was discovered on Walton Heath. Numbers remained low and there was no proof of breeding within the London Area between 1956 and 1960, though the presence of pairs and occasionally juveniles may indicate that nesting sometimes occurred undetected. An improvement in 1961 to at least three pairs was short-lived and after the severe winter of 1962-63 the Stonechat was not seen again as a breeding species until 1966.

The Atlas survey showed a slightly more encouraging picture. There was a concentration of records from the Thames marshes as far upstream as Erith Marsh, and in Surrey the Stonechat was found on Banstead Downs, Epsom Common and Headley Heath. Mitcham Common, though surrounded by suburbia, continued to be occupied and two pairs may have nested there in 1973. In the north, breeding reports came from the Broxbourne and Hoddesdon areas. Since the Atlas survey numbers have increased further, reaching nine pairs in 1973, of which seven definitely bred, including a pair in Richmond Park for the first time since 1939. This was followed by a remarkable jump to some 25 pairs in 1974, about 15 of which were proved to have nested. Actual numbers may have been even higher as there was no information from northern localities.

Magee (1965) considered that habitat changes had a more permanent effect than climate on the Stonechat population. Thus in parts of the London Area the loss of the Rabbit may have allowed scrub to become too dense, but human disturbance may be another factor accounting for the reduction in Stonechats in some localities such as the North Downs. Aided by mild winters, however, the species has returned to the population level of the 1930s. If these climatic conditions persist the present expansion may well continue, as in addition to its favoured gorse habitats many unoccupied areas of open scrub with bushy cover for nesting still remain.

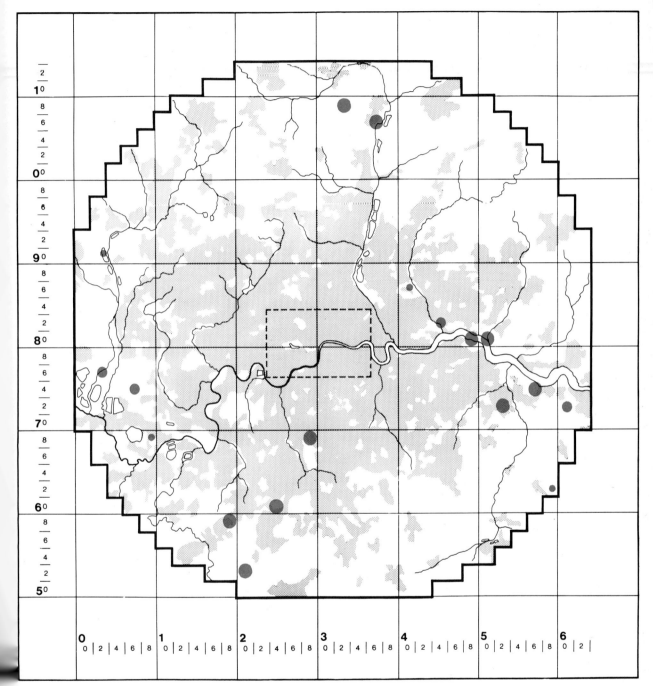

WHINCHAT

Saxicola rubetra

Breeding numbers of this summer visitor have greatly decreased in the London Area and reports are now down to single figures annually.

At the beginning of the century the Whinchat was locally common, especially in the northern part around Enfield. Suitable nesting sites were found on unused land and rough grassland as well as the sides of railway embankments. South of the Thames it nested sparsely on gorse-covered commons and banks of reservoirs. During the second quarter of the century there was a gradual decline in numbers, particularly in Surrey where there were no breeding records from 1940, when the species disappeared from Richmond Park, until 1951. By the 1950s breeding distribution was limited mainly to the river valleys, principally the Thames to the east of London, the Lea and the lower stretches of the Colne. From a population of about 45 pairs in 1955 numbers continued to fall until the early 1960s, since when there have been fluctuations between two and eight pairs, generally along the Thames marshes.

Breeding records during the Atlas survey came from nine tetrads, which was only one less than the Stonechat, but unlike that species, the Whinchat is not showing any signs of increasing. Over the five years the number of pairs reported reached a low of only two in 1970, increasing to seven in 1972, but then dropping back again to three in 1973 after the end of the survey. In the Lea valley it was found in the upper reaches around Ware and Hertford and further east there was a record from Great Parndon in 1970. Only south Essex and the marshes on both sides of the Thames showed any concentration of records. Rainham is still a regular locality, but there were also Atlas records from Hornchurch, Barking and near Dagenham. South of the River birds were recorded from Woolwich to Erith, but surprisingly, not from further downstream.

Although destruction of habitat through building development and changes in farming practices, particularly increased cultivation, may have contributed to the decline which has affected much of lowland England, Parslow considered that the rate of decrease in the Whinchat exceeded habitat losses and therefore other unknown factors must also be involved. There seems little chance that the species will ever again be classed as common in the London Area, but in spite of the changes, many former haunts still exist. Should the decline be reversed the Area could support a much higher breeding population than the remnant that now remains.

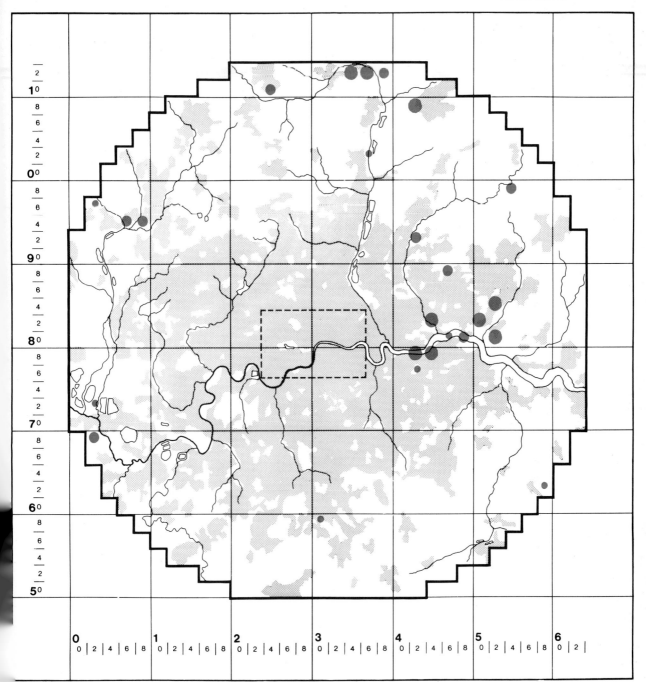

REDSTART

Phoenicurus phoenicurus

Although there have been periods of stability and even occasional increase in the summer population in the London Area, the general trend has been downward and the Redstart now has a very patchy distribution.

In contrast to the present scattered rural records, the Redstart used to breed earlier this century in such inner localities as Finchley and Bromley, but by the mid-1950s it had already declined. Numbers in Richmond Park dropped from 20-25 pairs in 1935 and 1936 to only nine in 1953, and elsewhere it was described as local and confined to well timbered habitats. Since then the population has fallen even further, though the pattern is difficult to trace accurately as not all regular haunts, such as Epping Forest, are thoroughly searched each year. In 1960 the London Area held a minimum of 35 breeding pairs, of which almost half were in Northaw Great Wood and Broxbourne Woods. More were reported the following year, but numbers were down in 1962 when six pairs in Northaw Great Wood were described as the lowest ever recorded there. In 1963, however, at least 90 cocks held territory in the Area and up to 59 pairs attempted to breed, thus emphasising the wide annual fluctuations at that time. Epping Forest with 56 singing males held the biggest concentration. The level of that year has never again been achieved.

Parslow considered that the widespread marked decrease ceased about the 1940s, followed in some areas by an increase. Records from Surrey outside the London Area supported this (Parr 1972), but within the Area there was no indication that the increases were other than temporary. Certainly evidence in this country indicates a recent dramatic decline and figures from the BTO Common Birds Census, though based on a very small sample, show a population index down from a base of 100 in 1966 to only 39 in 1974 after sinking to 23 in 1973 (B & M 1976). The Redstart is one of several species that winter in West Africa and drought conditions there over several years may have caused high mortality (Winstanley *et al.* 1974).

During the Atlas survey records came from only 71 tetrads, in 42 of which breeding or probable breeding occurred. Epping Forest remained the main stronghold with as many as 17 singing males in 1970 and Broxbourne Woods held seven pairs in 1968. In the south, the Ashtead area and the Surrey/Kent Lower Greensand hills around Limpsfield held a few pairs. Nearer London the only signs of the Redstart's former suburban existence were the reports of breeding in Richmond Park, though of no more than two pairs, and of a pair with juveniles on Wimbledon Common in 1968.

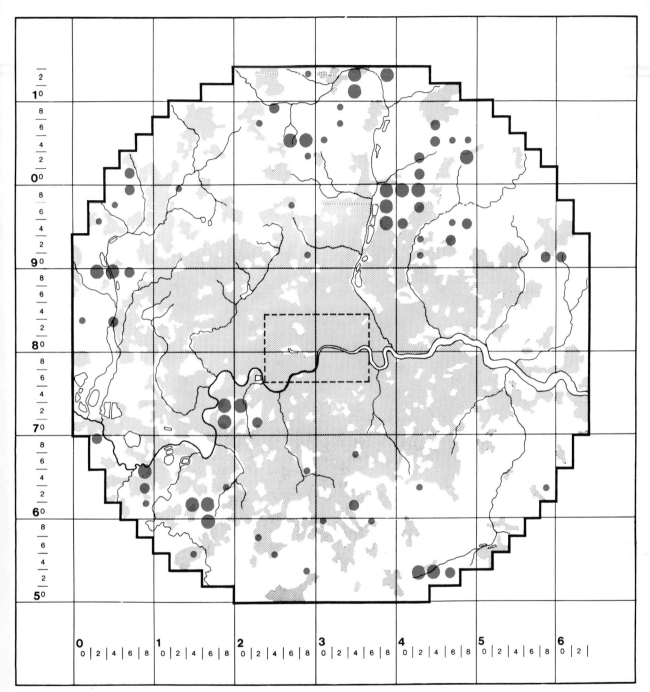

BLACK REDSTART

Phoenicurus ochruros

Added to the list of London's breeding species only this century, a few pairs of Black Redstarts now nest annually, mainly at industrial sites along the Thames and the River Lea and in parts of built-up suburbia.

Regular reports of nesting in Britain date from 1923 (Fitter 1965), with the first records from the London Area three years later. A site at Wembley was used annually until the end of 1941 when numbers began to expand elsewhere. For the next decade the Black Redstart was particularly associated with bombed sites of central London. As rebuilding progressed in the 1950s the number of birds reported declined. Renewed interest in the mid-1960s produced evidence of breeding pairs in several industrial localities never before explored by ornithologists, which raised doubts as to whether these records represented a shift in the population or whether they had been previously overlooked. Meadows (1970) showed the numbers of territorial males, including definite breeding pairs, in the London Area up to 1969 and in Figure 3 these are extended to 1974. Britain is on the edge of the Black Redstart's range and most breeding pairs are confined to east and south-east England. Those in the London Area thus represent a significant proportion of the total British population which only reached 53-55 territorial males in 1950-52 and may have since declined (Parslow).

Though described by Voous (1960) as primarily a bird of rocky slopes and cliff-faces, the Black Redstart in London has principally colonised industrial sites. Meadows (1970) listed power-stations, gas-works, railway sidings, warehouses, timber-yards, building and bombed sites, to which can be added the disused Surrey Docks, where four pairs, possibly five, bred in 1972. Most records during the Atlas survey came from the central area, extending east along the Thames to Northfleet and west to Heathrow Airport. Sites at Croydon have long been used and there were also records from Welwyn Garden City and Harlow, both in industrial localities. Suitability of these sites appears to be connected with the abundant supply of insect life, especially diptera (non-biting midges) hatching out of polluted, warm streams. In this way these eyesores can maintain a small population of one of our rarest breeding species.

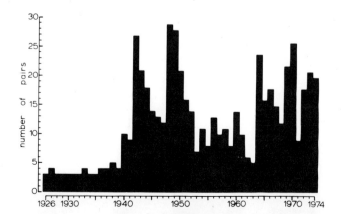

Fig. 3. Breeding season population (based on singing males holding territory) of Black Redstarts in the London Area, 1926 to 1974.

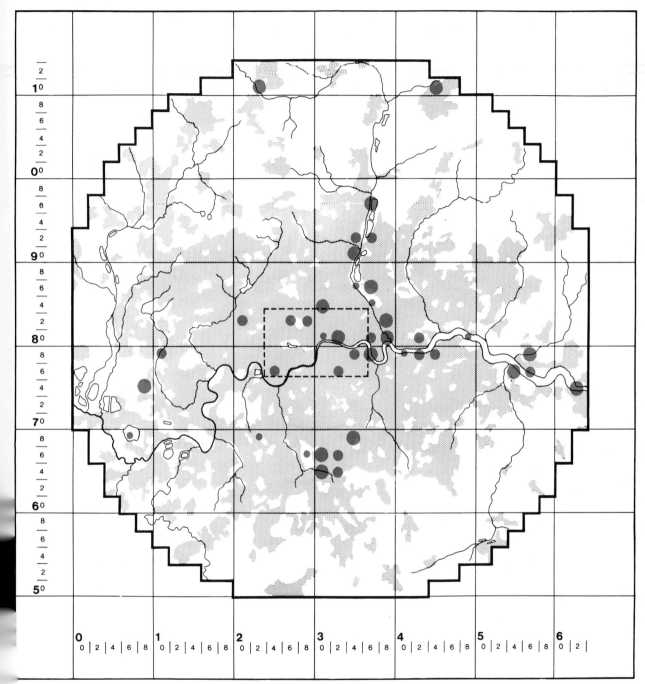

NIGHTINGALE

Luscinia megarhynchos

A serious decline has occurred since the 1950s and, while the Nightingale still has a widely scattered distribution in rural habitats, there is no longer the density that used to be found in some localities.

Once known to nest in Hyde Park and Regent's Park, the Nightingale had already disappeared as a breeding species from most of the inner zone by the turn of the century, though even as late as 1950 it was still nesting close to the centre at Wimbledon Common. In 1961 a total of 129 singing males was located in Broxbourne Woods and Epping Forest. By 1963 there were signs of a decline and only four pairs were recorded at Northaw Great Wood where previously the population had usually numbered about 20. Epping Forest also seemed to be affected and by 1964 the Nightingale was absent from many former breeding sites.

A Gloucestershire study, showing a sharp fall in 1957-59 and no recovery, typified many localities (Parslow) including Kent, Herts and Surrey. In the London Area, loss of hedgerows and small copses, as well as more disturbance, may be having some effect. Why numbers have dropped so heavily in largely unchanged woodlands, however, is not known and may be due to adverse conditions in other parts of the Nightingale's range.

Records during the Atlas survey came from 89 tetrads. Breeding was reported in only 21 and probable breeding in 49, though several of the latter were based on the presence of singing males which may have been migrants remaining in a suitable habitat for a short period before moving on. This was probably so with a bird recorded in the Richmond Park area which is now well outside the Nightingale's London range.

In the north of the London Area, main breeding localities were Northaw Great Wood, Broxbourne and Hertford Heath with smaller numbers in Epping Forest and at Hainault. Surrey held most of the birds in the southern part, though Ashtead Common, where there were 11 singing males in 1960, had none by 1969 (Parr 1972) and only one in 1971. Of the other principal habitats, Princes Coverts, Oxshott, contained the largest population with at least ten pairs in 1969, and 39ha of scrub at Bookham held five singing males in 1970 and 1972.

Reports since the survey from areas such as Epping Forest, where none was heard in 1973 and Bookham, where only one singing male was present in 1974, indicate that the London population may still be decreasing, creating fears that even the patchy distribution shown on the map will not be maintained.

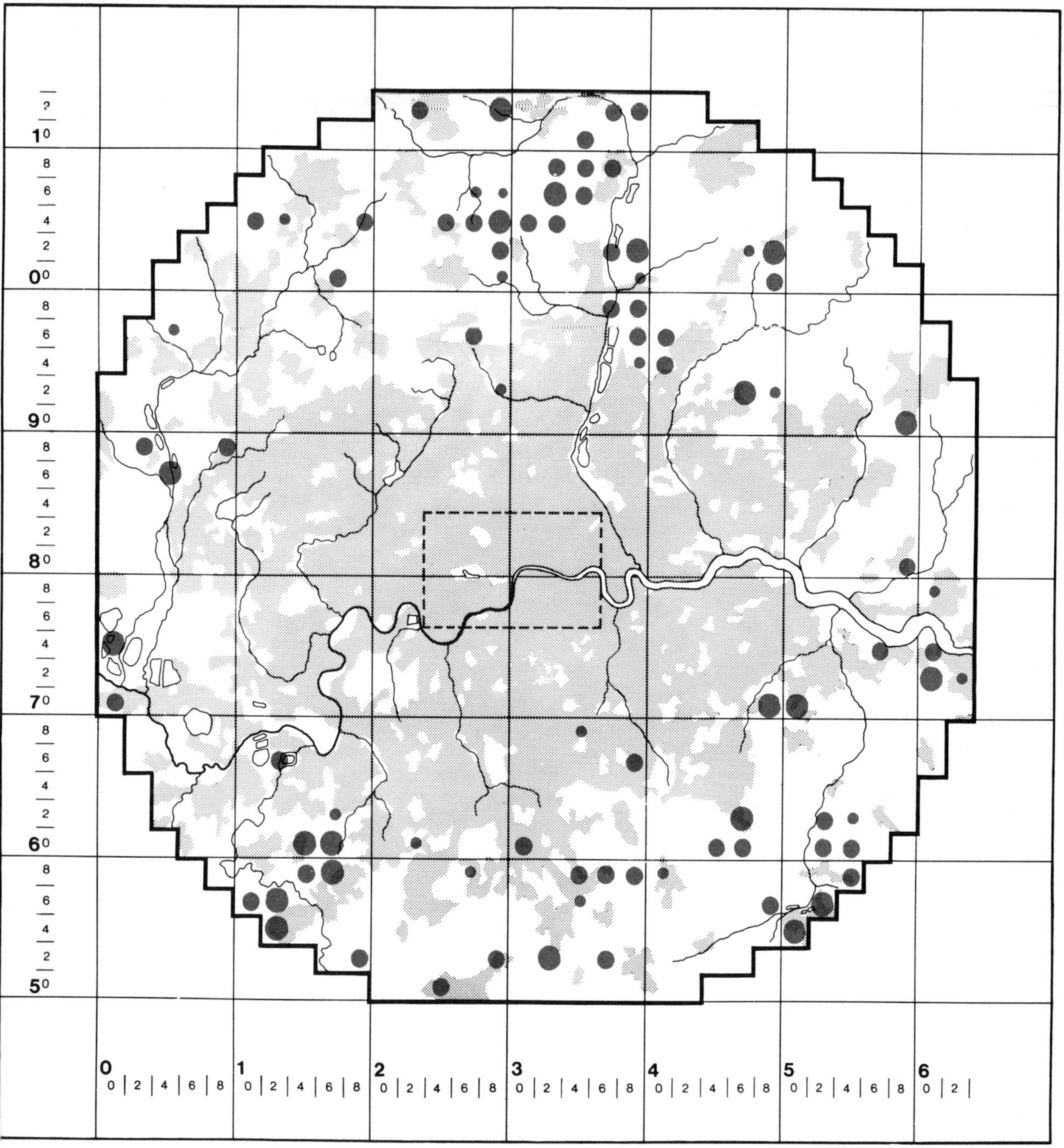
2
1⁰
8
6
4
2
0⁰
8
6
4
2
9⁰
8
6
4
2
8⁰
8
6
4
2
7⁰
8
6
4
2
6⁰
8
6
4
2
5⁰
0 0 2 4 6 8
1 0 2 4 6 8
2 0 2 4 6 8
3 0 2 4 6 8
4 0 2 4 6 8
5 0 2 4 6 8
6 0 2

ROBIN

Erithacus rubecula

Unlike its European counterpart, the British race of the Robin nests commonly in urban areas and is a familiar bird of the London scene. It is widespread and numerous except in the most densely built-up districts and in localities where marsh or open country lack suitable cover.

In rural habitats a slight setback followed the winter of 1962-63, as with many other ground feeders. Some woodland Robins disperse after breeding on to more exposed ground where prolonged frost can prevent them obtaining enough food. Numbers seemed to recover quickly and in Bookham oakwood at least, the losses had been made good by 1964 (Beven 1976).

Little information is available for suburban areas, but random observations suggest that the breeding population remains at a fairly constant level. This generally static pattern of distribution in London reflects the national position which Parslow considered had not altered significantly over roughly the last hundred years. Cats and possibly the Grey Squirrel are the two serious predators of a bird which for nesting will adopt any well hidden crevice around dwellings from a secluded hollow in a cultivated bank to crannies in walls or in dense creeper. Simms (1962), however, found that in suburban Dollis Hill the Robin did not often build in private gardens because suitable nest sites were not available.

In central London, where the Robin is mainly confined to the larger parks and gardens containing patches of undisturbed low cover, it is firmly established and may even have increased. Cramp & Tomlins (1966) put the Inner London population at 50-60 pairs. Later records show that by 1968 numbers in Regent's Park had risen to 20 pairs from only 14 in 1959 (Wallace 1974) and in Hyde Park/Kensington Gardens there were 25 pairs in 1973 and 30 in 1974 against 16 in 1968. Holland Park held between eight and 12 pairs during the years of the Atlas survey and other breeding reports came from Walton Street, SW3, where a juvenile was seen being fed on cheese in 1968, and Battersea Park and Brompton cemetery in 1971. Buckingham Palace Gardens were certainly occupied and birds were present in St James's Park in 1971 and bred there in 1973 and 1974. Over the London Area as a whole there were breeding records from 681 tetrads, amounting to 80% of the total.

Despite the prediction by Hudson (1898) that the Robin would disappear from the large central parks, which he considered were then mismanaged from a bird-lover's point of view, it has in fact remained in them in some numbers and luckily its London niche is still secure.

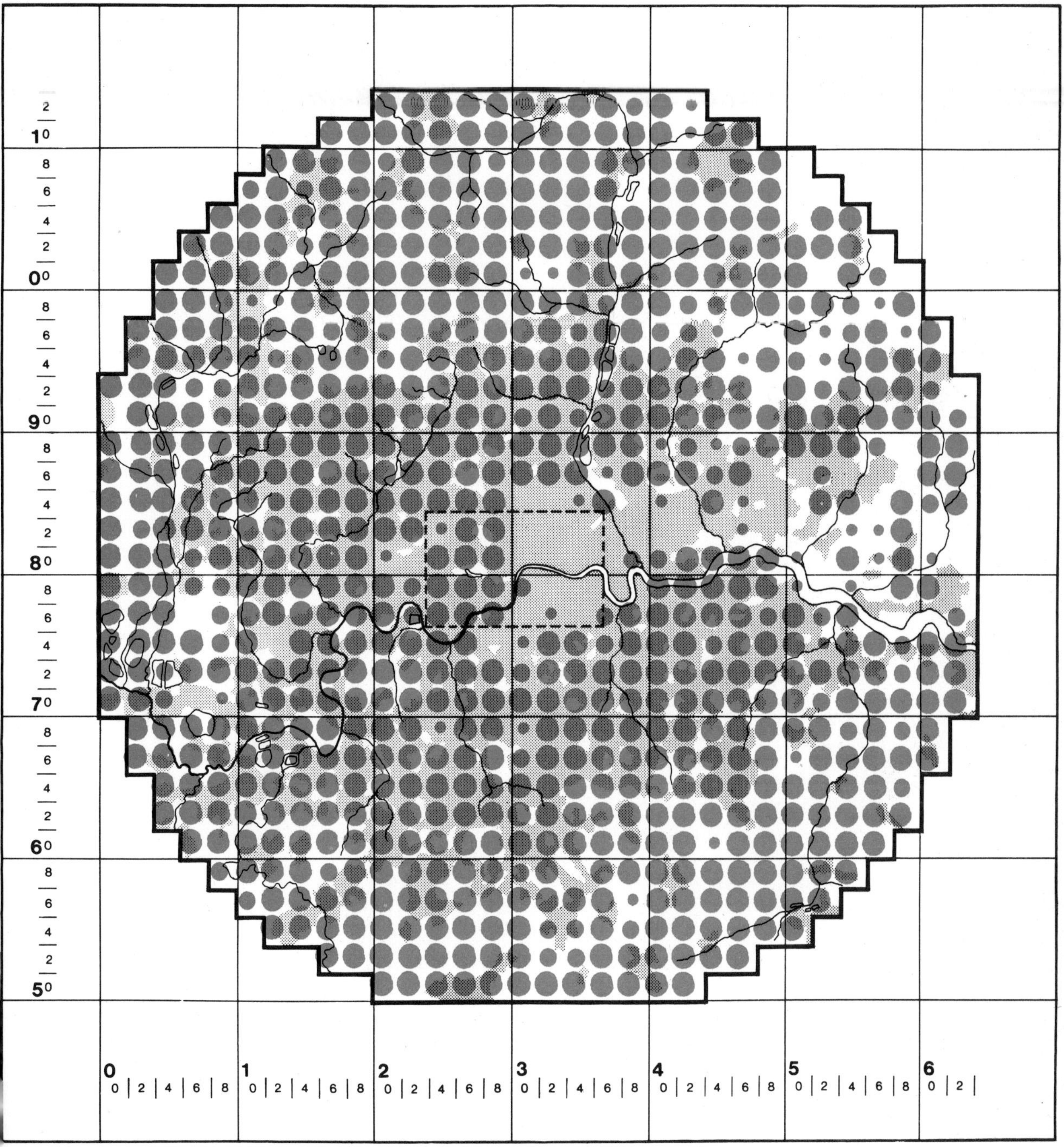
2
1 0
8
6
4
2
0 0
8
6
4
2
9 0
8
6
4
2
8 0
8
6
4
2
7 0
8
6
4
2
6 0
8
6
4
2
5 0
0 0 2 4 6 8
1 0 2 4 6 8
2 0 2 4 6 8
3 0 2 4 6 8
4 0 2 4 6 8
5 0 2 4 6 8
6 0 2

GRASSHOPPER WARBLER

Locustella naevia

This is one of the scarce summer migrants of the London Area. Records are quite widely scattered in rural habitats, but both numbers and distribution vary considerably from year to year.

Because of its mainly skulking habits and shifting population, changes in the status of the Grasshopper Warbler are difficult to follow. Numbers are thought to have decreased this century and by the 1950s there were only about three localities where birds were heard regularly. These were Bookham Common, Ashtead Common and the Colne valley between Uxbridge and Rickmansworth. From that low level numbers improved, so that by 1959 up to 50 singing males were reported in the London Area. Then followed more lean years, with only ten records in 1963, but by 1971 there were as many as 90 singing males reported from 37 localities. After this numbers dropped again slightly in the following two years.

With such fluctuations, a five-year distribution map may well show a pattern of greater abundance than for any one summer. Records of breeding or probable breeding came from 105 tetrads and were well in excess of the number for any single year of the Atlas survey. Of this total, breeding was reported from only 22 tetrads, which shows the difficulty of accurately establishing the status of this species.

Most of its regular haunts are still in Surrey, where annual totals at Bookham Common reached a maximum of six singing males between 1968 and 1972 and there were up to ten pairs at both Ashtead Common and Prince's Coverts, Oxshott. By 1954 there had been only one record from Kent in twenty years, but an improvement has evidently occurred since with Atlas records from 27 tetrads. The species remains scarce in Essex and is virtually absent from Middlesex, though there was an isolated breeding record from the Brent Reservoir in 1964 and a singing male occurred there during the Atlas survey.

Destruction of habitat is a possible cause of desertion of breeding sites, such as Broxbourne Woods in 1961, though these were recolonised by 1966. Conifer plantations are now important habitats for this species (Parslow) and a rotation of planting and felling which maintains areas of rough, low scrub while the trees are small provides suitable breeding habitat. As trees become too high and dense birds move into newly cleared areas as happened at Prince's Coverts (Parr 1972). Such places, fenced off to prevent trampling of young trees, provide sanctuaries for a few years, but other favoured areas such as tussocky, brambly heath or marshy scrub are more vulnerable to disturbance or clearance.

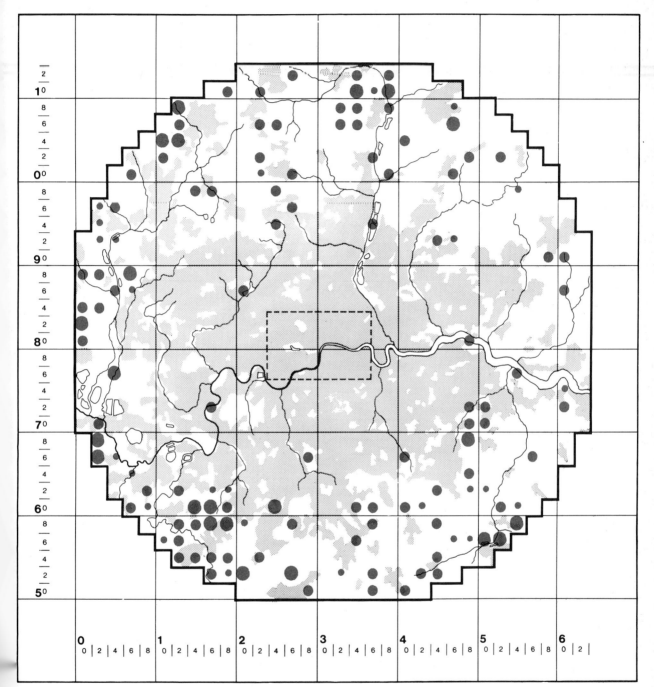

REED WARBLER

Acrocephalus scirpaceus

In the west of the London Area the Reed Warbler's status appears substantially unchanged this century, but numbers have declined in the east through loss of habitat, particularly resulting from changes in land use along the Thames marshes.

Breeding distribution of the Reed Warbler is often determined by the presence or absence of the Common Reed along rivers and ditches or at lakes, gravel pits and, to some extent, at old-style sewage farms. Any local variations in this species of reed, especially its wholesale clearance by man, will lead to corresponding fluctuations in breeding numbers of Reed Warblers.

Earlier records for the London Area showed that these birds were fairly common throughout the length of the Colne and Lea valleys and the lower Thames, with scattered records elsewhere. Little additional information has been added, but results of the Atlas survey indicated that these river valleys still held the greatest concentrations. Density at some of the bigger sites varies and at Rye Meads, for example, numbers rose from 11 pairs in 1961 to 20 pairs in 1972. Nowhere, however, approached the 130-150 pairs in a 4ha reedbed at Abbey Wood recorded in 1949. Since that time there has been a serious loss of habitat along the Thames, especially owing to the Thamesmead new town development.

Away from the main river systems breeding localities were rather scattered. Modernisation of Beddington S.F. has resulted in the loss of a breeding site in south London, but the foothold established at Barn Elms in the 1950s has been successfully maintained with generally at least one breeding pair. Other nesting areas during the Atlas survey included Richmond Park, Ruxley and south of the North Downs at Gatton, Godstone and Sevenoaks. North of the Thames there were suburban records from the Brent Reservoir, Bushy Park/Hampton Court and Hampstead. Records from only 118 tetrads altogether were considerably fewer than for the Sedge Warbler. As well as the more restricted distribution, there is some evidence that where both species occur the Reed Warbler is less numerous, as was reported in 1972 from Stocker's Lake/Springwell G.P., Rye Meads and Thamesmead.

There are no records of Reed Warblers ever nesting in Inner London, though migrants are regular visitors and a family party was seen in Regent's Park in 1959. One bird was seen on several dates in 1972 up to 28 June in Hyde Park/Kensington Gardens, but there was no indication of breeding.

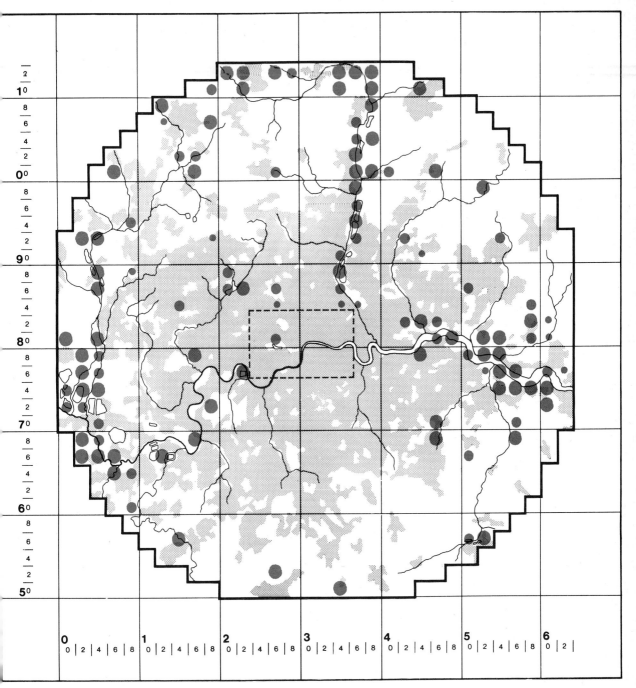

MARSH WARBLER

Acrocephalus palustris

As a breeding species, the Marsh Warbler has always been extremely rare in the London Area. There have been a number of reports from one site since 1959, but otherwise breeding season records over the years from other localities have been very few.

In contrast to the national pattern, London records have become more frequent than they were in the first half of this century. Between 1900 and 1911 only five definite breeding pairs were recorded, all in the western fringe of the Area at Harefield, Thorpe and Wraysbury. Twenty years elapsed before the next report, from Chalfont Park in 1931, and yet another twenty years before a pair was found nesting at Swanscombe Marsh in 1952. The fact that these, the only breeding records of the Marsh Warbler in forty years, were scattered over a distance of some 60km perhaps emphasises the sporadic nature of its occurrence.

From 1958 records began to increase. In that year two birds were located at·Gatton Park and behaviour suggested that they were feeding young (Parr 1972), while a single male near Sevenoaks was the forerunner of a remarkable series of records extending into the 1970s. Apart from a bird at Sundridge in 1964, all these were at the Sevenoaks G.P. reserve where, according to Harrison (1974), birds were present during the breeding season in four of the ten years up to 1968, with one pair nesting successfully in 1963. Thereafter, he reported the establishment of a small colony in 1971, but by 1974 records were down to singing males on only single dates in May and July.

In England as a whole the Marsh Warbler has declined over the last thirty years, particularly since about 1950, and breeding is now confined to a few localities, mainly in Gloucestershire and Worcestershire (Parslow). It has always been a marginal species in Britain, although Voous (1960) stated that there was a northward expansion of its European range in the early part of this century.

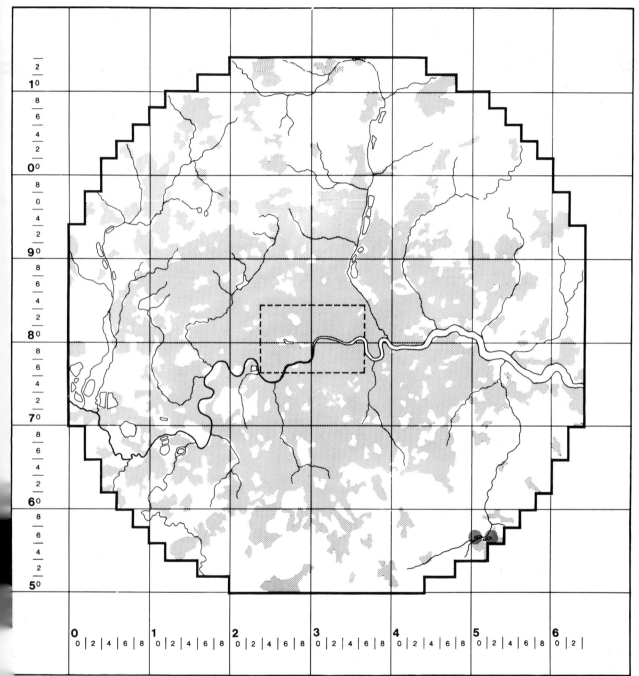

SEDGE WARBLER

Acrocephalus schoenobaenus

Being generally restricted to the vicinity of water, the Sedge Warbler has a patchy distribution in the London Area, though because of its less specialised requirements it is more widespread than the Reed Warbler.

While the status of the Sedge Warbler has probably not changed greatly since the mid-1950s, there are signs of decreases in some areas, partly as a result of loss of habitat through drainage and further urban expansion. National figures taken from the BTO Common Birds Census show, despite quite wide variations, a continuing downward trend, until in 1974 the population index was only 41% of that in 1966 (B & M 1976). A long period of drought in the species' African wintering area resulting in heavy mortality was thought to be one reason for the widespread decline (Winstanley *et al.* 1974). At a more local level, reductions were reported in Surrey in the late 1960s and two gravel pits in Kent also showed some falling numbers. At Ruxley G.P. occupied territories for the years 1966-68 were 14, three and five and at Sevenoaks G.P. reserve the number of nesting pairs dropped from eight in 1970 to only four in 1973 (Harrison 1974). Rye Meads showed the opposite trend, with breeding pairs increasing from about 50 in 1971 to about 100 two years later.

Nevertheless the Sedge Warbler still appears to be commoner than the Reed Warbler, being found during the Atlas survey breeding or probably breeding in 176 tetrads, or 21% of the London Area compared with 13% for the Reed Warbler. The Sedge Warbler is most widespread in the Colne and Lea valleys where the river habitats are augmented by lakes and gravel pits with surrounding rough vegetation. It is also commonly found along the Thames valley to the east and west of London, as well as in the upper reaches of the River Roding and its tributaries. Suitable habitat in the suburbs is obviously scarcer, but during the Atlas years there were reports of breeding pairs at the Brent Reservoir, Walthamstow, Erith Marsh, Ruxley, Mitcham and Berrylands S.F.

Maintenance of the Sedge Warbler's present wide distribution ,probably depends upon preservation of undisturbed scrub around gravel pits and along rivers. In some parts of Britain, however, birds are moving into drier habitats and have been recorded singing from fields of growing crops (Bonham & Sharrock 1974) and nesting in young conifer plantations (Parslow). While such sites are likely to be no more than marginal habitats, there is perhaps scope for expansion into new localities to counteract displacement by the spread of suburbia.

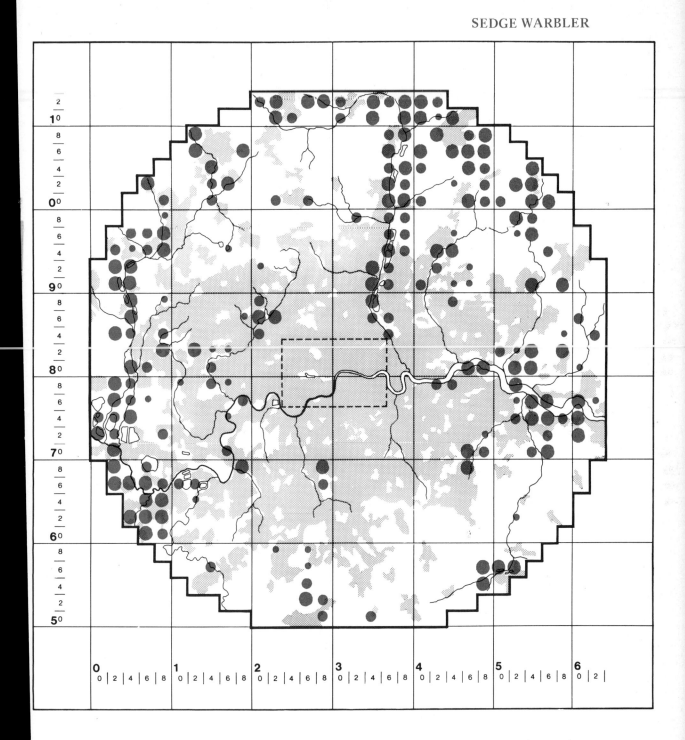

BLACKCAP

Sylvia atricapilla

Of the four *sylvia* warblers that breed in the London Area, the Blackcap has the widest distribution, being absent only from the open agricultural parts of south Essex and from densely built-up localities.

Probably little change in the population level has occurred since the 1950s. Most breeding data are from the regularly watched central London parks and the oakwood and scrub habitats at Bookham. Records from the parks appear to have increased in the late 1960s and the earlier statement (Cramp & Tomlins 1966) that warblers have been unable to find enough cover and freedom from disturbance for regular breeding is no longer true for this species. Blackcaps may have nested regularly in Holland Park before 1939 when the grounds were still private, but later records were lacking until 1960 when one pair reared young. There were two breeding pairs in 1961 and a single pair nested in most following years, increasing to two pairs in 1967 and probably three in 1969. In Kensington Gardens regular nesting ceased in the 1870s and was not recorded again until 1961 when a pair attempted to breed, but was unsuccessful (Fitter 1949, Sanderson 1968). Two pairs were present in 1966 and breeding proved again in 1967. A few pairs are now recorded annually.

Table 12 shows the numbers of occupied territories at three Inner London parks and at Bookham Common for the years 1966-74. With the provision of sanctuaries, the parks can now obtain densities comparable with more rural localities. For the London Area as a whole records covered 71% of the tetrads compared with 43% for the Garden Warbler. The Blackcap accepts a wider range of habitats and does not require such dense cover as the Garden Warbler, though the presence of trees is necessary.

Some of the gaps on the map may simply indicate lack of sufficient coverage, but in central London, away from the parks, there are few suitable nesting areas. To the east, the countryside just north of the Thames beyond the dense suburban developments is mainly open farmland with low hedges and few patches of woodland. This area probably offers little to attract the Blackcap, which elsewhere is clearly still well established.

Table 12.   Occupied territories of Blackcaps at selected
localities in the London Area, 1966-74

		66	67	68	69	70	71	72	73	74
Bookham	— oakwood	7	6	3	6	1	3	4	3	2
	— scrub	1	2	2	2	3	4	7	7	5
Inner London	— Holland Park	1	2	2/3	3	2	2/3	1	?	?
	— Hyde Park/									
	Kensington Gardens	2	3	8	7	8	2	8	7	4
	— Regent's Park	—	2	3	5	1	—	1	3	5

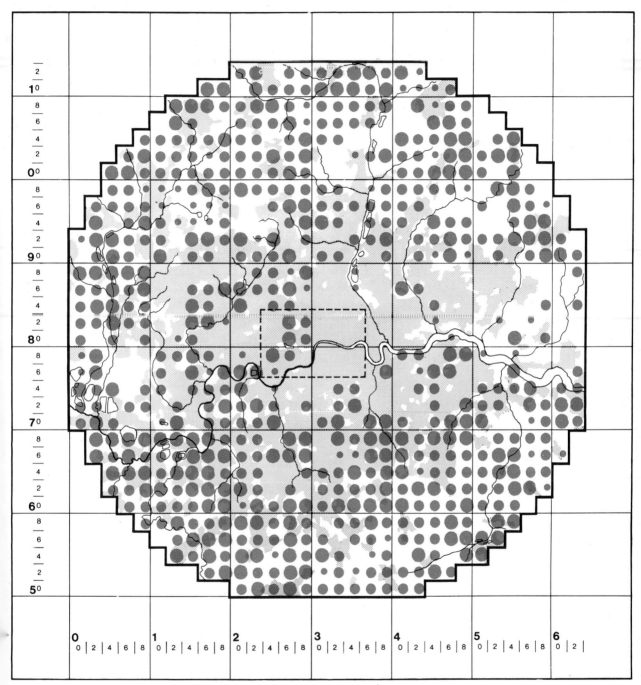

GARDEN WARBLER

Sylvia borin

Compared with the Blackcap, the Garden Warbler has a more restricted distribution in the London Area, indicative of its more exacting habitat requirements. Low dense cover, which it prefers, is found mainly in the outer suburbs and rural parts of the Area and its patchy distribution is closely related to the occurrence of woods, commons and scrub.

This is another species for which few references either to increases or decreases are available. Long-term surveys at Bookham Common have shown the relationship between the Garden Warbler and Blackcap, both of which occupy somewhat similar habitats in rural areas, though the latter is more closely associated with woodland, whereas the Garden Warbler tends to keep to lower, denser scrub, feeding chiefly in bushes. In 16ha of pedunculate oakwood at Bookham, the number of singing males holding territory over a period of twenty-four years averaged 2.4 per annum for the Garden Warbler (15 per 100ha) compared with 3.5 for the Blackcap (22 per 100ha). Even allowing for considerable annual variations, since 1962 Garden Warblers have consistently been in the minority and have declined so much that none bred during 1971-73 (Beven 1974b & 1976).

Numbers of the two species were more even in 39ha of scrub at Bookham surveyed since 1964. In this habitat the Garden Warbler averaged 2.7 territories per annum against 3.1 for the Blackcap (seven and eight per 100ha respectively), though in later years, as the scrub and trees grew, Blackcap numbers increased (Beven 1974b).

BTO Common Birds Census studies have shown that numbers of both species in the breeding season have been very erratic. The Garden Warbler was also thought by Winstanley *et al.* (1974) to have suffered from the drought in its wintering areas in the Sahel region of Africa, though the extent of the decline in London has not been sufficient to cause comment.

Distribution of records shown on the map is almost entirely confined to the rural parts of the Area, with few pairs penetrating far into the suburbs and then only into localities with large gardens and a scattering of open spaces. The inner limits of Chislehurst, Eltham, Dulwich, Hendon, Hampstead Heath and Epping Forest are similar to those described in the 1950s. There are also records of breeding or probable breeding from the extensive open spaces at Wimbledon, Richmond Park and Kew. Although usually occurring in the Inner London parks only on migration, there was one breeding record for the Atlas survey when a pair was reported to have nested successfully in Regent's Park in 1972.

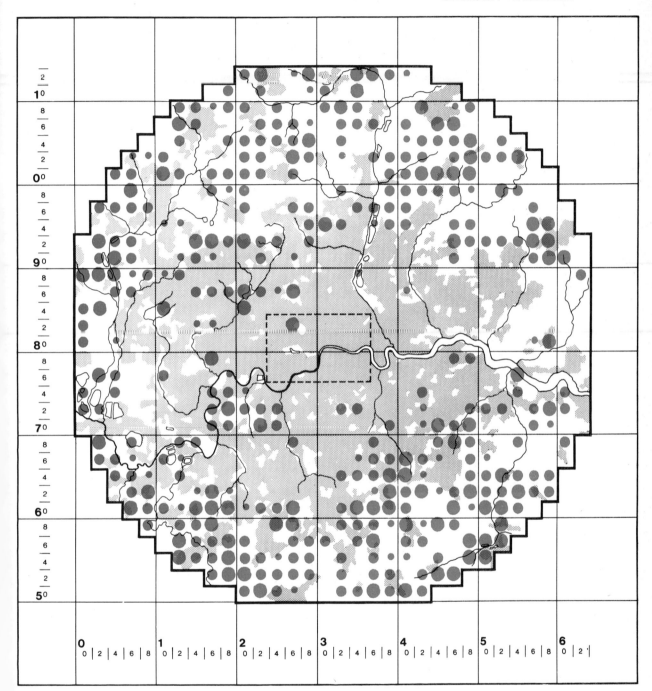

WHITETHROAT

Sylvia communis

From the map, the Whitethroat appears to be common and widespread in the London Area and indeed up to 1969 this seems to have been the position. The population then crashed while the survey was still in progress, but as tetrads were not censused both before and after the collapse, the map cannot show the extent of the losses. Recovery has been very slow and some localities occupied in 1968 may not yet have been recolonised.

At Bookham Common the number of territories of singing males in 39ha of scrub and grassland during 1964-73 varied between 11 and 22. The highest figure was in 1967, dropping to 16 in 1968 and 11 in 1969, then gradually rising to 17 in 1973 (Beven 1974a). In this locality the fall was evidently not as dramatic as in other parts of the London Area. Ten observers who gave comparable figures reported 33 pairs in 1969 against 145 the previous year and on Common Birds Census plots in London occupied territories were down to 18 compared with 89 in 1968. These two comparisons indicate a reduction of between 77% and 80% in the breeding population.

Analyses of Whitethroat territories shown by the BTO Common Birds Census for the country as a whole show similar results. In 1968 the population index on farmland for this species reached its highest level since the census began in 1962 and then dropped by over 70% the following year (B & M 1976). The failure of Whitethroats to reappear in the spring of 1969 in anything like their former numbers and their continuing low level has been the subject of considerable investigation and appears to be related to the long drought in the species' wintering area on the southern fringe of the Sahara, resulting in greatly reduced winter survival (Winstanley *et al.* 1974).

A preference for low, rank vegetation with thick patches of bramble, nettle or gorse, means that many of the London parks are unsuitable for breeding Whitethroats and consequently they are absent from the central part of the London Area. There appear to be only three records of nesting in Inner London. In 1953 a pair successfully raised young in Regent's Park and attempted to do so in 1956, and in Holland Park in 1960 a bird was seen carrying food. The nearest records to central London reported during the Atlas survey were from Woolwich, Dulwich, Wimbledon, Chiswick, Hampstead Heath and down the Lea valley as far as Hackney.

Away from the centre, the Whitethroat can be found throughout most of the outer suburbs and rural parts of the London Area and, before the recent decline, was locally numerous. By 1972 Walton Heath was the only locality where reports suggested that numbers were back to former levels.

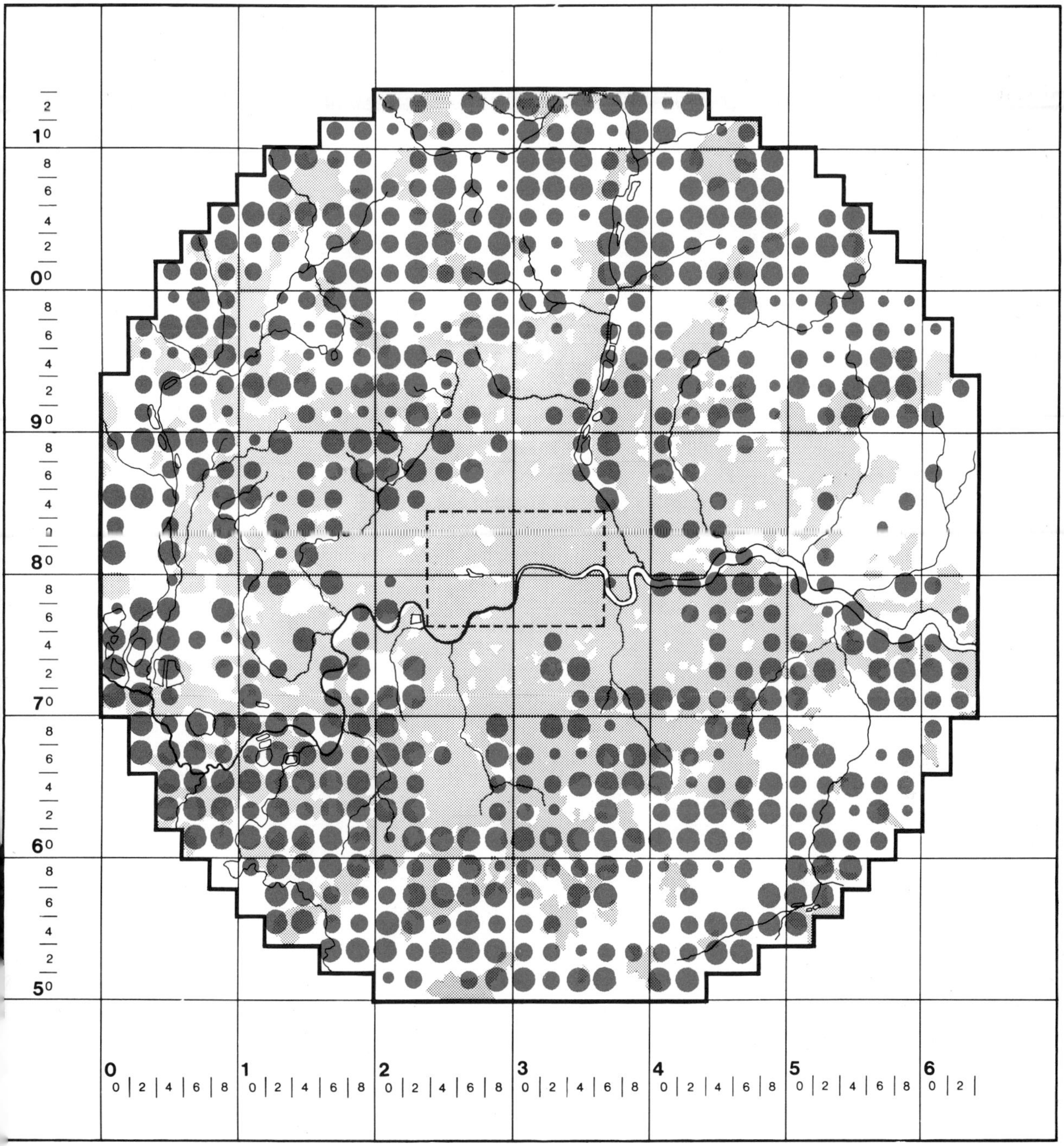
2
1 0
8
6
4
2
0 0
8
6
4
2
9 0
8
6
4
2
8 0
8
6
4
2
7 0
8
6
4
2
6 0
8
6
4
2
5 0
0 0 2 4 6 8
1 0 2 4 6 8
2 0 2 4 6 8
3 0 2 4 6 8
4 0 2 4 6 8
5 0 2 4 6 8
6 0 2

LESSER WHITETHROAT

Sylvia curruca

The Lesser Whitethroat is the least numerous of the *sylvia* warblers nesting in the London Area. Though widely scattered it has a very patchy distribution throughout the suburbs and rural zone.

Generally suspected of being under-recorded, the status of this species is particularly difficult to assess, though there is no evidence of significant changes during this century. In 1960 the Lesser Whitethroat was seen in 22 possible breeding localities and was considered at the time to be more numerous than usual. There was an increase in 1962, which included four pairs reported in Epping Forest, and a further slight rise in numbers over the next few years when observers were asked to pay more attention to this species. As with some other summer migrants, however, there was a drop in 1969, though not to the same extent as the Whitethroat. Compared with these reports, the total of 221 tetrads in which the Lesser Whitethroat was found breeding or probably breeding during the Atlas survey appears to represent a major expansion, but is more likely to have been the result of more thorough and systematic searching. Numbers reported fluctuate from year to year and in fact the only indication of a trend in the population is that the occasional breeding records from Inner London parks now seem to be entirely lacking.

Habitat requirements for this species are somewhat similar to the Whitethroat, though it prefers taller hedgerows and scattered trees as well as dense scrub. Much of the inner suburbs and Inner London are therefore unsuitable and the main concentration of Atlas records came from the rural parts of the London Area, particularly on the heaths and commons around Esher, Ashtead and further out towards Bookham Common. North of the Thames there were numerous records from the Colne valley and from Essex. Inner limits were very similar to those of the Garden Warbler and included Woolwich, Bromley, Dulwich, Wimbledon, Hendon and Chigwell. Though present on Hampstead Heath breeding was not proved during the survey years.

There were no records, other than of migrants, from Inner London though breeding has been recorded in the past. Singing males in Holland Park in many years up to 1940 suggest that breeding may have occurred there regularly up to that time, but the last definite breeding record appears to have been in Kensington Gardens as long ago as 1921.

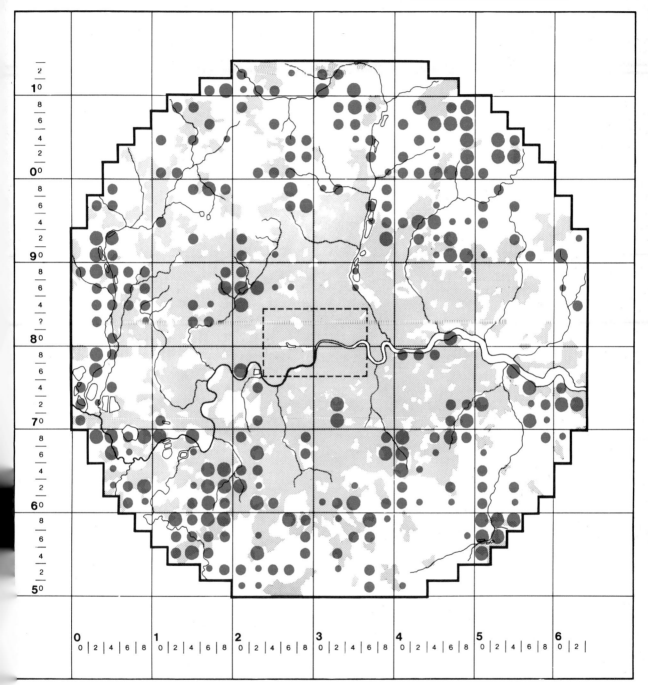

WILLOW
WARBLER

Phylloscopus trochilus

Being less restricted in its choice of habitat than either of the other two *phylloscopus* warblers breeding in the London Area, the Willow Warbler is both more widespread and more numerous. It is common in open woodland and birch scrub, but will also nest in large suburban gardens and occasionally in the parks in Inner London.

Loss of habitat through the continual spread of suburban London may have forced the Willow Warbler out of some former haunts, but overall there is no evidence of any major change in status this century. Long-term studies, as at Bookham Common, show fluctuations from year to year, though whether these are due to changes in breeding habitat rather than conditions during migration or in wintering areas is not clear. In a 39ha census plot at Bookham, where scrub and hawthorn had increased considerably in the 1950s, the number of territories occupied by Willow Warblers over the ten years up to 1973 varied from 20 in 1964 and 1973 to a maximum of 27 in 1967 and a minimum of 14 in 1965 and 1970 (Beven 1974a). An area of 16ha of oakwood, also at Bookham, showed a declining population from a maximum of 21 territories in 1950 down to only two in 1970 and none in 1971 to 1974 (Beven 1976). Birds may have moved into surrounding habitat which became more attractive as the wood itself became denser.

BTO Common Birds Census studies in Britain have not shown any marked change in numbers in woodland since 1964 when figures first became available, while on farmland the population index more than doubled between 1962 and 1970, fell by 20% in 1971 and then remained steady up to 1974 (B & M 1976).

Being fairly catholic in its choice of habitats, the Willow Warbler is found throughout most of the London Area and during the Atlas survey was recorded from 652 tetrads or 76% of the total. In suburban London the inner limits followed the stretch of woodland and parkland south of the Thames from Dulwich to Richmond Park and north of the River came as close to the centre as Hampstead Heath. Birds have also nested occasionally in some of the Inner London parks where the provision of sanctuaries has enabled them to breed undisturbed. Willow Warblers and Blackcaps have been the two most successful warblers nesting in Holland Park, even though there is no proof of the Willow Warbler breeding there successfully since 1960 in spite of regular spring records. During the survey years it was proved to breed in Hyde Park/Kensington Gardens in 1969, for the first time since 1923, and again in 1972. Breeding has also occurred in Regent's Park in 1954, 1955, probably in 1956 and was reported again in 1972.

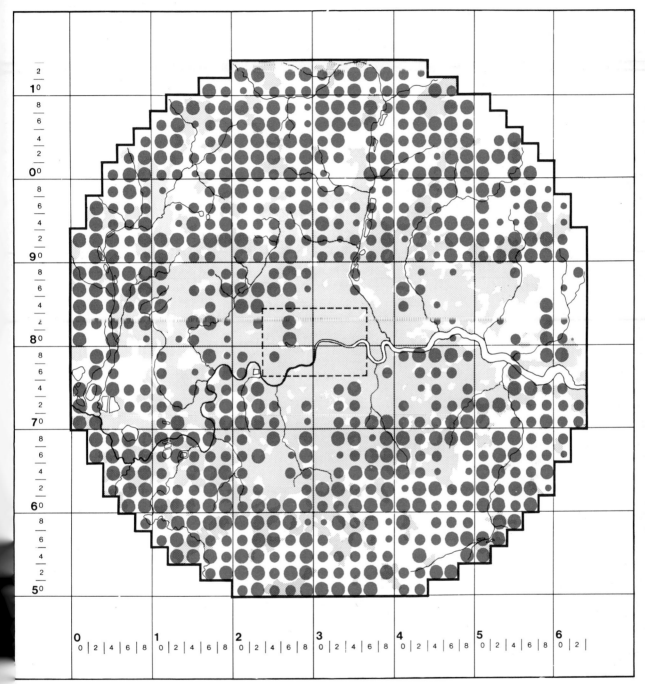

CHIFFCHAFF

Phylloscopus collybita

Like the Willow Warbler, the Chiffchaff is a widespread summer visitor to the London Area with a broadly similar breeding distribution. There are few records from the central area or densely developed suburbs, but the species can be found throughout most of the outlying districts.

The only detectable change this century has been some degree of retreat from localities that have become more densely built-up. Many of the records during the Atlas period refer to cases of probable breeding, often based on the presence of singing males. While it can be difficult to obtain definite proof of nesting, the distinctive song is easy to recognise. Nevertheless, the Chiffchaff was recorded in 38 fewer tetrads than the Willow Warbler. Its habitat requirements are more exacting, with a preference for taller trees as song posts, and it is found particularly in mature, fairly open woodland and woodland edge. In a census of 16ha of oakwood at Bookham Common from 1949 until 1959 Chiffchaffs averaged only three pairs annually compared with 13.8 for the Willow Warbler. As the wood became denser and the rides narrower, the Willow Warbler declined and was completely absent in 1971 to 1974, whereas the Chiffchaff has maintained its position with little change (Beven 1976).

BTO Common Birds Census analyses indicate that Chiffchaff numbers on farmland were low in 1962 and 1963 (B & M 1976). Since then the population index has shown a fairly rapid increase so that the average level during the Atlas years was nearly four times greater than that recorded in 1962. In woodland plots the increase has been much less marked and the five-year average was only 1.5 times greater than in 1964, the first year for which figures were available in this habitat.

Inner limits of regular breeding of the Chiffchaff in the London Area are comparable with other breeding warblers, corresponding with the more rural aspects of Dulwich, Wimbledon, Richmond and Kew south of the Thames and Hampstead Heath north of the River. It is a regular migrant through the Inner London parks and some birds stay for several weeks, so that during the Atlas survey singing males were reported from Holland Park, Hyde Park/Kensington Gardens and Regent's Park. Definite breeding records, however, have been few and the last in Holland Park was as far back as 1937, though a pair was reported to have nested in Regent's Park in 1972. Disturbance and the lack of any extensive areas of rough ground probably prevent the species from nesting regularly in these localities which may be only marginally suitable.

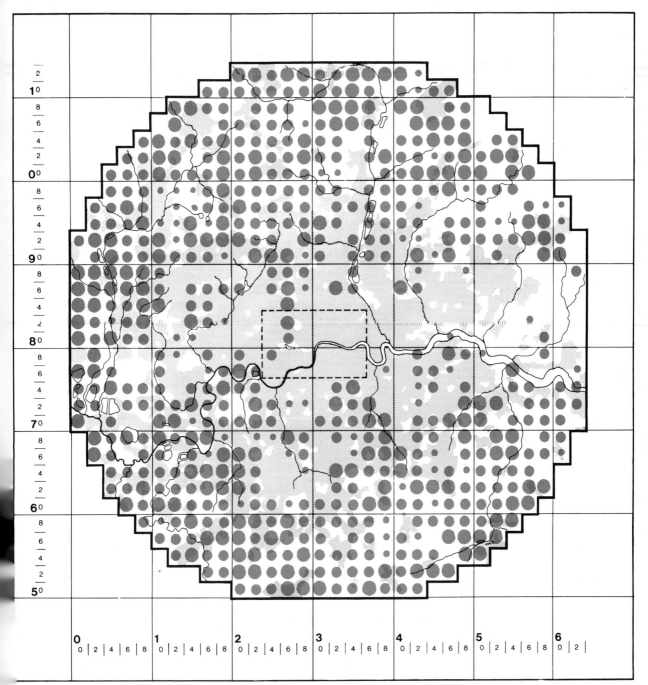

WOOD WARBLER

Phylloscopus sibilatrix

This is a fairly scarce breeding species in the London Area, found in scattered localities, but more frequently in the dry beechwoods and heaths in the south and south-west.

Its preference for woodland with little undergrowth must be a limiting factor in its distribution and increased disturbance may have led to a reduction in numbers since the 1950s when it was described as breeding in most suitable localities. In 1958 High Beach in Epping Forest was said to be a regular locality for the Wood Warbler, but the map shows a very sparse distribution in Essex during the Atlas survey and there is no indication that High Beach is any longer a favoured site. Human pressures on that part of the forest may be responsible for the decline. The *London Bird Report* for 1960 expressed the view that the status of the Wood Warbler as a breeding bird of the London Area was clearly insecure. This comment may have spurred observers to pay more attention to the species and in 1962 there were breeding season reports of 13 or 14 singing males, though only two pairs were known to have nested successfully. During the Atlas survey the Wood Warbler was reported from 82 tetrads, but whether this represents an increase is difficult to judge, as records were collected over five years. There are annual fluctuations and numbers appeared to be low in 1972 when once again only two pairs were known to have bred. This thin distribution is in keeping with its status elsewhere in the eastern half of England where it is a scarce and local breeding species (Parslow).

Many of the records on the map are based on the presence of singing males in suitable breeding habitats, though some may have been merely migrants. Breeding reports during the five years came from no more than 15 out of the total of 82 occupied tetrads. There were three from localities north of the Thames, at Stanmore Common, Hampstead Heath and Northaw Great Wood. South of the River, there was one record from Petts Wood, but all the others were in Surrey from Limpsfield westwards, with the main concentration of breeding records in the Banstead, Walton and Headley Heath areas. In the south London suburbs there were breeding records from the Shirley Hills near Croydon and from Wimbledon Common.

With records coming from such a limited number of localities the continued presence of the Wood Warbler is very much dependent on the maintenance of suitable, undisturbed habitat, in particular the preservation of mature woodland.

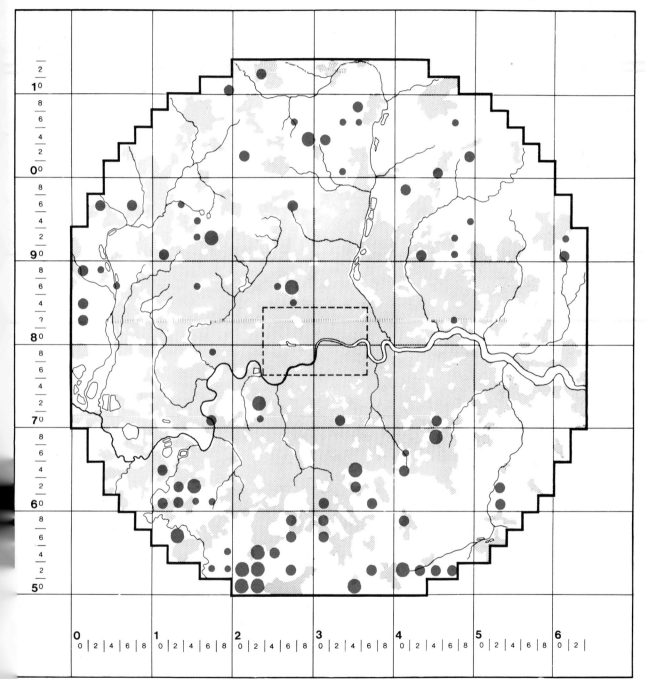

GOLDCREST

Regulus regulus

Clearly gaining a considerable benefit from a series of mild winters, the Goldcrest population has expanded and the species is now widespread in the London Area, especially in the southern and western parts.

In the mid-1950s the Goldcrest was considered to have a patchy and irregular breeding distribution, being most common on the Surrey heaths and slopes of the North Downs. It is particularly susceptible to severe weather and consequently numbers may fluctuate widely over a period of years. Two consecutive cold winters in 1962 and 1963 resulted in an enormous drop. Several reports in 1963 referred to drastic reductions or the complete absence of normal breeding populations in parts of the London Area and breeding season records for that year totalled no more than ten adults from only seven localities, all but one in Surrey. Recovery seemed to be slow, though there were insufficient reports in later years to allow the increase and spread to be followed in detail, but the losses have been made good and numbers now appear to be higher than for many years. A series of mild winters since 1963 has clearly aided this recovery, but the growth of conifer plantations in the London Area, as in many parts of the country, may be helping its expansion.

Through the years of the Atlas survey Goldcrests were recorded in a little under half the tetrads of the London Area. Most records came from south of the Thames where 57% of the Area was occupied compared with 38% north of the River. Records were absent from densely built-up urban and suburban habitats and from a wide stretch of country on both sides of the Thames east of London where much of the land is taken up by agriculture or industrial development. Looking at the map, the Lea valley also appears to be generally unsuitable. In Inner London birds were seen carrying food in Holland Park in 1971 and two broods were seen there the following year, when a pair was also present in Hyde Park/Kensington Gardens.

With the Goldcrest population increasing during the years of the Atlas survey the map shows distribution at a time when numbers were already high. Further mild winters have allowed the upward trend to continue and the species has probably expanded further, as indicated by analyses of BTO Common Birds Census results which show that in 1974 the Goldcrest was over ten times as common as it was in 1964 (B & M 1976).

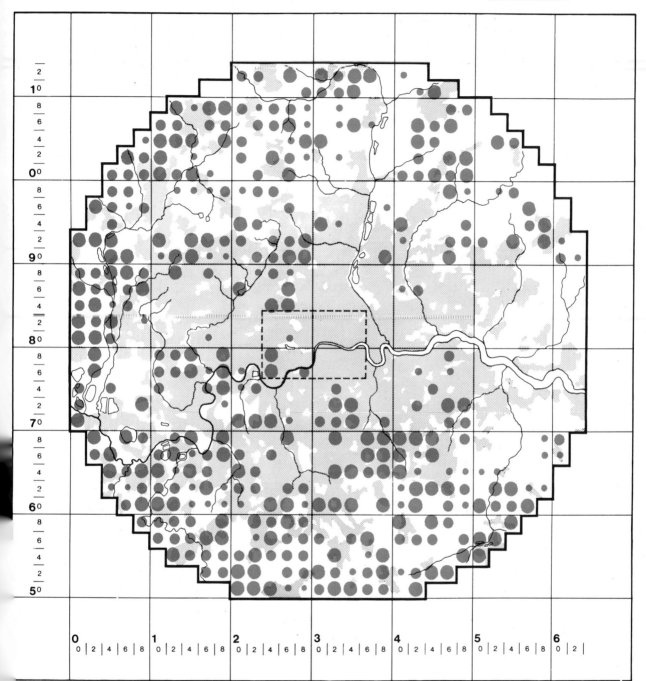

FIRECREST

Regulus ignicapillus

The Firecrest is a relative newcomer to the list of British breeding species. While there is no evidence that it has yet colonised the London Area, birds have been seen in May and even June in suitable habitat.

There were about 28 known occurrences of the Firecrest in the London Area up to 1954, all between September and April. Records were more regular in the following years with birds seen annually from 1955 to 1967, except during 1962-64 when two severe winters may have affected continental populations. From 1967 the Firecrest became more familiar. In that year seven birds were seen, one of which on Hampstead Heath on 8 May seems to have been the first record for that month. There was a minimum of eight each year throughout the Atlas period and perhaps as many as 13 in 1971. Most records were still outside the breeding season, but included one in May 1968 and 1970 and two in May and one in June 1971.

This pattern of increasing regularity coincided with the discovery of breeding populations in the New Forest, Hampshire, in 1962 (Adams 1966) and at Wendover Forest, Bucks, in 1971. Since then the species has also nested in Dorset, Somerset and possibly Bedfordshire and singing males have been recorded in other mainly southern counties (Batten 1973a).

Of the breeding season records in the London Area, those in Kent were all of singing males, but the birds did not remain in the same locality for more than one or two days and with no sign of accompanying females. In the Westerham area single birds were recorded on 30 April 1967 and 11 May 1968, while in Petts Wood two singing males were present in the same group of pines on 1 and 2 May 1971. Also in 1971 there was a record from Coopersale, near Epping, where on 12 June a male Firecrest was caught and ringed after one had been heard singing the previous week. Again there was no indication of breeding, though the Coopersale site appeared to be suitable habitat comprising Scots pine, spruce and larch that already held a large breeding population of Goldcrests. Batten (1973a) suggested that Norway spruce was the most favoured tree, but the Firecrest can also occur in a variety of conifers and even in predominantly broad-leaved woodland.

Two further May records occurred in 1973, a bird singing at Potters Bar on the 19th and one singing and feeding in hawthorn in Kensington Gardens on the 11th, where one was also recorded on 21 May 1974. All the evidence so far suggests that before long the Firecrest will colonise the London Area, but with the amount of potentially suitable habitat available the species could very easily be overlooked.

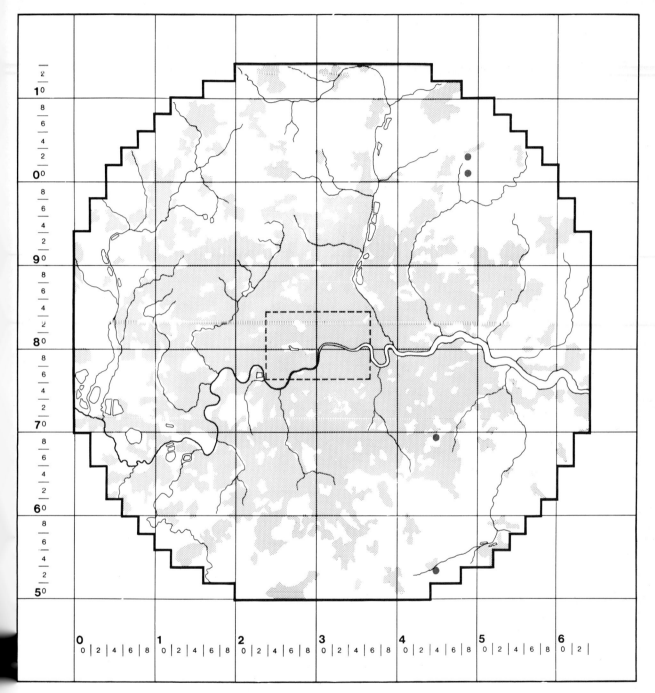

SPOTTED FLYCATCHER

Muscicapa striata

As a widespread summer visitor, the Spotted Flycatcher is found throughout almost the whole of the London Area. Though not abundant, it is only absent from places where trees or hedges are scarce.

Because it is a familiar bird it fails to attract comment and there is little published information on breeding numbers. Most of the detailed records are from Inner London where Cramp & Tomlins (1966) considered the Spotted Flycatcher to be one of the few summer migrants breeding regularly and estimated the population at ten to 20 pairs. As well as the parks, it has nested in St John's Wood, Bloomsbury and less frequently in Chelsea and Lambeth. A slight increase in numbers may have occurred in recent years as shown by counts in Hyde Park/Kensington Gardens given in Table 13. Except for 1967, birds have nested annually in Holland Park since 1959 up to 1973 and three pairs were present in 1971. In Regent's Park the average annual breeding population during 1959-68 was 7.6 pairs (Wallace 1974). With each pair producing an average of 1.4 broods of 1.9 young each year, this species had the highest success rate of any passerines nesting in the Park, probably because of freedom from competition for nest sites and colonisation of underexploited habitat.

BTO Common Birds Census analyses indicate that the population was lower during the years 1970-74 than in the previous five years, particularly on farmland (B & M 1976). Counts in Hyde Park/Kensington Gardens have tended to show the reverse with high numbers in 1972 and 1973, but dropping to only six in 1974, which was the lowest figure for ten years.

During the Atlas survey distribution was similar to other widely spread insectivorous species with the inner limits ranging from Greenwich Park, Dulwich, Clapham, Kew, Hampstead Heath and Wanstead, but with a greater density of Inner London records. Less atmospheric pollution in recent years in central London, following the introduction of clean air legislation, may have resulted in an increase in the quantity of insects, thus making food more readily available for feeding young. The fact, too, that the Spotted Flycatcher nests in holes in trees and in creeper on trees or buildings, making it less dependent on ground cover than the warblers, may aid its survival in London parks and gardens.

Table 13.   Occupied territories of Spotted Flycatchers in
Hyde Park/Kensington Gardens, 1966-74

	66	67	68	69	70	71	72	73	74
Hyde Park/Kensington Gardens	8	7	8	10	8	7	11	15	6

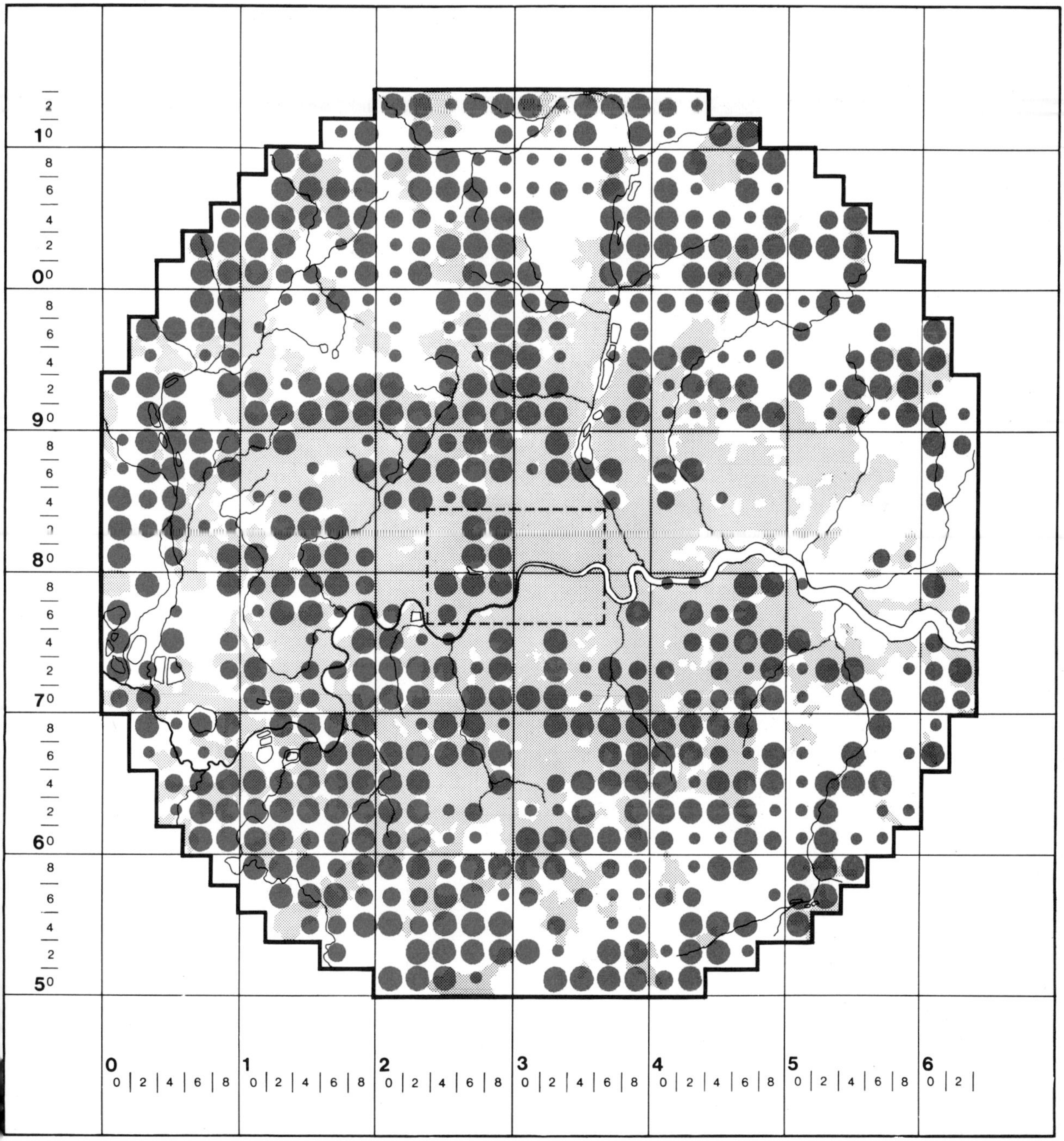
2
1 0
8
6
4
2
0 0
8
6
4
2
9 0
8
6
4
2
8 0
8
6
4
2
7 0
8
6
4
2
6 0
8
6
4
2
5 0
0 1 2 3 4 5 6
0 2 4 6 8

DUNNOCK

Prunella modularis

The Dunnock is one of the most common species in the London Area and, though unobtrusive, is widely recorded.

Its status does not appear to have changed during the present century. Unlike some other species which have retreated towards the rural fringe before the advance of suburbia, the Dunnock has become a familiar bird of parks and gardens. Cramp & Tomlins (1966) stated that in Inner London in 1965 it was more numerous than the Robin and had a breeding population of 100-120 pairs. During the Atlas survey records came from 93% of the tetrads over the whole of the London Area and breeding was reported from 70%. There was a lack of records from some central localities where indeed it may be absent from the most heavily developed parts, and from several tetrads in south Essex where observer coverage was poor.

A comparison of breeding season censuses from Hyde Park/Kensington Gardens in Inner London and Bookham Common near the south-west boundary of the Area, shown in Table 14, indicates a decline in the rural habitat, particularly in the oakwood, and an increase in urban parkland, though such trends may not necessarily apply elsewhere. In fact numbers in Regent's Park showed little change over the years 1959-68 with an annual average of 51.2 pairs (Wallace 1974). Breeding success in the Park was very low and over the ten year study period an average of only 0.4 fledged young per pair was recorded. To maintain the population there must have been recruitment from outside or remarkably low adult mortality.

As a resident species generally feeding on the ground, the Dunnock might be thought to be particularly susceptible to the effects of prolonged frost and snow in severe winters. There is little direct evidence of this in London though in suburban habitat at Dollis Hill numbers declined from about 48 pairs in 1962 to 25-30 pairs in 1963 after the harsh conditions in the early months of that year. In Regent's Park (Wallace 1974) the reduction in breeding numbers was insignificant.

Table 14. Occupied territories of Dunnocks at Bookham Common
and Hyde Park/Kensington Gardens, 1965-74

	65	66	67	68	69	70	71	72	73	74
Bookham — oakwood	5	4	8	6	6	3	2	1	—	3
— scrub	15	13	18	12	12	13	10	13	9	14
Hyde Park/Kensington Gardens — parkland	13	16	23	29	28	33	32	26	24	22

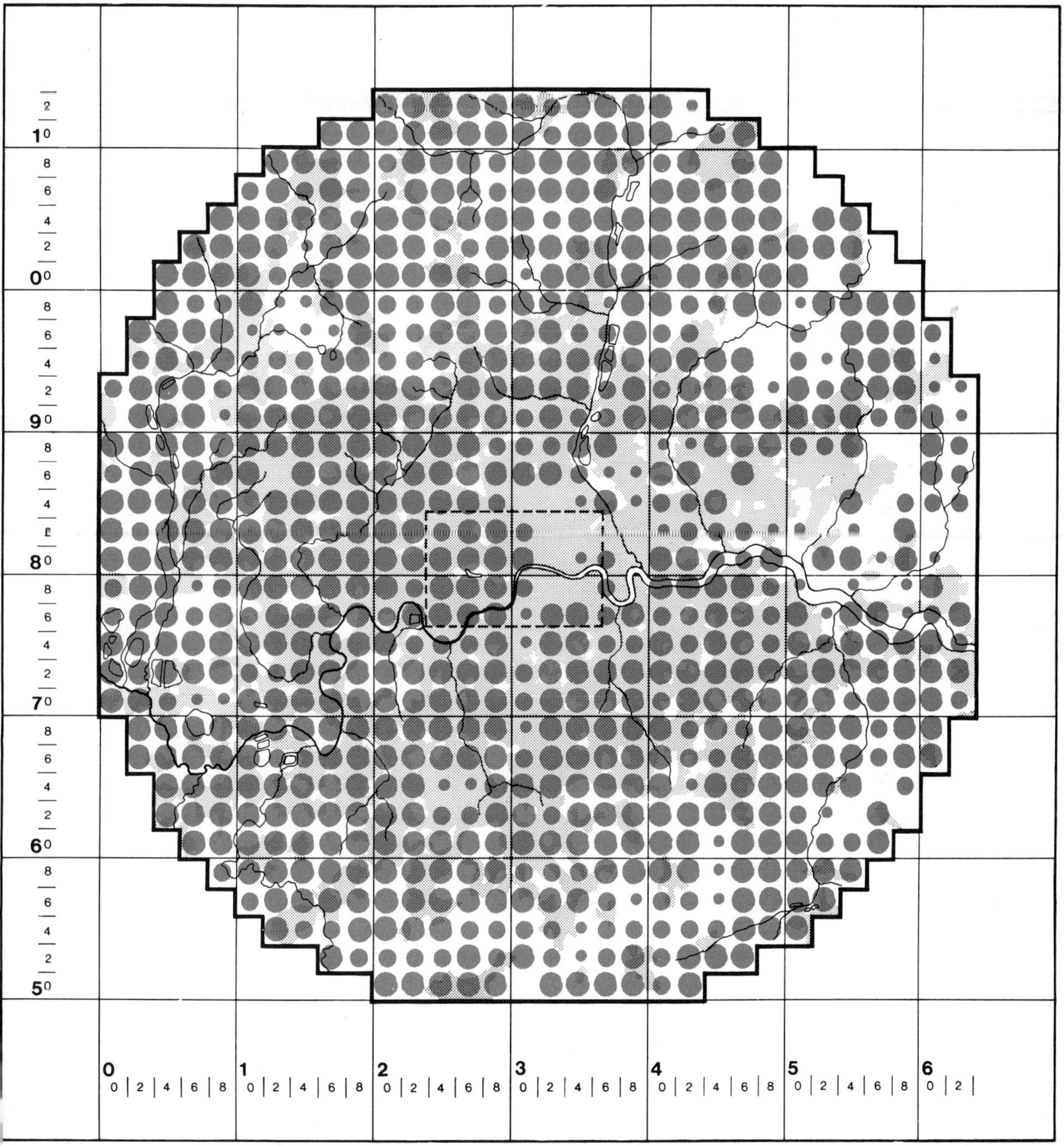
1
0
9
8
7
6
5
0
1
2
3
4
5
6
0 2 4 6 8

MEADOW PIPIT

Anthus pratensis

This species has a scattered distribution in the London Area where it is limited by the lack of open country. Isolated breeding records from such localities as the disused Elmers End S.F. and at Beddington S.F. suggest that birds will continue to occupy traditional sites in spite of changing conditions provided the areas remain relatively undisturbed.

As with many other passerines, there have been few previous studies of the Meadow Pipit. Numbers have perhaps increased during the present century, though up to the 1950s it was still a scarce and local nesting species in the Area. Since then there may have been a further slight increase. While a survey of the breeding population in 1957 was incomplete and the results can be regarded as conservative, the figures indicated that about 80 pairs were present in the Area in approximately 30 localities (Homes *et al.* 1960). Comparison with the Atlas results, even bearing in mind that the latter covered five years, suggests that Meadow Pipits are now more widespread, even if some records of probable breeding on the map, based on the presence of singing males, could relate to migrants. During the years 1968-72 breeding reports came from 72 tetrads out of a total of 194 in which the species was recorded. As in the earlier survey, breeding habitats were broadly divided into two main categories of heath or waterside. On the heaths the Meadow Pipit occurs typically in areas of fairly short grass with scattered scrub, but the growth of trees seems to cause a decline as the habitat becomes less open.

Of areas where the species was found in 1957, Rainham and Thurrock, north of the Thames, and the rough ground bordering the south bank from Plumstead and Erith eastwards remain largely undisturbed and continue to be occupied by Meadow Pipits, but there has been some loss of habitat, as at Thamesmead new town development. Atlas records also showed the species was still present on the Surrey heaths, particularly Banstead, Walton and Headley. Other favoured localities included commons and parklands such as Wimbledon and Richmond Park and the grassy surroundings of reservoirs and gravel pits, including the lower part of the Colne valley.

With people visiting the Surrey heaths in greater numbers, the most secure breeding localities of the Meadow Pipit are probably those near water. The continuing spread of gravel pits within the London Area may open up new localities from time to time to compensate for losses elsewhere, but preservation of some at least of the remaining Thames marshes is also important.

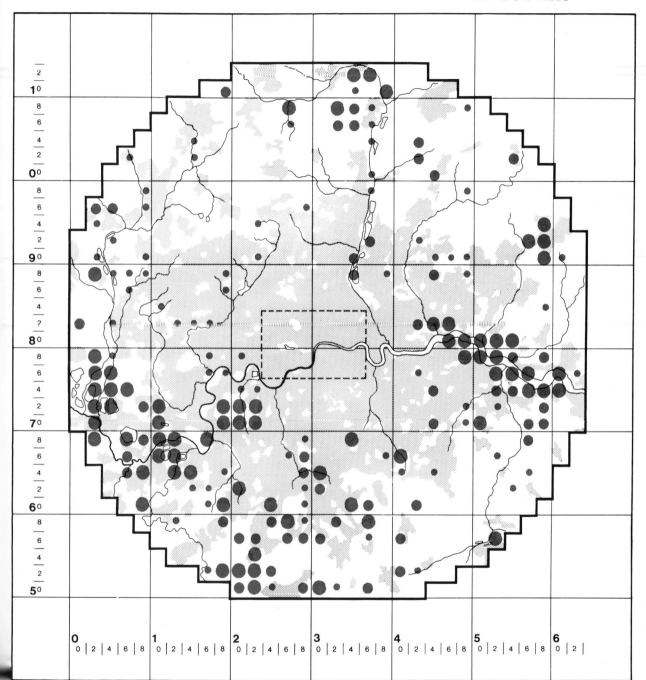

TREE PIPIT

Anthus trivialis

Compared with the Meadow Pipit, this species is much more a bird of the countryside beyond the built-up suburbs and, with only few exceptions, the records are largely concentrated on the heaths, commons and woods.

During the Atlas survey the Tree Pipit was recorded from 192 tetrads, only two less than the Meadow Pipit, and there were records of breeding from 68, only four fewer. With suitable habitat more than one pair may occur within a tetrad, so that in numbers of pairs the Tree Pipit could still be the commoner of the two species as suggested earlier by Homes. As with the Meadow Pipit, some records of probable breeding shown on the map are based on the presence of singing males which could have been migrants lingering in the Area without eventually nesting.

References to changes in breeding distribution over the years may reflect nothing more than shifts in local populations as some habitats become unsuitable. In scrub at Bookham Common, for example, where the Tree Pipit used to nest regularly with 12 pairs or more in 1948, breeding ceased after 1954, probably due to growth of the scrub and bracken (Beven 1969). A pair took up territory in 1968 in a partly burnt area where there had also been some clearance of scrub and singing males have been recorded in some other years, but so far the species has failed to re-establish itself in this locality. One area where numbers rose was Hainault Forest, where having remained fairly constant at three to four pairs from 1965 to 1969, the population increased from 1970 onwards reaching ten pairs in 1972 and 1973. Preferred habitat seems to be open plantations, clearings and woodland edge, so that reafforestation, at least in the early stages of growth, is likely to benefit this species, but is also likely to cause local fluctuations unrelated to national trends. At the time the population in Hainault Forest was expanding the BTO Common Birds Census index was showing a slight decline (B & M 1976).

Within the London Area, the Tree Pipit is more likely to be found on the higher ground and there were few Atlas records from river valleys. Neither does it penetrate very far into the suburbs and the only records close to the centre were from Joyden's Wood, Wimbledon Common and Richmond Park, and an isolated record from Barn Hill near the Brent Reservoir. There were no Inner London records, though in 1972 a bird was singing in Hyde Park in May and one was present there in June. These were most likely late migrants as there is probably insufficient rough, undisturbed habitat in the central parks to encourage this species to breed.

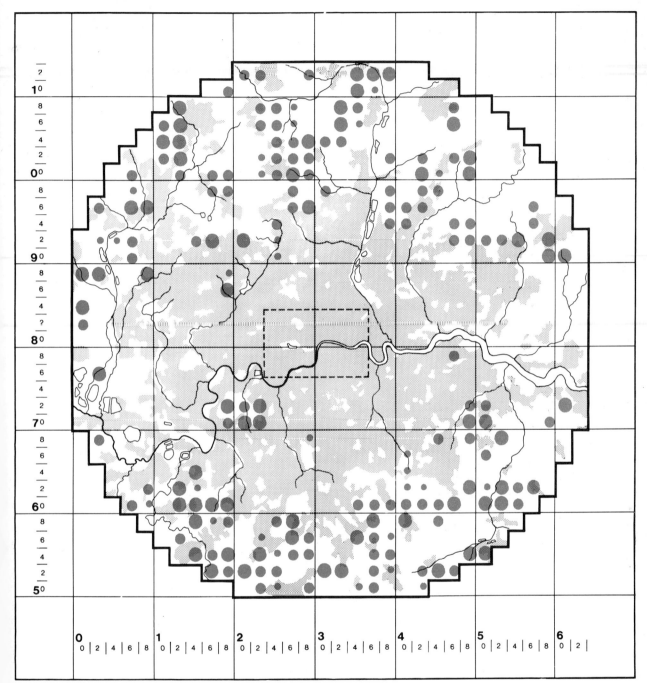

PIED WAGTAIL

Motacilla alba

This is the most numerous and widespread of the three species of wagtail nesting in the London Area. It occurs in a wide variety of habitats, usually near water, but it will also sometimes breed in dry, urban localities.

There is no evidence of any significant change in status in the London Area this century and, though Parslow refers to a report that numbers in Sussex may have been reduced to only half their level of thirty years earlier, the national trend, too, for this species seems broadly unchanged. In the London Area there were Atlas records from 647 tetrads, representing 76% of the total, and it was absent only from the driest or most densely built-up localities. Lack of adequate coverage in places may well account for some of the blank spaces on the map.

Only in the thirty years since 1946 has the Pied Wagtail become a regular breeding species in Inner London. After the second world war it was found nesting amongst bombed sites and occasionally in the parks. Additionally two pairs nested in the garden of Buckingham Palace from 1961 to 1964 and had probably done so in previous years (Cramp & Tomlins 1966). Breeding reports during the Atlas survey came from such localities as Brunswick Square in 1968, which was the first record for Bloomsbury, and also from Charterhouse Square, Smith Square, Clerkenwell, the bombed and redevelopment area of Cripplegate that had been occupied for several breeding seasons after the war, and the Strand, where a pair nested at the foot of a ventilator on Shell-Mex House in 1970. Birds seen carrying food to the roof of Apsley House at Hyde Park Corner in 1968 probably included part of Hyde Park within their territory. Pied Wagtails have nested occasionally in Hyde Park/Kensington Gardens and more frequently in Regent's Park, not usually more than one pair, but in 1972 Hyde Park/Kensington Gardens had three occupied territories.

Further away from the centre, most Pied Wagtails probably nest near or within a short flying distance of water and pairs can be found in parks, at gravel pits, reservoirs, sewage farms and along the borders of rivers, streams and canals. In drier areas, quite small ponds can be sufficient to attract a breeding pair. Where conditions are specially favourable and food probably plentiful several pairs may nest in close proximity, as at Hersham S.F. in the early 1960s when between ten and 20 pairs nested regularly (Parr 1972). The nests were built in the clinker walls of the sprinklers, in trees, buildings and even abandoned cars.

THAMES POLYTECHNIC LIBRARY

GREY WAGTAIL

Motacilla cinerea

This species breeds in fairly small numbers in a scattering of localities almost entirely in the western half of the London Area where streams and gravel pits are more numerous.

Early this century there were very few breeding records of the Grey Wagtail and all were closely connected with rural streams mainly to the south of the Thames. Since then numbers have increased gradually and the species has spread to other streams as well as to some of the suburbs and occasionally into central London. In 1952 a pair nested in Cripplegate on a bombed site and in 1960 and 1961 a pair nested successfully on a brewery in Whitechapel, rearing two broods each year.

By the early 1950s the Grey Wagtail was breeding annually in small numbers in widely separated localities. An annual average of about 13 breeding pairs was reported during the years 1955-62 with a maximum of 16 in 1958 and 1961. A setback occurred in 1963, probably as a result of two successive hard winters, but losses appear to have been made good by the time of the Atlas survey and the number of pairs recorded reached 18 in 1971. Altogether over the five-year survey Grey Wagtail breeding records came from 55 tetrads, the main concentration being in the south-west where there are numerous lakes, gravel pits and streams, and extending north along the Colne valley. Birds were also found around the Brent Reservoir and the upper part of the Lea valley. In Essex, away from the Lea valley, the species appears to have remained quite unknown as a breeding bird. There were a few records from the south and south-east of the Area during the Atlas years, mainly from the Darent Valley at Lullingstone and near Westerham and also from the Cray valley, Petts Wood, Beddington S.F. and the Oxted district.

Because of its close association with streams at all times of the year, the Grey Wagtail is very vulnerable to prolonged periods of frost and snow and the winters of 1962 and 1963 resulted in severe losses throughout south-east England (Dobinson & Richards 1964). Since then there has been a succession of mild winters and the population in the London Area may now be at a higher level that any previously recorded. This could account for the recent recolonisation of Inner London. At least two pairs nested in the centre in 1975, one pair rearing two broods on a building site, and three pairs bred in 1976. There is evidence, too, that the Grey Wagtail is spreading in other parts of Europe and extending its range to the north-west (Voous 1960) so that the population in the London Area could be further augmented by immigration.

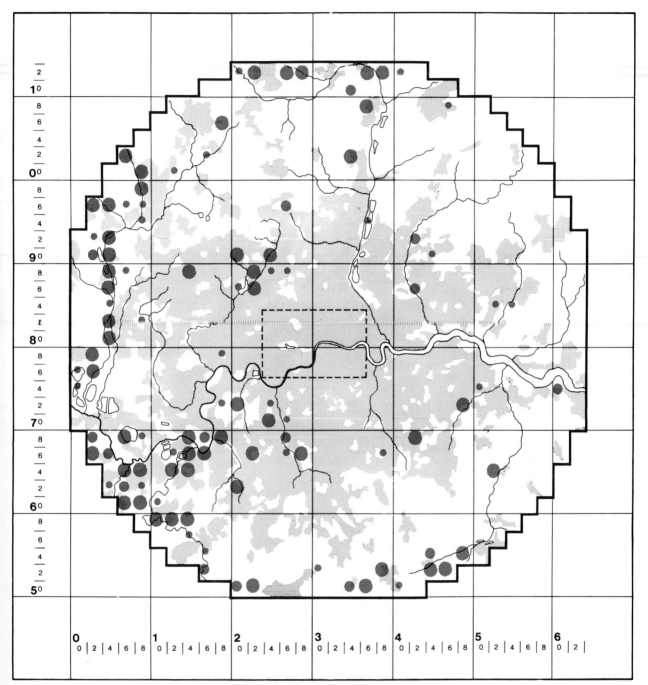

YELLOW WAGTAIL

Motacilla flava

Being primarily a bird of low-lying marshy ground and water meadows, the Yellow Wagtail's distribution follows the main river valleys in the London Area, especially the Thames east of London, the Lea and the Colne.

There appears to have been little change in status since the 1950s though land drainage may have led to loss of some breeding localities. While there have been occasional records of birds nesting in dry habitats, the importance of rivers or streams is evident from the map. As well as the Thames marshes and the Lea and Colne valleys, breeding records came from gravel pits and sewage farms, with several pairs at suitable sites. In 1955, for example, there were 20 pairs at Beddington S.F., though recent modernisation has made the area less suitable and by 1973 breeding numbers were much reduced. The species is still numerous in several parts of the London Area and records during the survey included about 34 pairs at King George V and William Girling Reservoirs in the Lea valley in 1968, about 11-12 pairs on the Thames marshes from Greenwich to Dartford in 1969 and six pairs at Fairlop G.P. in 1972, though numbers there were declining as the rubbish dump expanded.

During the 1968-72 survey records came from 157 tetrads and in 102 of those there was evidence of breeding. In view of some of the densities already mentioned these figures give no indication of the total population in any one year.

Burton (1972) considered that the Yellow Wagtail was a characteristic bird of waste ground in otherwise built-up areas and that nesting records in such places represented opportunistic breeding at temporary sites. This may explain the occasional nesting in Inner London. Regent's Park was briefly colonised during the second world war and there were records from two localities during the Atlas survey. In 1968 a pair was seen near Vauxhall Bridge feeding a juvenile scarcely able to fly and two pairs nested there in 1970 (Cornelius 1971). Surrey Docks were quickly occupied after being closed in 1970; the following year seven or eight pairs were present and in 1972 about six pairs (George 1974).

The race of the Yellow Wagtail breeding in Britain is *M.f. flavissima*, but birds resembling *M.f. flava*, the Blue-headed Wagtail, occur in the London Area almost annually. Possibly they interbreed, as hybrids or birds similar to some of the other European races are occasionally reported. *Flava* was only recorded three times up to 1930, but it may simply have been overlooked earlier and not necessarily have increased recently.

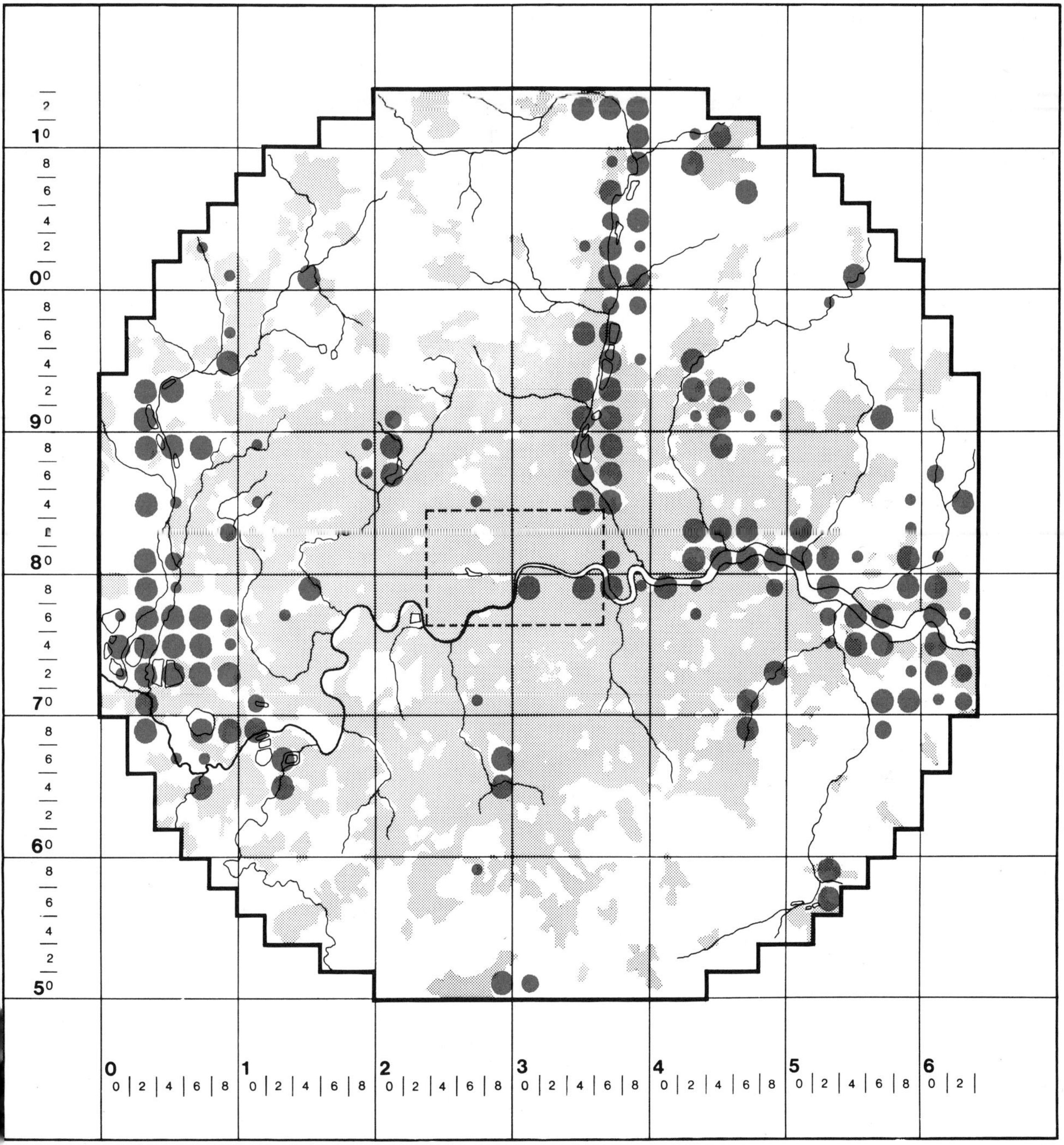
2
10
8
6
4
2
00
8
6
4
2
90
8
6
4
2
80
8
6
4
2
70
8
6
4
2
60
8
6
4
2
50
0 | 0 2 4 6 8
1 | 0 2 4 6 8
2 | 0 2 4 6 8
3 | 0 2 4 6 8
4 | 0 2 4 6 8
5 | 0 2 4 6 8
6 | 0 2

RED-BACKED SHRIKE

Lanius collurio

Annual breeding numbers of this species reported during 1968-72 varied from one to three pairs, corresponding with its continuing decline in Britain.

In the first decade of this century the Red-backed Shrike was well distributed in suitable habitats such as open land with tall bushes, tall hedgerows and overgrown quarries. At that time birds bred as close to central London as Dulwich, Barnes Common and Hampstead Heath. There appears to have been a downward trend ever since, which accelerated in the 1950s and 1960s. From an estimated 61 pairs in 1952 the population was thought to have fallen the next year to 32 pairs, of which nine were in Essex, two in Herts, five in Middlesex and 16 in Surrey. There were still two pairs at both Mitcham Common and Wimbledon Common and as many as four at Ruislip. By 1958 only 12 pairs were reported and, though there was a slight recovery with 24 pairs still present in 1962, numbers again fell steeply. Figures for the years 1955 to 1974 are given in Table 15 and show a rapid decline to the present precariously low level.

Parslow has described the general fall in numbers of the Red-backed Shrike in southern England. As in London, the decrease and contraction of range has been most marked since the early 1950s, especially outside the species' main strongholds. A national census in 1971 indicated a breeding population of 81 pairs, of which only 22 were outside Norfolk and Suffolk (Bibby 1973). Various factors may have been responsible for the reduction in numbers, but the major cause may be linked with climatic changes leading to a much reduced supply of large insects which form the bulk of the Shrike's food. With such a low population, other causes such as habitat changes and egg collecting can have a critical effect.

Demand for building land and clearance of marginal land for agriculture have reduced the suitable habitats of the London Area, but there are still numerous commons or patches of scrub available to the Red-backed Shrike. That it is tolerant of disturbance is shown by successful breeding in the past at such central sites as Mitcham and Putney Vale, much used for leisure activities. Bibby (1973) concluded, however, that it was unlikely to remain as a regular British breeding bird for very much longer and certainly in the London Area it retains only a very tenuous hold.

Table 15.   Numbers of pairs of Red-backed Shrikes
reported in the London Area, 1955-74

55	56	57	58	59	60	61	62	63	64	65	66	67	68	69	70	71	72	73	74
31	26	19	12	20	24	23	24	12	16	8	2	–	3	1	1	1	1	2	1

236

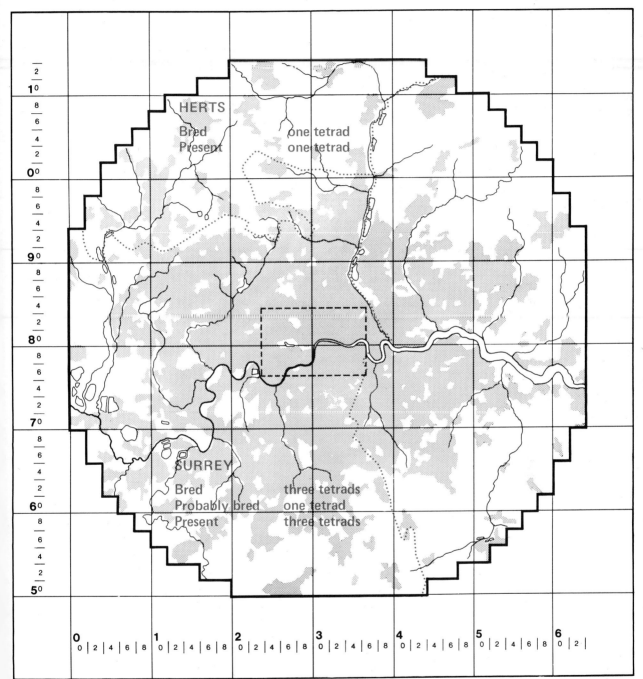

HERTS

Bred   one tetrad
Present   one tetrad

SURREY

Bred   three tetrads
Probably bred   one tetrad
Present   three tetrads

STARLING

Sturnus vulgaris

This is one of London's commonest resident breeding birds, not only exploiting a wide variety of nesting sites and food made available by the activities of man, but equally able to maintain itself in all types of rural habitat wherever a suitable nesting hole is available.

The Starling was probably equally widespread at the beginning of the century. In fact numbers in some of the Inner London parks even seem to have fallen in recent years. As it is a thrusting species able to take advantage of any favourable circumstances which may occur, any local reductions are likely to be associated with loss of nest sites.

Results of an earlier ringing programme showed that the majority of adults present in the breeding season were sedentary. Up to the end of 1953, out of 96 adults ringed in the London Area in summer, 92 were recovered where ringed, and out of 239 ringed in winter and recovered in summer, 230 were at or near the place of ringing. Recoveries of Starlings hatched in London suggested that some, perhaps a third, move away for their first winter, but very few travel any distance once fully adult.

Little information is available on numbers breeding at any one locality, but approximate densities can be calculated from some published studies. Dollis Hill, in the inner suburban zone, showed a density in the 1950s of about 123 pairs per 100ha (Simms 1962). In Inner London, Regent's Park with the surrounding large gardens and houses held 41 pairs per 100ha in 1963 (Wallace 1974), though only about half that figure by 1969, while in Hyde Park/Kensington Gardens occupied territories numbered five per 100ha in 1973. These figures show a wide range from the low level in parkland where most Starlings would have to find natural nest-holes in the scattered trees, to a very high density in a suburban locality where some 75% of the habitat comprised residential or industrial development containing a plentiful supply of artificial nest sites. The average figure for dense oakwood at Bookham Common during 1965-74 fell between these two extremes at 51 pairs per 100ha.

Overall there can be few places where a pair of Starlings cannot find a nest-hole in a tree or building, and gaps shown on the map are surely due only to inadequate coverage. Occupied nests are not difficult to locate as the young are very noisy towards the end of the fledging period. With man supplementing, albeit unintentionally, the Starling's supply of natural nest sites, it is not a species expected to require any further assistance to maintain its presence throughout London.

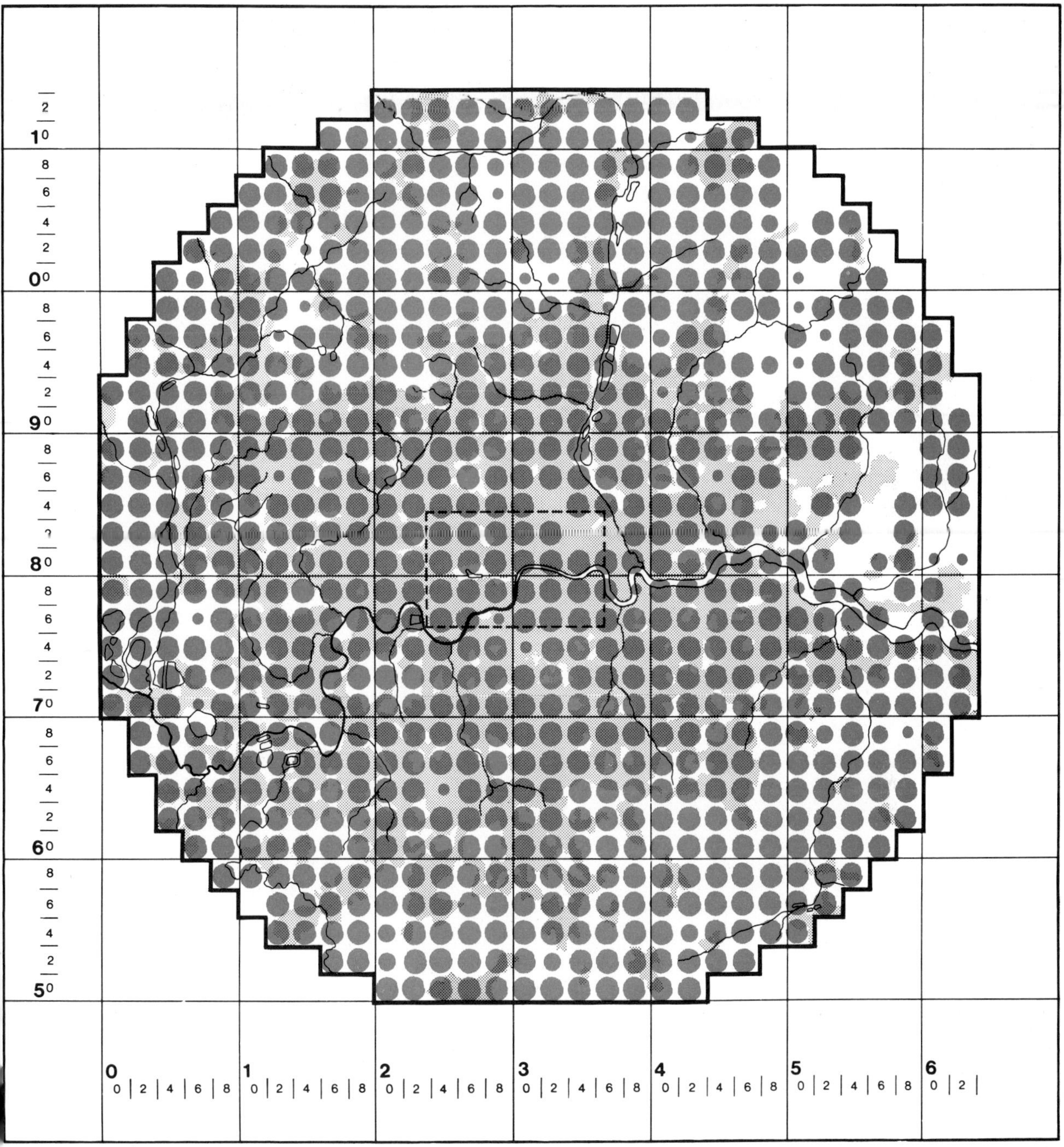

10
00
90
80
70
60
50
0
1
2
3
4
5
6

HAWFINCH

Coccothraustes coccothraustes

While the Hawfinch appears to be a scarce and local breeding species in the London Area, its secretive behaviour, particularly in the breeding season, can easily result in its being overlooked.

Homes concluded that the Hawfinch population fluctuated more widely than many other species, though a review of published breeding season records for the years 1959-61 indicated that the species was widespread at that time in suitable habitat. Pairs or small parties were seen during that period in six localities in Essex, two in Herts, 12 in Middlesex, five in Kent, ten in Surrey and one in Inner London.

The Hawfinch is principally a bird of broad-leaved woodland, characteristic of ancient European oak/hornbeam forest (Voous 1960). In the London Area perhaps the most notable locality of this type is Epping Forest which continues to be a regular haunt of the Hawfinch. In fact it was there that the species was first recorded as breeding in Britain in 1832. There is no proof of nesting in Inner London, though it may have done so in Regent's Park or the adjoining large gardens of St John's Wood. Adults were seen feeding young in the Park in 1951, 1952 and 1956, carrying nesting material in 1954 and juveniles were recorded in 1960 and 1962 (Cramp & Tomlins 1966). Kew Gardens remains the nearest breeding site to central London and there, too, hornbeams are the main attraction.

Atlas records, though perhaps not representative of any one breeding season, came from 78 tetrads, but reports of breeding from only 14, which indicates the problems posed by a breeding survey of this species. Of these 14 records, nine were from north of the Thames, including Epping Forest, Parndon and Broxbourne Woods as well as near Harlow, Cheshunt, Hatfield and Ruislip. Only five were south of the Thames, including Lullingstone, Keston, Kew and the Reigate area.

References to the elusiveness of the Hawfinch and to marked variations in numbers were also made by Parslow in relation to the national distribution, but, as in the London Area, no long-term trends have been identified. Mountfort (1957) considered that the main period of range expansion, after the first Epping Forest record, extended from approximately 1835 to 1915 and that it continued subsequently at a much slower pace.

In the London Area many woodlands are subject to some degree of disturbance, but preservation of stands of mature trees should enable the Hawfinch at least to maintain its present distribution even though there may not be sufficient suitable habitat to allow it to spread to any great extent.

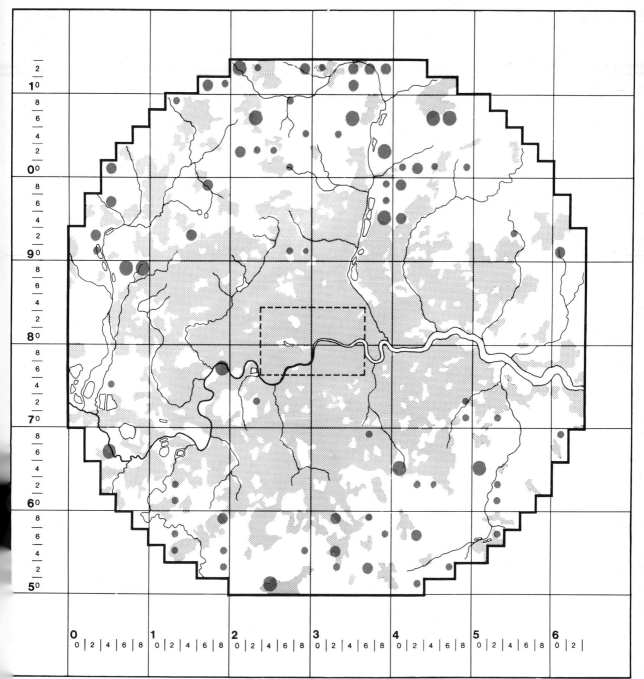

GREENFINCH

Carduelis chloris

This is one of the commonest resident breeding species of the London Area, favouring gardens, hedgerows, bushy places and woodland edge.

At the beginning of this century the Greenfinch was less common than it is now and was only a winter visitor to Inner London. Since then the population has expanded and it has become a familiar bird, especially in the suburbs where it ranks as the most numerous of the finches. It is also widely distributed in rural areas and is likely to be entirely absent only from the most densely built-up localities. In Inner London, Greenfinches breed regularly in Holland Park, Hyde Park/Kensington Gardens, Regent's Park and occasionally in other parks as well as in areas like Bloomsbury and parts of Chelsea where small gardens or squares sometimes provide suitable nesting sites.

Cramp & Tomlins (1966) considered that the Inner London population increased markedly in the early 1960s. This was the case in Kensington Gardens where there were no certain breeding records between 1952 and 1956 (Sanderson 1968), but numbers subsequently built up to a level in Hyde Park and Kensington Gardens combined ranging from 22 to 31 occupied territories during the Atlas survey years of 1968-72. The higher figure was in 1970 when 24 out of the 31 territories were in Kensington Gardens and the remaining seven in Hyde Park. In Regent's Park about 30 pairs were reported in 1968 and 1969.

There was no evidence that the severe winter of 1962-63 had any serious effect on the breeding strength of the Greenfinch (Dobinson & Richards 1964). The population index for farmland based on BTO Common Birds Census analyses, however, more than doubled from 1963 to 1966, since when it has remained almost constant (B & M 1976). On woodland census plots numbers have recently been at a lower level than in the mid-1960s. Suburban populations may not necessarily correspond with either of these patterns and it is possible that in such habitat numbers are continuing to increase. Food, particularly peanuts, provided by householders in many areas throughout the winter months may encourage birds to remain in favourable localities, resulting in higher densities in some of the suburbs than in more rural areas.

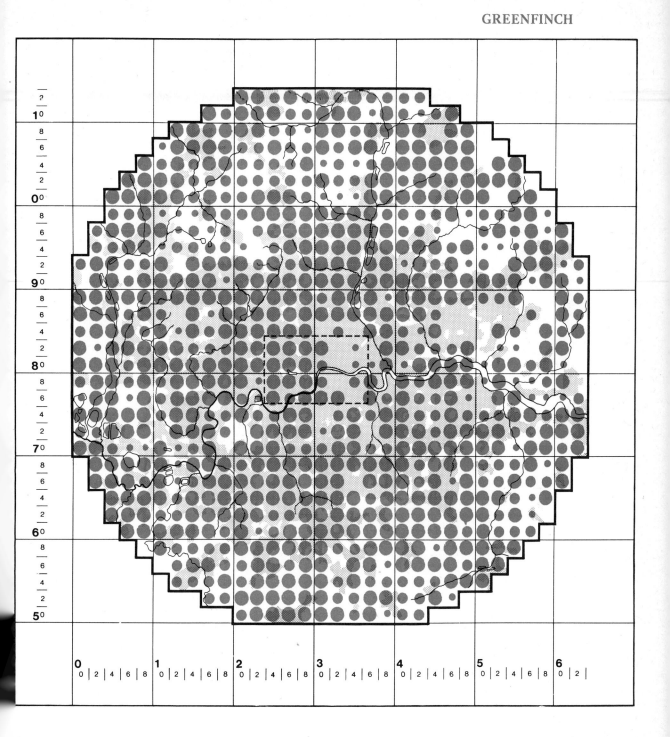

GOLDFINCH

Carduelis carduelis

Though less numerous than the Greenfinch, the Goldfinch is a common and widespread breeding resident in the London Area associated particularly with suburban habitat.

Starting this century with a very low population, probably because of the activities of bird-catchers, the Goldfinch began to recover by about 1907-08, no doubt aided by the introduction of protection measures. Apart from short-term or local fluctuations, numbers have continued to increase, especially in suburban London, and it is now well distributed in parks and gardens, avoiding only the most densely urban areas. Even here, however, it will colonise industrial sites if there is undisturbed waste ground with an abundance of seeding weeds to provide food.

A similar pattern of expansion has occurred in other parts of the country (Parslow), though the BTO Common Birds Census population figures (B & M 1976) show a levelling off after 1966 until a large increase in 1973 took the index well above any point previously reached since the census began in 1962.

While the Goldfinch is considered pre-eminently a suburban bird, the Atlas map suggests that it is evenly distributed throughout the Area. There are few localities around London totally devoid of gardens, trees or hedgerows, so that suitable breeding habitat is widely available. Small numbers now seem to nest regularly in Inner London, though the first record was not until 1945 when young were seen in Regent's Park. Since then birds have nested in several Inner London localities and in 1965 the population was put at five to ten pairs (Cramp & Tomlins 1966).

During the Atlas survey, Regent's Park remained the major central breeding site with up to six pairs in 1968. Of all species nesting in the Park during the period 1959-68, the Goldfinch was rated second in terms of breeding productivity and its success was attributed to colonisation of previously underexploited habitats (Wallace 1974). Elsewhere in Inner London there were Atlas records of juveniles in Hyde Park/Kensington Gardens in 1971 and 1972 and subsequently in 1973, but the birds may have hatched from nests just outside the parks. Surrey Docks were successfully colonised in 1971 and in 1973 there were at least three pairs.

Flocks of several hundred birds are seen outside the breeding season, especially in autumn. Unfortunately there were fears that bird-catchers were active again in 1969 when an observer felt obliged to request that the locality of a flock of about 400 birds should not be disclosed.

244

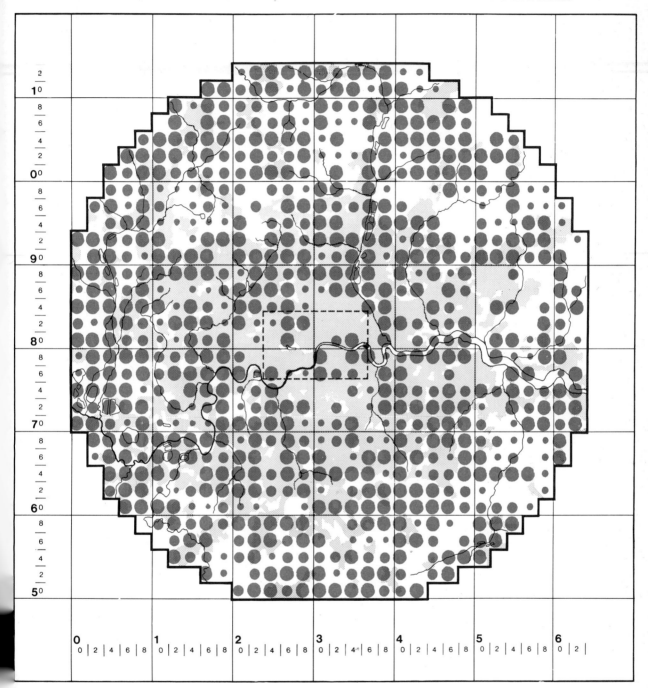

SISKIN

Carduelis spinus

While the Siskin is familiar in some localities as a winter visitor and passage migrant, commoner in some winters than others, there is still no definite evidence that it has ever nested successfully in the London Area.

There were three breeding season records up to 1954. The first was of a pair found building a nest at Sundridge Park, near Bromley, in April 1901, but the nest was destroyed and it was not known whether eggs were laid. The other records date from May and June 1924 when a bird was heard singing at Weybridge, and from the end of July 1941 when ten birds were discovered in Bushy Park.

While the majority of Siskins have left the London Area by late April, there is an increasing number of records of birds remaining into the first week of May and in 1969 there were as many as 25 at Epsom Common on the 2nd. More unusual was a report of three at Banstead on 13 and 18 July 1969 and Parr (1972) refers to an adult pair in the Weybridge area from July to September 1970. Finally the one large dot shown on the map relates to a party of fledged juveniles seen late in the breeding season in the northern part of Epping Forest during the course of the Atlas survey.

Parslow considered that the increase in summering and nesting records in England and Wales, though partly attributable to increased observation, was largely connected with the expansion of coniferous woodland. Breeding has already been recorded in counties as close to London as Suffolk, Kent and Hampshire. The Epping Forest birds may possibly have been reared locally, but equally they may have wandered into the London Area from East Anglia.

Wintering flocks are now tending to be larger than formerly and the provision of artificial food, again principally peanuts, is attracting Siskins into gardens in many parts of the Area. In a garden at Weybridge, where a large number of Siskins have been ringed, a total of 466 birds was caught in 1970 and as many as 101 different individuals were handled in a single day (Spencer & Gush 1973). With such high numbers present in the early months of the year and a scattering of records in May and occasionally later, proof of a pair nesting successfully in the London Area may well follow before long.

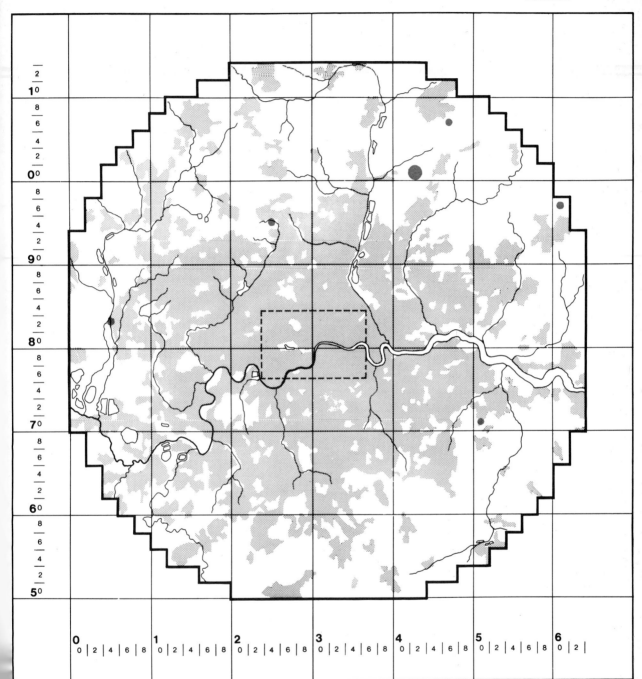

THAMES POLYTECHNIC LIBRARY

LINNET

Acanthis cannabina

This species is a fairly common breeding bird in the London Area mainly in the rural parts and outer suburbs. Typically a bird of gorse-covered heaths and commons, though also found widely around patches of scrub and thick vegetation as well as overgrown hedgerows in agricultural areas, the Linnet does not readily nest in gardens and is therefore somewhat restricted in its distribution in the heavily built-up inner suburban zone.

In the first ten to twenty years of the present century numbers began to increase, an important factor probably being the virtual cessation of bird-catching. There is no evidence of any major change in status in recent years and decreases are generally due to the destruction of suitable breeding habitats.

As the map shows, records during the Atlas survey were concentrated in the outer part of the London Area. Observer coverage in south Essex was not complete and there it was probably overlooked in some tetrads. Its absence from the inner built-up zone is likely to reflect the true situation and breeding tends to be confined to waste land and overgrown rough ground as in the Lea valley and along the borders of the Thames.

Nesting in Inner London is unusual. A pair bred in Hyde Park in 1918, but fifty years elapsed before the next record when in 1968 there were probably two pairs in Regent's Park, one of which nested and reared two young. Since then Surrey Docks have provided another Inner London breeding site. Following their closure in 1970, the Docks quickly attracted a wide variety of birds. Linnets first bred there in 1971 when three or four pairs were present, and they have continued to do so up to 1974 when at least one pair nested successfully. This is likely to be only a temporary site, however, as the habitat will disappear when the land is eventually redeveloped. Perhaps by that time Linnets will have returned to the parks where the sanctuaries created in recent years may eventually provide the necessary seclusion for nesting. Birds were seen in Hyde Park/Kensington Gardens in the spring of 1973 with up to five birds on four dates from 10 April to 2 May, and in 1974 there were records from Regent's Park up to 9 May.

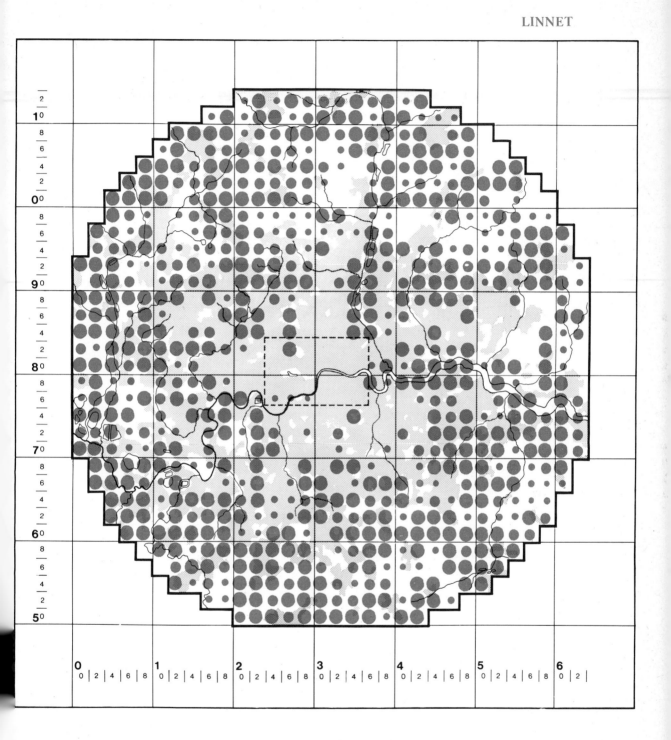

REDPOLL
Acantbis flammea

Though the map shows a scattered and somewhat local distribution for the Redpoll, numbers are increasing and it is expanding into new areas.

As with some other cardueline finches, the Redpoll, too, probably benefited from a reduction in bird-catching early this century, but after the initial increase little change was reported up to the mid-1950s when it was considered widespread, but sparse and rather local. A noticeable expansion has occurred recently and the Redpoll is now less confined to heaths and commons and adjacent large gardens. Breeding pairs do not normally penetrate far into the built-up suburbs or urban London and the inner limits have remained more or less unchanged, represented by Wimbledon Common south of the Thames and Hampstead Heath to the north.

Dobinson & Richards (1964) considered that the Redpoll was not greatly affected by the hard winter of 1962-63 and in fact breeding numbers the following spring were probably slightly higher than the previous year. Figures from the BTO Common Birds Census analyses show the size of the subsequent increase, with the 1974 population index more than four times the level of 1964 (B & M 1976). A particularly large rise was recorded in 1969 and again in 1972, in which year the Redpoll showed the greatest population increase of all species examined (Batten 1973b). Parslow dated the start of the national expansion in both numbers and range from about 1950, aided largely by the widespread planting of conifers. In the London Area birds are now seen more often in deciduous woodland, on farmland and in gardens, so other unknown factors are probably also involved.

With the population still growing when the Atlas survey ended, the Redpoll's range has almost certainly extended further as it has continued to colonise new localities. During 1968-72 it was recorded from only 29% of the tetrads within the London boundary, but such a dynamic species is easily overlooked in new and perhaps unexpected habitats so the map may understate the position. Furthermore the map does not indicate density. In suitable areas several pairs can be found in close proximity and any assessment of the overall population is additionally confused by the loose territorial, almost colonial, behaviour of breeding pairs.

Heaths and commons on dry, light soil with birch and conifers are more numerous south of the Thames, especially in Surrey, than they are north of the River. This no doubt explains why, during the survey, the Redpoll was found in 37% of tetrads in the south and only 24% in the north, but its continuing expansion may well lead to a more even distribution.

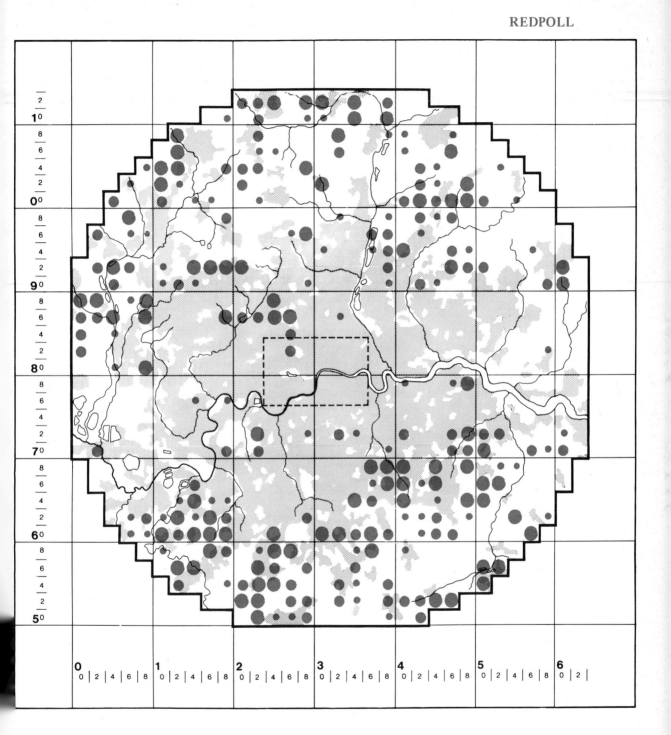

BULLFINCH

Pyrrhula pyrrhula

The Bullfinch is a common and widespread breeding bird in the London Area except in some central parts that are too heavily built-up and some of the open country lacking cover, as along stretches of the Thames marshes.

Its status appears to have remained stable in the first half of this century, except for a slight retreat towards the country as the large gardens of the inner suburbs were built over. It was also said to shun Inner London more than most woodland birds. Since then the population has grown and not only have numbers increased in rural parts of the Area, but the Bullfinch is now more familiar in suburban London. It is still absent from much of the central part, as would be expected in a species that generally nests in thickets, thick hedgerows and shrubberies, but reversing the earlier move outwards there were breeding records during the Atlas survey from Greenwich Park, Peckham, Camberwell, Wimbledon and Fulham as well as some of the Inner London parks.

This expansion in the London Area was concurrent with an increase in many other parts of the country which began about 1955 and resulted in numerous reports of Bullfinches moving into new habitats including gardens and town parks and also into more open country in rural areas (Newton 1972, Parslow).

Cramp & Tomlins (1966) listed the Bullfinch as a recent arrival in Inner London and the first proof of nesting was in Regent's Park in 1959. Numbers there increased to three pairs in 1963 to 1967 and then in 1968 and 1969 the breeding population jumped to seven pairs. In Hyde Park/Kensington Gardens a pair probably nested in 1966 (Sanderson 1968) and definitely did so in 1969. Holland Park was first colonised in 1967 and was also occupied again in 1969. Since then breeding pairs have been reported each year up to 1974 in Regent's Park and Hyde Park/Kensington Gardens and up to 1973 in Holland Park.

Bullfinches have long had a reputation for eating fruit buds and Newton (1972) quotes a reference dating from the sixteenth century. With the recent growth of the population outside woodland, orchards and gardens in some parts of the country have suffered serious damage. Fruit growers in the London Area, particularly where Bullfinches are numerous, can hardly have escaped their depredations, but there is no information to show how widespread the problem is within the Area or to what extent there are variations from year to year.

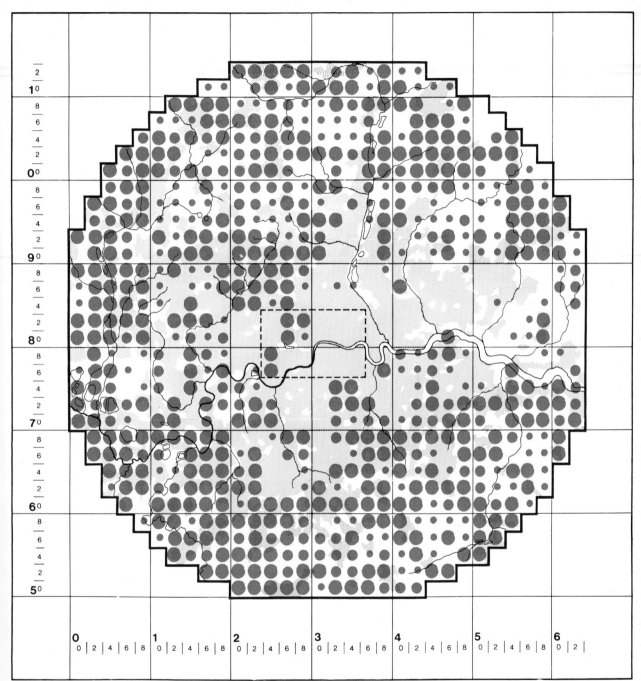

CROSSBILL

Loxia curvirostra

This is mainly an irruptive species in the London Area occurring irregularly in summer and autumn. Birds may remain in suitable localities where food is available and breeding is occasionally reported.

There is no evidence of a regular resident population in the Area. Crossbills were seen in twenty-nine of the fifty-five years up to 1954, but annually since 1956. Nesting pairs have been recorded much less frequently. A large irruption in 1909 was followed by breeding in 1910 at Gerrards Cross, Weybridge, Walton Heath, Keston, Croydon and Bostall Woods. Subsequent records were in 1914 at Walton Heath, 1926 at Addington, 1931 at Iver Heath, 1936 at Kew Gardens, and probably in 1943 when a pair was seen carrying material to a nest site on Reigate Heath though successful nesting was not proved. The next record was about twenty years later when a juvenile was seen being fed at Esher Common in 1962. Irruptions occurred in 1963 and 1966 and probably accounted for the single pairs suspected of breeding at Oaklands near St Albans and possibly at Panshanger in 1963 and the pair that nested successfully at Kew Gardens in 1967.

Only two breeding records were obtained during the Atlas survey, both in 1968. At Hosey Common at least five pairs were present and an adult was seen with a newly-fledged juvenile on 19 May. The other site was at St George's Hill, Weybridge, where a female was seen feeding three young on 11 May.

With breeding occurring annually in the Brecklands of East Anglia and in the New Forest, Hampshire, perhaps in parts of Surrey outside the London Area and in some other southern counties (Parslow), the Crossbill is likely to arrive in the Area more often as birds wander in search of food. Recent extensive planting of conifers has probably aided the establishment of this species in new localities and invasions from the continent, also related to food shortages, augment existing populations. The complicated relationship between Crossbills and conifer seeds, which is their main food source, has been fully discussed by Newton (1972).

Almost all breeding records from the London Area have come from south of the Thames where conifer woodland is more widespread than in the north. Even in the south, however, localities are widely scattered, though occasional nesting pairs could easily be overlooked. Nevertheless with the intensive five-year Atlas survey producing only two records there is no sign of the Crossbill becoming permanently established.

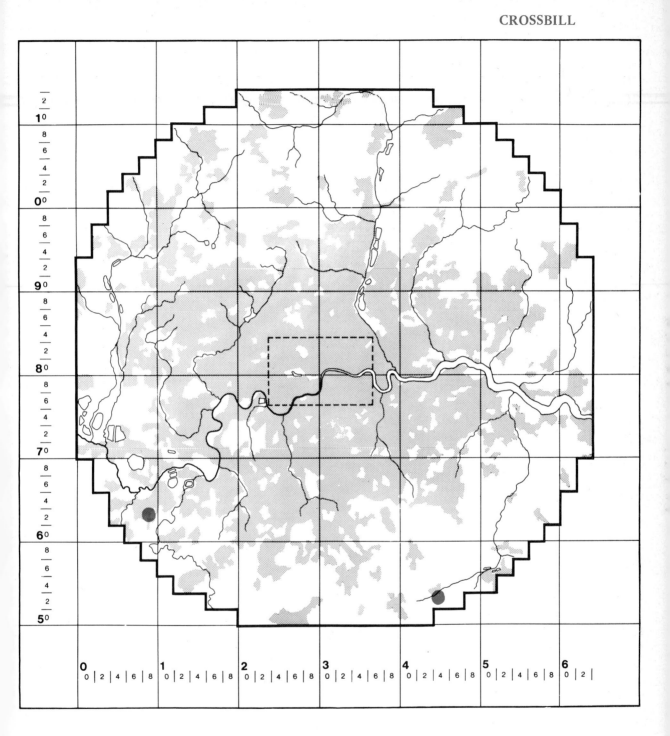

CHAFFINCH

Fringilla coelebs

Though the Chaffinch is one of the commonest breeding birds found almost throughout the London Area, the total population may have declined slightly in recent years.

There is no evidence that its status changed appreciably in the first half of the present century, though one or two comments since the 1950s have referred to decreases. The map shows, however, that the Chaffinch has maintained its wide distribution and was proved to be breeding in most localities in the London Area. Lack of adequate coverage in parts of south Essex could explain some of the gaps, but its absence from tetrads in urban central London, where the habitat is clearly less suitable, is doubtless genuine as the Chaffinch is easily identifiable both by appearance and song.

Beven (1976) has shown that in 16ha of oakwood at Bookham Common breeding pairs varied from 12 in 1951 to only one in 1974, though there were annual fluctuations and recent peaks of eight in 1965 and 1972. Figures from 39ha of scrub at Bookham between 1964 and 1973 were more stable, with between 12 and 14 pairs recorded in six out of the ten years (Beven 1974a). Parslow suggested that the main period of national decline began, as at the Bookham oakwood, in the late 1950s. Agricultural eastern England was particularly affected and the low point was reached about 1960-62 followed, according to the BTO Common Birds Census figures, by an increase over the next three years (B & M 1976). There was some evidence in 1969 of another reverse, however, when 15 census plots in the London Area showed a fall of 10% in the number of occupied territories compared with the previous year. Only one locality appears to have shown an increase and that was the Sevenoaks G.P. reserve where the Chaffinch along with other finches, benefited from the creation of new habitat (Harrison 1974).

Typically a woodland bird, the Chaffinch also frequents parks and gardens where trees are available to provide food and song posts. Some Inner London parks with their mature trees present suitable breeding localities in an otherwise densely built-up area, though Cramp & Tomlins (1966) found the Chaffinch doing less well in central London than elsewhere. In Regent's Park numbers reached a peak in 1962, but then fell steadily for the next four years, so that the Chaffinch was overtaken by the Greenfinch as the dominant finch (Wallace 1974). On the other hand the population in Hyde Park/Kensington Gardens between 1966 and 1973 showed little change, with occupied territories varying between 17 and 20, though dropping to 15 in 1974.

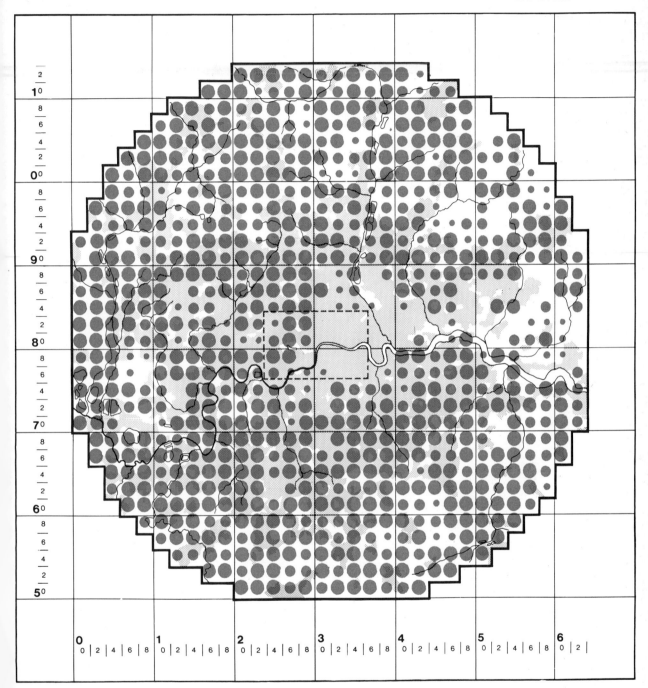

CORN BUNTING

Emberiza calandra

Essentially a bird of open agricultural land, the Corn Bunting inevitably has a patchy distribution in the London Area where such habitat is largely confined to the outer zone.

It is a difficult species to census, being found in some areas, yet absent from others that look equally suitable. Numbers in Essex were thought to be increasing in the early 1950s, though Surrey appeared to have suffered a catastrophic decline even on the North Downs that had not been built over. Well established breeding localities at that time were in Herts, along the Thames marshes and in the west Middlesex plain.

Parslow also found the status of the Corn Bunting difficult to assess and though reports more often referred to decreases than increases, he doubted whether overall there had been any marked decline. BTO Common Birds Census figures for farmland plots showed an increasing trend from 1962, when analyses began, up to 1967, followed by a fall until 1972 and then an increase of 25% in 1973 (B & M 1976).

Results of the Atlas survey suggest that, except for local fluctuations, distribution has changed little since the 1950s. There were relatively few reports from the Thames marshes which, with records like twenty singing males at Rainham in 1951, were once well populated. Habitat loss with the new town development of Thamesmead on the south side of the Thames may account for some of the changes, but reasons for the apparent absence of birds from further down the River are unknown. Records in Kent from both sides of the Darent valley provide the widest distribution south of the Thames. Breeding numbers have increased in Surrey since 1950 (Parr 1972) and records on the western boundary of the Area include small colonies at Chertsey and Thorpe. In Essex, Hainault, Fairlop and Thurrock are regular haunts. A census in 1964 produced totals of ten pairs at the two former localities and 23 singing males at the last. Continuing development is likely to reduce suitable Corn Bunting habitat in Middlesex though birds still nest at Osterley Park and near Stanwell. Most records during the Atlas survey came from Herts, where there is a sequence of breeding localities west of the Colne valley from Uxbridge northwards and along much of the lower slopes of the Chilterns.

In total during the Atlas survey there were records from 144 tetrads. Probable breeding was reported from 85, but evidence of confirmed breeding came from only 27, reflecting a widely held view that, of all species, nests of the Corn Bunting are amongst the most difficult to find.

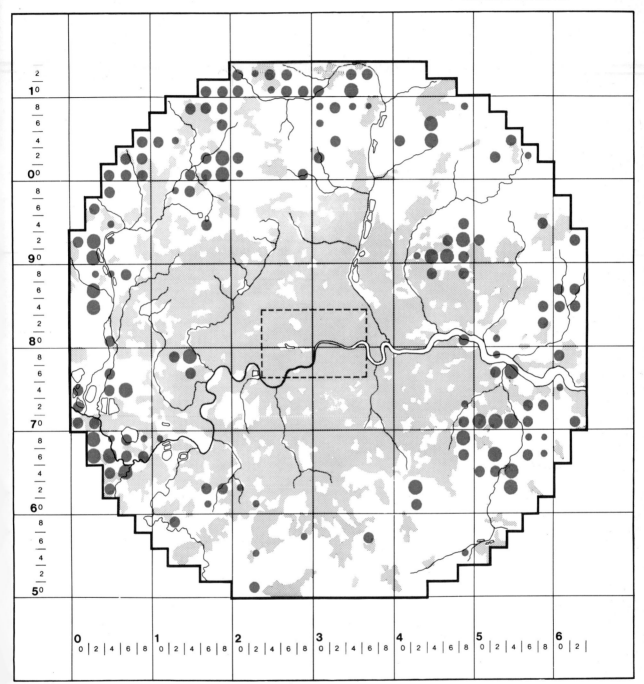

YELLOWHAMMER
Emberiza citrinella

There are a few scattered breeding records in the inner suburbs, but otherwise the Yellowhammer is a bird of the countryside where it is fairly common and widespread.

Homes considered that the principal change in distribution of this species in the present century was its retreat from many suburban districts and commented that the presence of Yellowhammers was a good test of a locality's retention of country status. This is still broadly true, although some records indicate that the country need not be of any great extent to satisfy the Yellowhammer's requirements. Favoured habitats are commons, heaths, open scrub and along hedgerows on farmland, all of which persist to some extent in the outer suburbs. Though the inner limits given by Homes may have been pushed slightly further out, breeding localities still include some that are largely surrounded by suburbia, as at Joyden's Wood, Bromley Common, Banstead, Chessington, Hillingdon, Ruislip and Harrow. Closer to the centre there is little suitable habitat. At Wimbledon Common and Richmond Park breeding was reported during the Atlas survey from five tetrads and there were records from Kingsbury and the Brent Reservoir and also Hampstead Heath, which provided the nearest record to central London. Two pairs bred there successfully in West Meadow at Ken Wood in 1959, the first report for at least thirty years. There were two pairs again the following year and one in 1961, after which nesting appears to have again become sporadic.

There is no recent evidence of any change in the population level in the London Area, but Parslow found that in parts of eastern England numbers fell sharply in the late 1950s and singled out Essex as a county where the decline was most marked and where birds disappeared entirely from areas in which they had previously been common. Loss of hedgerows and the introduction of persistent organochlorine pesticides were both cited as possible causes in some areas. Whether that part of Essex within the London Area was affected is unknown; there is a wide distribution shown on the map in the northern part, but in the south the Yellowhammer may have been overlooked.

Overall the Yellowhammer was recorded in 507 tetrads, representing 59% of the London Area and breeding or probable breeding was noted in all but 67 of those. Whether this level of distribution can be maintained will depend on the continued existence of patches of countryside within suburban London and the preservation of the Green Belt.

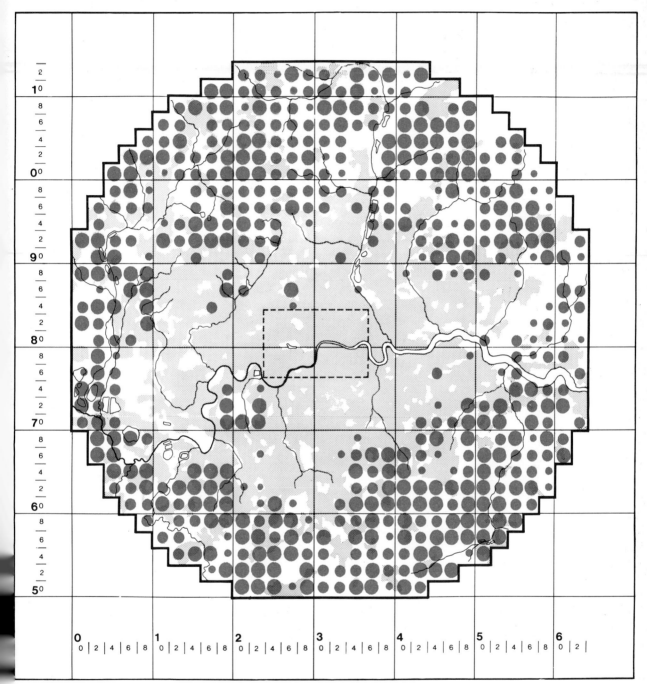

CIRL BUNTING

Emberiza cirlus

This species remains very scarce in the London Area. Breeding has not been proved since 1949, though a pair is likely to have nested in 1965.

The Cirl Bunting has always had an extremely local breeding distribution throughout this century with only 16 nests on record up to 1954, of which ten were on or near the North Downs. Other breeding records came from Weybridge and the only site north of the Thames at Harrow. With such small numbers present, isolated nesting pairs could have been overlooked though there have been occasional scattered records of singing males.

Voous (1960) described the Cirl Bunting as the southern European ecological counterpart of the Yellowhammer. England is on the north-west edge of its range and though formerly more widespread, the Cirl Bunting is now virtually confined to counties south and south-west of the Thames, with a few pairs extending north into west Herts (BOU 1971). Its principal habitat, often on Chalk slopes, is more or less open country with bushes, trees and hedges. There is no shortage of this type of habitat round the edge of the London Area, so its absence must be due to other factors. Whether they are related to summer temperatures or competition with the similarly mainly sedentary Yellowhammer is unknown.

From 1955 to 1967 Cirl Buntings were recorded between May and mid-August in seven of the thirteen years. Of the localities involved only two were mentioned in more than one year. A singing male was reported from Godstone in 1961 and 1962, though at different sites, and at Wimbledon Common in 1965 and 1967. In the latter year birds were heard between 21 March and 25 July. Other records of singing males were from Cobham in 1956, Chipstead (Surrey) in 1960, Orpington in 1967 and from north of the Thames at Hilfield Park Reservoir in 1959. There was also a report of a female at Old Parkbury in 1962. The only evidence of breeding was in 1965 when a male was seen carrying food at Brands Hatch.

During the Atlas survey there were no more than a few isolated records, including a report of a singing male in the Orpington area again in 1968. Singing males were also reported from two other sites, at Lullingstone and at Pebblecombe where two were present on 2 May 1969. These records and the other three reports of birds present may all have related to migrants on passage through the Area. Clearly there is a possiblity that an odd pair might again nest in the London Area, but with such a scattering of sites any proof of the Cirl Bunting doing so will depend almost certainly on a chance discovery.

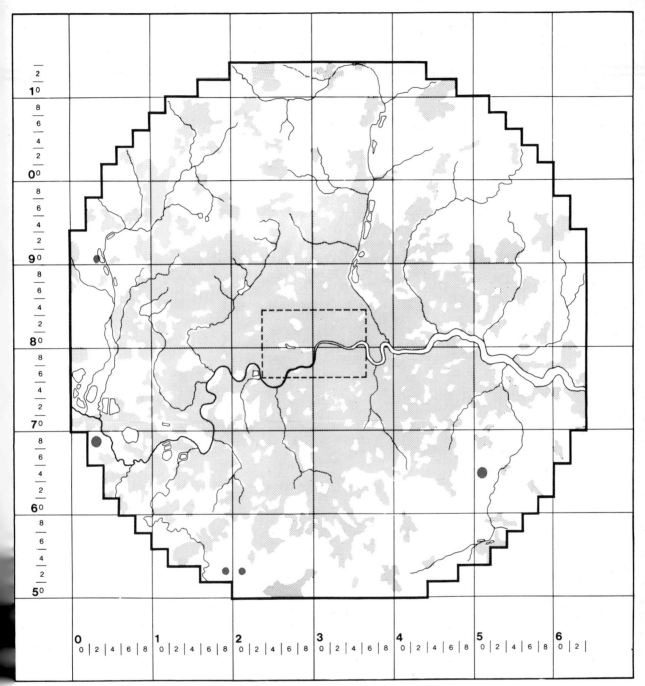

REED BUNTING

Emberiza schoeniclus

A breeding bird of mainly damp areas, the Reed Bunting nests fairly commonly in the London Area, where, as in certain other parts of the country, there has recently been some expansion into drier habitats.

Evidence of nesting away from the immediate vicinity of water dates from 1960 when birds were discovered on arable farmland north of Epping Forest and three pairs nested in fairly dry grass on Ashtead Common. This trend continued and in 1968 the Reed Bunting was reported to be a very common breeding species around Potters Bar where many territories were in cornfields away from water. In some cases the change of habitat may be related to drainage, as at Mill Hill where disturbance of marshland was considered to have been the cause of Reed Buntings moving out onto a golf course and parkland.

Witherby *et al.* (1940) indicated a fairly clear distinction between breeding habitats of the Reed Bunting and the Yellowhammer. More recently, however, Kent (1964), at a Nottinghamshire site, found Reed Buntings breeding in typical Yellowhammer habitat and suggested that the species was embarking on a phase of ecological expansion. Birds have also been recorded nesting alongside Corn Buntings in barley fields (Williamson 1968) and alongside Yellowhammers on the dry Chilterns outside the London Area (Williamson 1975). In contrast, Summers-Smith (1968) found Reed Buntings on a Yorkshire farm increased from two pairs in 1963 to 14 pairs in 1968 while the Yellowhammer disappeared as a breeding bird.

Despite these moves away from traditional habitats, the Reed Bunting remains generally associated with areas of wetland. Thus the widest distribution shown by the Atlas survey of the London Area is north of the Thames and in the west where there are more rivers and gravel pits than in the south and south-east where the largely dry North Downs still prove unattractive to this species. Patches of suitable habitat within the suburbs allow the Reed Bunting to breed at the Brent Reservoir, Hampstead Heath, the lower parts of the Lea valley and along the Thames towards central London as far as Barking, Erith and Plumstead. There were records from Wimbledon Common and Richmond Park and also Barn Elms Reservoirs, where breeding was not proved though birds have nested there in the past.

Since the end of the survey Inner London has been colonised by birds moving into the old Surrey Docks. Two males were present in 1971 and a pair summered in 1972 (George 1974). Breeding was established in 1973 when one, possibly two pairs, were successful in raising young and one pair bred in 1974.

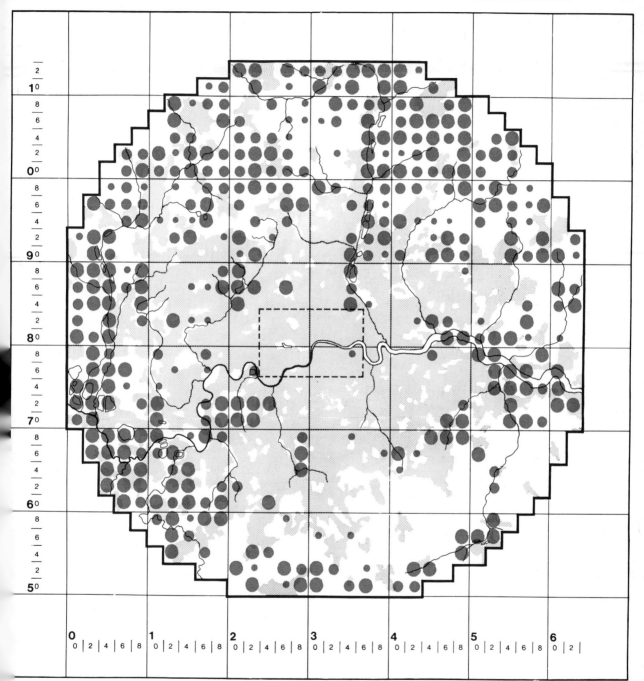

HOUSE SPARROW

Passer domesticus

From its close association with man, the House Sparrow, of all species, might be expected to breed in all tetrads in the London Area and the most likely explanation of the few blanks on the map is surely lack of adequate coverage rather than lack of House Sparrows.

Spillage from the nose-bags of horses provided urban House Sparrows with one ready source of food into the early years of this century. A decline in numbers in central London, coinciding with the disappearance of horse-drawn traffic, was thought to be related to the loss of feeding opportunities, but in fact the population continued to drop long after the introduction of motor transport. Counts in the Bloomsbury squares showed a 39% fall between 1950 and 1965 (Cramp & Tomlins 1966). Predators, of which the cat is perhaps the most important, were not considered to have been the cause nor was the increased competition for food from Woodpigeons, Feral Pigeons or, to some extent, Blackbirds. In fact observations suggested that supplies of bread generally exceeded demand. Also from Inner London, a decline was reported in Kensington Gardens to the extent of about 25% in the eighteen years between 1948 and 1965. (Sanderson 1968). In this locality the felling of a large number of old trees used as nesting sites may have been a contributory cause.

Summers-Smith (1963) showed that up to the early 1960s the greatest density of House Sparrows was in the urban, mainly built-up habitat of central London. It is not clear whether this still holds good as the decline in the centre appears to be still continuing. Density in the suburbs has not been monitored to the same extent, but there is no evidence here of any similar decreases, although expansion may sometimes be limited by a shortage of suitable nest sites which are usually in holes in buildings, in ivy or other creepers and less often in trees or bushes. In rural habitats the population is lower, even though farmland provides favourable feeding grounds at certain times of the year, especially after harvest.

Results of the five-year Atlas survey still left 32 tetrads without records of House Sparrows. Of the 824 tetrads where birds were reported, evidence of breeding came from 783, or 91% of the London Area. There is little doubt that further searching of the remaining area would have revealed that there, too, the ubiquitous House Sparrow was nesting successfully.

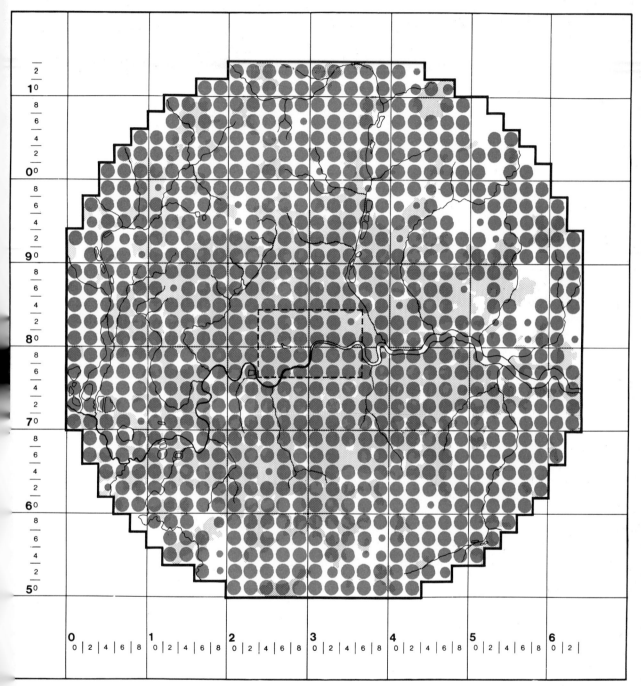

TREE SPARROW

Passer montanus

Unlike its much more familiar relative, the Tree Sparrow is a difficult species to survey. Though widespread it has a somewhat patchy distribution in the London Area.

A census in the Area in 1961 and 1962 indicated an absolute minimum population of 745 pairs of Tree Sparrows from some 115 sites (Sage 1963). Results of the much more thorough Atlas survey are not strictly comparable, but support the view that since then the population has increased. Similar reports of higher numbers have come from other parts of the country. Nest-box populations rose enormously from 1961 to about 1964, and also beginning in 1961 there was a remarkable explosive increase in range (Parslow).

An analysis of the records from both London surveys, by counties, is given in Table 16. Details of the earlier survey have been taken from Sage (1963); Atlas survey figures are approximate as the recording basis was the national grid tetrad which does not correspond with the much more irregular county boundaries. Atlas records showed that the Tree Sparrow was breeding in 329 tetrads and was found in a further 202, totalling altogether 62% of the London Area.

With increasing numbers, birds have colonised localities nearer central London. Breeding records during the Atlas survey came as close to the centre as Camberwell, Wandsworth, Fulham and Willesden. The Fulham site is only just outside the Inner London boundary and, with apparently suitable breeding habitat available in some of the parks, the species may soon be added to the list of those nesting in Inner London where at present birds are occasionally seen outside the breeding season.

Table 16. Numbers of breeding pairs of Tree Sparrows recorded in the London Area, 1961-62 and analysis of sites by counties, 1961-62 and 1968-72

		Essex	Herts	Middlesex & Bucks	Kent	Surrey	Total
1961-62	Breeding pairs	101	308	101	47	188	745
(Sage 1963)	Number of sites	17	33	31	9	25	115
1968-72 (Atlas data)	Total number of tetrads with breeding records	75	64	69	52	69	329

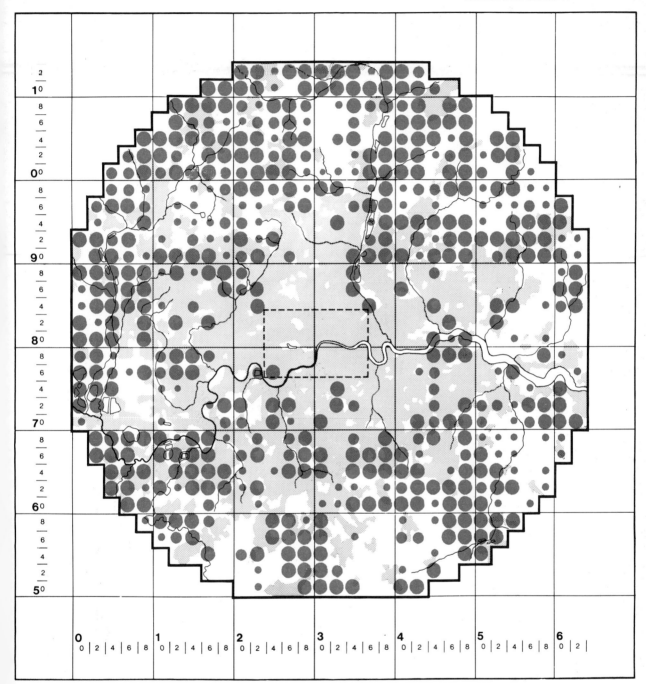

Appendices

Appendix I

(Opposite) Numbers of species recorded in each tetrad of the London Area during the 1968-72 Atlas survey, shown in four zones — Inner London, inner suburban London, outer suburban London and rural London.

Average numbers of species recorded within the four zones and the overall average

	Number of tetrads within zones	Total number of records	Average per tetrad
Inner London	24	521	22
Inner suburban London	200 (1)	7,360 (2)	37
Outer suburban London	260 (8)	11,122 (29)	44
Rural London	372 (19)	18,346 (21)	52
	856 (28)	37,349 (52)	45

Note: Columns 1 and 2 include all tetrads and all records shown on the species maps. For Inner London the average is calculated from these figures. In arriving at the average for the other three zones and the overall average, tetrads with less than ten species recorded (i.e. inadequate observer coverage) have been excluded. The total tetrads and records thus excluded are shown in brackets.

```
                    73 69 40 62 67 64 16 73 77 72 58 51
                    48 68 41 56 46 38 57 61 53 75 45 63 57 36 45 29
                 74 56 52 59 42 47 61 57 51 38 63 67 65 60 48 52  2 57 57
                 22 70 34 43 62 47 58 46 60 44 44 53 57 50 47 52 56 66 47
              50 59 53 52 47 54 52 46 50 61 64 46 52 31 50 56 60 58 55 49 55   48 55
              72 58 61 50 46 55 47 59 58 58 58 56 41 39 39 71 61 46 56 47 53 68 49 60 58  1
              57 66 61 51 56 53 64 60 46 61 49 67 44 29 30 27 59 66 58 60 62 65 67 38   46 34
           43 52 57 29 39 38 60 59 46 45 56 47 41 55 58 11 60 63 41 41 39 46 44 39 63 54 38 36
           71 71 64 69 32 27 41 37 31 31 34 41 64 63 46 46 56 57 63 45 30 24  1 49 36 43 59 44 51
           44 44 41 60 34 33 43 45 41 39 37 47 35 40 46 47 24 63 64 64 40 50 54 40 35 32 49 58 51 43
        47 84 83 39 35 47 36 53 44 54 58 36 50 33 43 34 33 36 45 49 32 56 47 76 50 55 36 62 47 54 35 24
        68 58 33 35 45 40 47 40 31 43 44 48 42 40 31 33 44 40 44 47 56 65 71 58 29 39 35 44 59 68 40
     62 76 74 69 67 44 38 28 29 39 37 36 41 41 34 25 26 56 20 29 30 34 41 33 34 20 18 24  3    30 38
     45 51 69 54 53 37 10 43 33 51 61 46 38 51 32 30 34 52 31 18 59 44 20 21 12  7  7  1  2    58 36
     63 64 60 42 44 46 22 33 35 20 40 32 27 51 21 11 16 24 38 16 16 13 33 19     5 44 37  1 41 29 41
     66 34 80 35 57 24 39 49 50 26 23 22 19 46 35 17  9 10 12 17 12 21 31 39 15 13 14 12 14 47 24
     57 46 74 40 42 29 34 44 33 26 18 18 20 46 24 16 12 11 19 15 13 20 21 48 50 19 36 39 27 50 32  6
     29 63 48 24 22 48 43 58 48 34 36 22 30 27 24  6  9 18 20 35 42 46 52 48 27 30 25 14 47 36
     42 75 61 36 27 40 35 52 49 56 42 41 31 21 29 16 22 13 14 35 23 40 35 36 19  8 35 56 25  8 30 48
     70 61 69 40 34 47 15 35 42 40 27 19 26 17 41 35 17 22 22 34 54 33 36 36 50 56 34 65 30
     59 58 33 37 50 29 24 35 53 64 53 56 45 33 36 16 50 45 21 26 29 40 36 45 68 47 41 42 35 46 61 42
     57 54 38 30 19 55 38 29 46 51 51 56 41 29 28 30 43 38 29 39 27 41 52 66 69 44 14 49 61 47 40 39
     89 67 76 60 57 60 63 57 46 22 38 38 42 50 14 41 46 50 38 34 42 62 44 49 25 29 35 47 40 48
     58 72 57 56 56 51 47 55 41 39 48 30 46 52 29 27 37 51 62 58 49 43 34 42 45 40 41 38 46 48
        69 73 68 42 63 53 59 50 46 38 21 30 54 38 47 49 42 63 51 36 35 49 48 57 46 45 39
        56 70 71 50 66 61 65 82 59 46 20 29 36 39 35 37 34 33 51 61 56 53 50 45 57 47 43 51
           65 71 60 60 64 68 67 43 54 42 46 43 46 42 57 54 56 56 53 48 55 42 53 57 49 34
           44 57 69 65 61 56 48 51 52 64 45 35 44 29 57 48 51 36 42 48 37 40 54 42
           26 74 65 52 42 48 51 50 57 57 59 15 55 46 35 44 41 36 40 61 74 81
              56 51 49 60 54 67 54 53 49 34 51 32 43 49 42 30 44 24 63 49
              60 55 59 58 47 68 60 56 55 42 67 63 48 57 71 58
              57 73 55 48 65 54 56 72 64 46 50 58
```

Left axis: 2, 10, 8, 6, 4, 2, 00, 8, 6, 4, 2, 90, 8, 6, 4, 2, 80, 8, 6, 4, 2, 70, 8, 6, 4, 2, 60, 8, 6, 4, 2, 50

Bottom axis: 0 | 0 2 4 6 8 | 1 | 0 2 4 6 8 | 2 | 0 2 4 6 8 | 3 | 0 2 4 6 8 | 4 | 0 2 4 6 8 | 5 | 0 2 4 6 8 | 6 | 0 2 |

Appendix II

Codes used by observers in completing Atlas record cards (given in ascending order of importance from least to most definite evidence of breeding).

● **Possible breeding**

✓ Bird recorded in breeding season in possible nesting habitat, but no other indication of breeding.

For this category, breeding season taken as 1 April to 31 July for most resident species and 1 May to 31 July for summer visitors with following exceptions: pigeons and doves, April-August; owls, February-July; Mistle Thrush, March-June; Crossbill, January-mid-May; Corn Bunting and Yellowhammer, April-August.

Birds excluded were Grey Heron where it was known no heronry existed, migrant waders and summering, non-breeding gulls.

● **Probable breeding**

S Singing male present or breeding calls heard on more than one date in same place.
T Bird, or pair, apparently holding territory.
D Courtship and display, agitated behaviour or anxiety calls from adults suggesting probable presence of nest or young nearby; or brood-patch on trapped female.
N Visiting probable nest site.
B Nest-building, including excavating nest-hole.

Definite evidence of breeding for most species, and in final analysis records were upgraded to BB (Breeding) except for birds of prey, waders, gulls, terns, owls, Carrion Crow, Rook, Jackdaw, Wren, *acrocephalus* and *sylvia* warblers.

● **Breeding**

[BB Nest-building, including excavating nest-hole. Upgraded from B in second category except for species listed above.]
DD Distraction display or injury feigning.
UN Used nest found.
FL Recently fledged young.
FS Adult carrying faecal sac.
FY Adult(s) with food for young.

Not to be confused with courtship feeding.

ON Adult(s) entering or leaving nest site in circumstances indicating occupied nest.

Merely prospecting for nest site would be N in second category.

NE Nest and eggs, bird sitting and not disturbed or egg-shells found away from nest.
NY Nest with young, or downy young of ducks, gamebirds, waders, etc.

Cuckoo's egg or young in a nest qualified as NE or NY respectively for both Cuckoo and fostering species.

Appendix II
Definition of 'tetrad'

A tetrad is a 2x2-km square formed by the even-numbered lines of the Ordnance Survey national grid system and can be described by a combination of letters and numbers that are readily derived from Ordnance Survey maps. Firstly, two letters define the 100-km square and, for the 10-km square, are followed by two numbers corresponding to the first digit shown against grid lines forming the west and south edges of the square. A letter 'T' and two further numbers are added for the tetrad reference, the numbers being the second digit shown against the even-numbered grid lines forming the west and south edges of the tetrad.

For example, the tetrad reference for St Paul's Cathedral is: TQ38 T/20.

Appendix III

Scientific names of plants and animals other than birds mentioned in the text.

Plants

Beech *Fagus sylvatica*
Birch *Betula* spp
Bracken *Pteridium aquilinum*
Bramble *Rubus fruticosus* agg

Elm *Ulmus* spp

Fumitory *Fumaria officinalis*

Gorse *Ulex* spp

Hawthorn *Crataegus* spp
Heather *Calluna vulgaris*
Hogweed *Heracleum sphondylium*
Hornbeam *Carpinus betulus*

Ivy *Hedera helix*

Larch *Larix* spp

Mugwort *Artemisia vulgaris*

Nettle *Urtica* spp

Oak *Quercus* spp
—, Pedunculate *Q. robur*

Pine *Pinus* spp
—, Scots *P. sylvestris*
Plane *Platanus acerifolia*

Reed, Common *Phragmites australis*

Sallow *Salix* spp
Sedge *Carex* spp
Spruce *Picea* spp
—, Norway *P. abies*

Insects

Ant *Hymenoptera: Formicidae*
—, Meadow *Lasius flavus*
—, Wood *Formica rufa*

Animals

Bat, Noctule *Nyctalus noctula*

Frog, Common *Rana temporaria*

Mouse, Wood *Apodemus sylvaticus*

Rabbit *Oryctolagus cuniculus*

Squirrel, Grey *Sciurus cardinensis*

Appendix IV

GAZETTEER

	Grid		Grid		Grid
Abbey Wood	TQ47	Bough Beech		Chipstead, Kent	TQ45/55
Acton	TQ28	Reservoir	TQ44	Chipstead, Surrey	TQ25
Addington	TQ36	Bourne, River	TQ06	Chislehurst	TQ46/47
Addlestone	TQ06	Bow Creek	TQ38	Chiswick	TQ27
Aldenham	TQ19	Brands Hatch	TQ56	Clapham	TQ27
Archbishop's Park,		Brasted Chart	TQ45	Clerkenwell	TQ38
Lambeth	TQ37	Brent Park	TQ28	Cobham	TQ15/16
Ashford	TQ07	Brent Reservoir	TQ28	Collier Row,	
Ashtead	TQ15	Brentwood	TQ69	Romford	TQ49/59
Aveley Marsh	TQ57	Bromley	TQ46/47	Coopersale	
		Brompton		Common	TL40
Badger's Mount	TQ46/56	Cemetery	TQ27	County Hall	TQ37
Banstead	TQ25/26	Brooklands S.F.	TQ06	Cripplegate	TQ38
Barking	TQ48	Broxbourne	TL30	Crossness	TQ48
Barn Elms	TQ27	Brunswick Square	TQ38	Croydon	TQ36
Barnes	TQ27	Buckingham		Crystal Palace	TQ37
Barn Hill	TQ18	Palace	TQ27		
Battersea	TQ27	Bushy Park	TQ16/17	Dagenham	TQ48/58
Bayswater	TQ28			Dartford	TQ57
Bean	TQ57	Camberwell	TQ37	Dollis Hill	TQ28
Beckenham	TQ36	Cannon Street		Dulwich	TQ37
Beddington S.F.	TQ26	Station	TQ38		
Bedfont G.P.	TQ07	Carshalton	TQ26	East Molesey	TQ16
Belsize Park	TQ28	Cassiobury Park	TQ09	Edmonton	TQ39
Belvedere	TQ47	Caterham	TQ35	Egham	TQ07
Berrylands S.F.	TQ16	Chalfont Park	TQ08/09	Elmers End	TQ36
Berwick Pond	TQ58	Charterhouse		Elstree	
Bishop's Park,		Square	TQ38	Reservoir	TQ19
Fulham	TQ27	Chelsea	TQ27	Eltham	TQ47
Blackheath	TQ37	Chertsey	TQ06	Enfield	TQ39
Black Park	TQ08	Cheshunt	TL30	Epping	TL40
Bletchingley	TQ35	Chessington	TQ16	Epping Forest	TQ49/TL40
Bloomsbury	TQ28/38	Chevening	TQ45	Epsom	TQ26
Bookham	TQ15	Chigwell	TQ49	Epsom Common	TQ16
Borehamwood	TQ19/29	Chingford	TQ39	Epsom Downs	TQ25
Bostall Woods	TQ47	Chipping Ongar	TL50	Erith	TQ57

	Grid		Grid		Grid
Erith Marsh	TQ47/48	Hillingdon	TQ08	Leicester Square	TQ28
Esher	TQ16	Hoddesdon	TL30	Lewisham	TQ37
Eynsford	TQ56	Holland Park	TQ27	Limpsfield	TQ45
		Holmethorpe	TQ25	Lincoln's Inn	TQ38
Fairlop G.P.	TQ49	Hornchurch	TQ58	Lullingstone	TQ56
Finchley	TQ29	Hornsey	TQ28/38		
Finsbury Circus	TQ38	Horton Kirby	TQ56	Maple Cross S.F.	TQ09
Finsbury Park	TQ38	Hosey Common	TQ45	Marlborough Place,	
Fishers Green	TL30	Hyde Park/Ken-		NW8	TQ28
Foots Cray	TQ47	sington Gardens	TQ27/28	Mickleham	TQ15
Fulham	TQ27			Mill Hill	TQ29
		Ilford	TQ48	Mitcham	TQ26
Gatton Park	TQ25	Imperial College	TQ27	Morden	TQ26
Gerrards Cross	TQ08	Imperial War			
Godstone	TQ35	Museum	TQ37	Natural History	
Great Parndon	TL40	Islington	TQ38	Museum	TQ27
Green Park	TQ27/28	Iver Heath	TQ08	Navestock	TQ59
Greenwich	TQ37/47			Nazeing G.P.	TL30
Gunnersbury	TQ17	Joyden's Wood	TQ47/57	Neasden	TQ28
				Northaw Great	
Hackney	TQ38	Kelsey Park	TQ36	Wood	TL20
Hadley Wood	TQ29	Kempton Park	TQ16/17	Northfleet	TQ67
Haileybury	TL31	Kensington			
Hainault	TQ49	Gardens	TQ27/28	Oaklands	TL10
Hammersmith	TQ27	Ken Wood,		Old Ford	TQ38
Hamper Mill	TQ09	Hampstead	TQ28	Old Parkbury	TL10
Hampstead	TQ28	Keston	TQ46	Ongar	TL50
Hampton Court	TQ16	Kew	TQ17	Orpington	TQ46
Harefield	TQ08	Kilburn	TQ28	Osterley Park	TQ17
Harlow	TL40/41	King George V		Otford	TQ55
Harrow	TQ18	Reservoir	TQ39	Oxshott	TQ16
Hatfield	TL20	King George VI		Oxted	TQ35
Havering	TQ58	Reservoir	TQ07		
Hayes Common	TQ46	Kingsbury	TQ18/28	Paddington	TQ28
Headley Heath	TQ15/25	King's Cross		Panshanger	TL21
Heathrow Airport	TQ07	Station	TQ38	Park Downs	TQ25
Hendon	TQ28	Kings Langley	TL00	Park Langley	TQ36
Hersham S.F.	TQ16	Kingsmead G.P.	TQ07	Parndon	TL40
Hertford	TL31			Pebblecombe	TQ25
High Beach, Epping		Ladbroke Grove	TQ28	Peckham	TQ37
Forest	TQ49	Lambeth	TQ37	Perivale	TQ18
Highgate	TQ28	Langley	TQ07	Perry Oaks S.F.	TQ07
Hilfield Park		Leatherhead	TQ15	Petts Wood	TQ46
Reservoir	TQ19	Lee	TQ37/47	Plumstead Marsh	TQ47/48

	Grid		Grid		Grid
Potters Bar	TL20	Shirley	TQ36	Uxbridge	TQ08
Primrose Hill	TQ28	Shooters Hill	TQ47		
Prince Albert Road	TQ28	Shoreham	TQ56	Vauxhall Bridge	TQ37
Prince's Coverts	TQ15/16	Smith Square	TQ37	Victoria Park	TQ38
Purfleet	TQ57	Southall	TQ17/18	Victoria Station	TQ27
Putney	TQ27	South Kensington	TQ27	Virginia Water	SU96
Pymmes Park	TQ39	South Ockendon	TQ58		
		South Weald	TQ59	Waltham Abbey	TL30
Queen Elizabeth II		Staines	TQ07	Walthamstow	TQ38
Reservoir	TQ16	Stanborough		Walton Heath	TQ25
Queen Mary		Reedmarsh	TL21	Walton Reservoirs	TQ16
Reservoir	TQ06/07	Stanmore	TQ19	Walton Street,	
Queen Mother		Stanwell	TQ07	SW3	TQ27
Reservoir,		Stanwellmoor	TQ07	Wandsworth	TQ27
Datchet	TQ07	Stepney	TQ38	Wanstead	TQ48
		Stocker's Lake/		Wapping	TQ38
Radlett	TQ19/	Springwell G.P.	TQ09	Ware	TL31
	TL10	Stoke D'Abernon	TQ15	Warlingham	TQ35
Rainham Marsh	TQ57/58	Stoke Newington	TQ38	Watford	TQ09/19
Redhill	TQ24/25	Stone	TQ57	Welwyn Garden	
Regent's Park	TQ28	Strand, The	TQ38	City	TL21
Reigate	TQ24/25	Stratford	TQ38	Wembley	TQ18
Richmond Park	TQ17/27	Streatham	TQ27/37	Westbourne Grove	TQ28
Rickmansworth	TQ09	Sundridge	TQ45	Westerham	TQ45
Riverhead	TQ55	Sundridge Park	TQ47	West Ham	TQ48
Roehampton	TQ27	Surrey Commercial		West Hyde	TQ09
Romford	TQ58	Docks	TQ37/38	West Thurrock	TQ57
Ruislip	TQ08	Swanscombe		Weybridge	TQ06
Rush Green	TQ08	Marsh	TQ67	Whitechapel	TQ38
Russell Square	TQ38			Whitehall	TQ37/38
Ruxley G.P.	TQ46/47	Tatsfield	TQ45	Willesden	TQ28
Rye House Marsh	TL30/31	Temple	TQ38	William Girling	
Rye Meads	TL30/31	Thamesmead	TQ47/48	Reservoir	TQ39
		Thorndon Park	TQ69	Wimbledon	TQ27
St Albans	TL10	Thorpe	TQ06	Windsor Great	
St George's Hill,		Thurrock	TQ68	Park	SU97
Weybridge	TQ06	Tilbury	TQ67	Woldingham	TQ35
St James's Park	TQ27	Tilehouse G.P.	TQ08	Wood Green	TQ39
St John's Wood	TQ28	Tooting	TQ27	Woolwich	TQ47
St Paul's Cathedral	TQ38	Trafalgar Square	TQ38	Wormwood Scrubs	TQ28
Selsdon	TQ36	Tring	SP91	Wraysbury	TQ07
Sevenoaks	TQ55			Wrotham Park	TQ29
Shepperton	TQ06	Upminster	TQ58		

Bibliography

ADAMS, M.C. 1966. 'Firecrests breeding in Hampshire', *Brit. Birds,* 59: 240-6

ALEXANDER, W.B. and LACK, D. 1944. 'Changes in status among British breeding birds', *Brit. Birds,* 38:62-9

ATKINSON-WILLES, G.L. (Ed.) 1963. *Wildfowl in Great Britain,* Nature Conservancy Monograph No:3, HMSO, London

BATTEN, L.A. 1972. 'Bird population changes for the years 1970-71', *Bird Study,* 19: 241-8

— 1973a. 'The colonisation of England by the Firecrest', *Brit. Birds,* 66:159-66

— 1973b. 'Bird population changes for the years 1971-72', *Bird Study,* 20:303-7

BATTEN, L.A. and MARCHANT, J.H. 1975. 'Bird population changes for the years 1972-73', *Bird Study,* 22:99-104

— 1976. 'Bird population changes for the years 1973-74', *Bird Study,* 23:11-20

BEVEN, G. 1963. 'Population changes in a Surrey oakwood during fifteen years', *Brit. Birds,* 56:307-23

— 1964. 'Survey of Bookham Common: the effects of the severe winter', *Lond. Nat.,* 43: 84-5

— 1965. 'The food of Tawny Owls in London', *Lond. Bird Rep.,* 29:56-72

— 1969. 'Survey of Bookham Common: population studies — scrub and grassland', *Lond. Nat.,* 48:132-3

— 1973. 'Survey of Bookham Common: the status of the Marsh and Willow Tits on Bookham Common', *Lond. Nat.,* 52:79-80

— 1974a. 'Survey of Bookham Common: population studies — scrub and grassland', *Lond. Nat.,* 53:76

— 1974b. 'Survey of Bookham Common: the status of the Blackcap and Garden Warbler on Bookham Common', *Lond. Nat.,* 53:76-8

— 1976. 'Changes in breeding bird populations of an oakwood on Bookham Common, Surrey, over twenty-seven years', *Lond. Nat.,* 55:23-42

BIBBY, C. 1973. 'The Red-backed Shrike: a vanishing British species', *Bird Study,* 20: 103-10

BONHAM, P.F. and SHARROCK, J.T.R. 1974. 'Sedge Warblers singing in fields of rape', *Brit. Birds,* 67:389-90

BRITISH ORNITHOLOGISTS' UNION 1971. *The Status of Birds in Britain and Ireland,* Blackwell, Oxford

BROWN, E.P. 1972. 'Studying wildlife in Holland Park', *Lond. Nat.,* 51:7-19

BURTON, J.F. 1972. 'The Yellow Wagtail in London', *Lond. Bird Rep.,* 36:92-3

CAMPBELL, B. and FERGUSON-LEES, I.J. 1972. *A Field Guide to Birds' Nests,* Constable, London

CORNELIUS, L.W. 1971. 'Yellow Wagtails breeding in Inner London', *Lond. Bird Rep.,* 35:92

CRAMP, S. 1957. 'The census of Mute Swans, 1955 and 1956', *Lond. Bird Rep.,* 21: 58-62

Bibliography

CRAMP, S. 1963. 'Toxic chemicals and birds of prey', *Brit. Birds,* 56:124-39

— 1971. 'Gulls nesting on buildings in Britain and Ireland', *Brit. Birds,* 64:476-87

— 1972. 'The breeding of urban Woodpigeons', *Ibis,* 114:163-71

— 1975. 'The influence of cleaner air on the breeding birds of Inner London', *Lond. Bird Rep.,* 38:65-72

CRAMP, S. and GOODERS, J. 1967. 'The return of the House Martin', *Lond. Bird Rep.,* 31:93-8

CRAMP, S. and TEAGLE, W.G. 1952. 'The birds of Inner London, 1900-1950', *Brit. Birds,* 45:433-56

CRAMP, S. and TOMLINS, A.D. 1966. 'The birds of Inner London, 1951-65', *Brit. Birds,* 59:209-33

DIXON, C. 1909. *The Bird-Life of London,* Heinemann, London

DOBBS, A. 1964. 'Rook numbers in Nottinghamshire over 35 years', *Brit. Birds,* 57:360-4

DOBINSON, H.M. and RICHARDS, A.J. 1964. 'The effects of the severe winter of 1962-63 on birds in Britain', *Brit. Birds,* 57:373-434

FITTER, R.S.R. 1945. *London's Natural History,* Collins, London

— 1949. *London's Birds,* Collins, London

— 1965. 'The breeding status of the Black Redstart in Great Britain', *Brit. Birds,* 58:481-92

GEORGE, R.W. 1974. 'Birds at Surrey Commercial Docks, April 1971 to December 1972', *Lond. Bird Rep.,* 37:67-70

GLADWIN, T.W. 1963. 'A short account of Rye Meads, Herts. and its ornithology', *Lond. Bird Rep.,* 26:88-99

— 1976. 'Bearded Tits in Hertfordshire since 1959', *Trans. Herts. Nat. Hist. Soc.,* 27:Pt7:355-60

GOMPERTZ, T. 1957. 'Some observations on the Feral Pigeon in London', *Bird Study,* 4:2-13

GOODERS, J. 1968. 'The Swift in central London', *Lond. Bird Rep.,* 32:93-8

GOODWIN, D. 1957. 'Two cases of polyneuritis in Feral Pigeons', *Bird Study,* 4:13

GRANT, P.J. 1967. 'The birds of Greenwich Park and Blackheath', *Lond. Bird Rep.,* 31:64-92

— 1971. 'Birds at Surrey Commercial Docks', *Lond. Bird Rep.,* 35:87-91

HARRISON, C.J.O. 1961. 'Woodlark population and habitat', *Lond. Bird Rep.,* 24:71-80

HARRISON, J.G. 1974. *The Sevenoaks Gravel Pit Reserve,* WAGBI

HARRISON, J.G. and GRANT, P.J. 1976. *The Thames Transformed,* Deutsch, London

HINDLE, C.H. (Ed.) 1975. *The Kent Bird Report,* No:22, 1973, Kent Ornithological Society

HOMES, R.C. (Ed.) 1964. *The Birds of the London Area* (New revised edition), Hart-Davis, London

HOMES, R.C. 1976. 'Twenty-five years of duck counts in the London Area', *Lond. Bird Rep.,* 39:62-74

HOMES, R.C., SAGE, B.L. and SPENCER, R. 1960. 'Breeding populations of Lapwings, Coot and Meadow Pipits', *Lond. Bird Rep.,* 23:54-61

HORI, J. 1964. 'The breeding biology of the Shelduck *Tadorna tadorna*', *Ibis,* 106:333-60

HUDSON, R. 1965. 'The spread of the Collared Dove in Britain and Ireland', *Brit. Birds,* 58:105-39

HUDSON, W.H. 1898. *Birds in London,* Longmans, Green, London. New edition, 1969, David & Charles Reprints, Devon

HURCOMB, Lord 1962. *Bird Life in the Royal Parks, 1959-60:* Report by the Committee on bird sanctuaries in the Royal Parks (England & Wales), HMSO

KENT, A.K. 1964. 'The breeding habitats of the Reed Bunting and Yellowhammer in Nottinghamshire', *Bird Study,* 11:123-7

LACK, D. 1954. 'The stability of the Heron population', *Brit. Birds,* 47:111-19

— 1971. *Ecological Isolation in Birds,* Blackwell, Oxford

LONDON NATURAL HISTORY SOCIETY 1957. *The Birds of the London Area Since 1900,* Collins, London

LOUSLEY, J.E. 1969. *Wild Flowers of Chalk and Limestone,* Collins, London

LVPG – LEE VALLEY PROJECT GROUP (THE). *Birds of the Lee Valley 1975*

MACPHERSON, A. HOLTE 1929. 'A list of the birds of Inner London', *Brit. Birds,* 22: 222-44

MAGEE, J.D. 1965. 'The breeding distribution of the Stonechat in Britain and causes of its decline', *Bird Study,* 12:83-9

— 1972. 'Birds of Cassiobury Park, the West Hertfordshire Golf Course and Whippendell Woods, Watford', *Lond. Bird Rep.,* 36:67-74

MATHIASSON, S. 1973. 'Moulting grounds of Mute Swans *Cygnus olor* in Sweden, their origin and relation to population dynamics of Mute Swans in the Baltic area', *Viltrevy,* 8:399-452

MEAD, C.J. and PEPLER, G.R.M. 1975. 'Birds and other animals at Sand Martin colonies', *Brit. Birds,* 68:89-99

MEADOWS, B.S. 1970. 'Breeding distribution and feeding ecology of the Black Redstart in London', *Lond. Bird Rep.,* 34:72-9

— 1972. 'The recovery of the Kingfisher in London after the 1962-63 hard winter', *Lond. Bird Rep.,* 36:60-5

MELLUISH, W.D. 1957. 'The census of Great Crested Grebes 1946-55: final report and summary of results', *Lond. Bird Rep.,* 21:48-57

MILNE, B.S. 1956. 'A report on the bird population of Beddington Sewage Farm, 1954-55', *Lond. Bird Rep.,* 20:39-54

MITCHELL, A. 1973. 'Dutch elm disease and birds', *Bird Study,* 20:84-7

MONK. J.F. 1963. 'The past and present status of the Wryneck in the British Isles', *Bird Study,* 10:112-32

MONTIER, D.J. 1968. 'A survey of the breeding distribution of the Kestrel, Barn Owl and Tawny Owl in the London Area in 1967', *Lond. Bird Rep.,* 32:81-92

MOREAU, R.E. 1972. *The Palaearctic-African Bird Migration Systems,* Academic Press, London

MOUNTFORT, G. 1957. *The Hawfinch,* Collins, London

MURTON, R.K. 1965. *The Woodpigeon,* Collins, London

— 1971. *Man and Birds,* Collins, London

NAU, B.S. 1961. 'Sand Martin colonies in the London Area', *Lond. Bird Rep.,* 25:69-81

NEWTON, I. 1972. *Finches,* Collins, London

— 1973. 'Success of Sparrowhawks in an area of pesticide usage', *Bird Study,* 20:1-8

NOBLE, K. 1972. 'Oystercatchers breeding at Rainham Marsh, Essex', *Lond. Bird Rep.,* 36:91-2

OLIVER, P.J. 1975. 'Heronries in the London Area', *Lond. Bird Rep.*, 38:73-7

PARKER, A.C. 1970 'The decline of the Rook as a breeding species at Hainault, Essex', *Lond. Bird Rep.*, 33:87-95

PARR, D. (Ed.) 1972. *Birds in Surrey 1900-1970*, Batsford, London

PARRINDER, E.R. and E.D. 1975. 'Little Ringed Plovers in Britain in 1968-73', *Brit. Birds*, 68:359-68

PARSLOW, J.L.F. 1973. *Breeding Birds of Britain and Ireland*, Poyser, Berkhamsted

PEAL, R.E.F. 1965. 'Woodpigeons in a London suburb', *Lond. Bird Rep.*, 29:89-90

— 1968. 'The distribution of the Wryneck in the British Isles, 1964-66', *Bird Study*, 15:111-26

POTTS, G.R. 1970. 'Recent changes in the farmland fauna with special reference to the decline of the Grey Partridge', *Bird Study*, 17:145-66

PRESTT, I. 1965 'An inquiry into the recent breeding status of some of the smaller birds of prey and crows in Britain', *Bird Study*, 12:196-221

REYNOLDS, C.M. 1974. 'The Census of Heronries, 1969-73', *Bird Study*, 21:129-34

SAGE, B.L. 1963. 'The breeding distribution of the Tree Sparrow', *Lond. Bird Rep.*, 27:56-65

— (Ed.) 1966. *Northaw Great Wood: its history and natural history*, Herts. C.C.

— 1972. 'The decline of the Rook population of Hertfordshire', *Trans. Herts. Nat. Hist. Soc.*, 27:Pt4:190-206

SANDERSON, R.F. 1968. 'The changing status of birds in Kensington Gardens', *Lond. Bird Rep.*, 32:63-80

SIMMS, E. 1962. 'A study of suburban bird-life at Dollis Hill', *Brit. Birds*, 55:1-36

— 1965. 'Effects of the cold weather of 1962-63 on the Blackbird population of Dollis Hill, London', *Brit. Birds*, 58:33-43

— 1974. *Wild Life in the Royal Parks*, HMSO

SNOW, D.W. 1969 'Some vital statistics of British Mistle Thrushes', *Bird Study*, 16:34-44

SPENCER, R. and GUSH, G.H. 1973. 'Siskins feeding in gardens', *Brit. Birds*, 66:91-9

STAFFORD, J. 1962. 'Nightjar enquiry, 1957-58', *Bird Study*, 9:104-15

— 1971. 'The Heron population of England and Wales, 1928-1970', *Bird Study*, 18:218-21

STRANGEMAN, P.J. 1975. 'The breeding birds of Bishop's Park, Fulham, and its vicinity', *Lond. Bird Rep.*, 38:79-86

SUMMERS-SMITH, D. 1968. 'Buntings on a Yorkshire farm', *Bird Study*, 15:209-10

SUMMERS-SMITH, J.D. 1963. *The House Sparrow*, Collins, London

VOOUS, K.H. 1960. *Atlas of European Birds*, Nelson, London

WALLACE, D.I.M. 1964. 'Herring Gulls breeding in Inner London', *Brit. Birds*, 57:80-1

— 1974. 'The birds of Regent's Park, London, 1959-68', *Brit. Birds*, 67:449-68

WASHINGTON, D. (Ed.) 1975. *Surrey Bird Report*, No:22, 1974, Surrey Bird Club

WILLIAMSON, K. 1968. 'Buntings on a barley farm', *Bird Study*, 15:34-7

— 1975. 'The breeding bird community of Chalk grassland scrub in the Chiltern Hills' *Bird Study*, 22:59-70

WINSTANLEY, D., SPENCER, R. and WILLIAMSON, K. 1974. 'Where have all the White-throats gone?', *Bird Study*, 21:1-14

WITHERBY, H.F., JOURDAIN, F.C.R., TICEHURST, N.F. and TUCKER, B.W. 1940. *The Handbook of British Birds*, Witherby, London

List of names of observers

G.M. Abbott
R. Adamson
Mrs R. Adamson
R. Alderton
Miss P.E. Allan
Miss J. Allen
N. Allen
R. Allison
E.F. Anderson
M.S. Andrews
M.E. Antram
J.S. Armitage

L. Baker
P.F. Ball
B.P. Barker
E.V. Barker
R. Barker
G.M. Barratt
W.J. Barry
F. Bassnett
L.A. Batten
I.R. Beames
A.H. Beardsley
K. Bennet
F.K. Bennett
J.F.P. Bennett
Mrs P.A. Bennett
J.C. Benson
R.G. Bentall
Dr G. Beven
R.G. Bibby
M. Biggs
Miss S.A. Bills
Mr Birlison
C. Boase
R. Boddy
P.F. Bonham
S.G.E. Boucher
T.E. Bowley
C. Bowlt
D.F. Bowman
D.A. Boyd
R. Brighton
Miss L.M. Broome
A.G.W. Brown
Mrs A.G.W. Brown
Miss D.M. Brown

Miss E.P. Brown
Miss M.P. Brown
R.S. Brown
S.J. Broyd
C. Burgess
Dr R.R. Burn
G. Burness
P.S. Burns
R.M. Burrows
G.J.A. Burton
J.F. Burton
R.J. Buxton
R.W. Byrne

H.B. Camplin
F.R. Cannings
C.P. Carpenter
W.D. Carpenter
D. Carr
K. Carr
P.J. Casselton
Mr Chamberlayne
Mrs D. Chandler
A.G. Channer
E.A. Chapman
G.M. Chapman
Mrs J.K. Chesneau
R.D. Chesneau
A.K. Child
D. Christie
E. Clark
A.C. Clarke
N. Clarke
J.D. Clayden
J.R.H. Clements
J.A. Cocks
A.F. Coleman
B. Coleman
R.M. Cook
Miss J.C.L. Cooke
G. Cooper
J. Cooper
G.B. Corbet
G.T. Corley Smith
L.W. Cornelius
R.W. Cornelius
K. Costar
W. Coster

M.J. Cowlard
C.S. Crace
S. Cramp

R. Da Cunha
J.D. Daffarn
Dartford Ringing Group
B.R. Davies
M. Davies
Miss R. Davis
D. Dawe
D. Dean
M.K Dennis
R. Dennis
R.A. Dewey
Mrs B. Dobson
C.C. Dring
K.R. Drummond
A.G. Duff
C.K. Dunkley
D. Dunn
R.F. Durman

J. East
M. East
J.C. Eaton
R.D.M. Edgar
F.A. Edmunds
M. Edmunds
P.J. Edwards
G.D. Elcome
R. Ellis
P.A. Etheridge
G.C. Evans
M.C.W. Evans
P.G.H. Evans

Miss J. Farquharson
D.W. Faulkner
P.E. Feltham
B.W. Finch
J. Fitzpatrick
B.H. Fletcher
R.H.B. Forster
E.M. Forsyth
Mrs M.C. Foster
J.G. Francis
H.J. Freeman

S.W. Fremantle
D.V. Freshwater

C. Galey
N.E. Gammon
P.D. Gann
D.J. Garbutt
R. Gardner
A. Gasson
A. Gibbs
A.H. Gibson
D.C. Gilbert
E.H. Gillham
A.P. Goddard
K.A.J. Gold
J. Gooders
G.C.Gore
A.P. Gosling
M.G. Gotts
Mrs J.A. Gould
C.R. Grafton
P.J. Grant
C. Green
R.C. Green
A. Greensmith
S. Greenwood
D. Griffin
A.M. Griffiths
G.H. Gush

A. Hall
R. Hamilton
R.D. Harbird
Mrs B. Hardy
A.J. Harmer
D. G. Harris
M.A. Harris
Dr J.G. Harrison
Dr J.M. Harrison
J. Harrold
R.C.F. Hastings
J.A. Hazell
R.C. Headford
D.G. Henderson
J. Henderson
J.D. Henry
K.J. Herber
Miss D. Hersey

List of names of observers

Herts. Nat. Hist. Soc.
N.D. Hewitt
Miss P.J. Higgins
R.R. Higgs
L.E. Higson
Miss E.M. Hillman
G. Hinchon
G. Hockley
D.R. Hodge
A.J. Holcombe
J.M. Hollingworth
M.A. Hollingworth
D.J. Holman
F.J. Holroyde
R.C. Homes
S.D. Housden
N.G. Hudson
C. Hughes
D.J. Hughes
R.A. Husband
A.M. Hutson
A.J. Hyne

W.R. Ingram

J.A. Jobling
A.P. Johnson
C. Johnson
Lt. Cdr. D.H. Johnson
Mrs D.H. Johnson
I.G. Johnson
A.J. Johnston
P. Johnstone
J.C. Jones
Mrs B.M. Joslin
R.T. Joslin
P. Julian
M. July

A.S. Keith
Miss M.E. Kennedy
Kent Orn. Soc.
R.H. Kettle
F.R. Kilpatrick
F.M. King
Mrs King
P.K. Kinnear
S.J. Kirtland
A. Kogut

F.J. Lambert
J.W. Landells
W.N. Landells
Mrs Y.M. Laver
A.J. Lawrence
T.J. Lawrence

Mr Lea
B. Lee
R.F. Leighton
M.X. Lewin
D.A. Lilliman
Dr V.U. Lutwyche

F.G. McColl
W. McCubbin
R. McLaren
Dr D.A.C. McNeil
H. McSweeney
P. McSweeney
I.B. McWilton
J.W. Malster
I.G. Manklow
D. Manning
D.M. Mansell
W.B. Marrison
B.A. Marsh
F. Martin
G. Martin
Mrs J. Martin
J.H.N. Mason
Miss O. Maunder
N.A. May
C.J. Mead
J.V. Mead
B.S. Meadows
K.M. Meadows
W.G. Meadows
H.P. Medhurst
P. Meridith
Miss P.J. Messer
K.D. Metcalf
H. Miles
M.K. Miller
W.G.L. Miller
A.B.M. Mills
D.R. Mitchell
K.D.G. Mitchell
D.J. Montier
Mrs D.M. Montier
S. Moore
Mrs M. More
P.J. Morgan
K.W. Morris
L.P. Mulford
B.T. Mullins
Miss J.P. Muncaster
Maj. G.F.A. Munns
A.F. Mussellwhite
Mrs B.S. Mussellwhite

Mrs M. Newman

K. Noble

R.J. O'Connor
C. Ogston
B. Olby
P.J. Oliver
W.E. Olpin
K.C. Osborne

A.R.J. Paine
K.H. Palmer
R.A. Palmer
A.C. Parker
W. Parker
W.E. Parkinson
D. Parr
Mrs E.D. Parrinder
K.W. Parsley
R.W. Payne
Mrs E. Peal
R.E.F. Peal
R.G. Peal
J. Penry-Jones
D.J. Pezet
E. Phillips-Jones
D. Pitt-Pladdy
W. Plomer
S. R. Pomeroy
R.F. Powell
R. Price
Miss M.E. Pugh
A.H. Pulsford

M.J. Rayner
N. Redman
Miss H.M. Reed
F.C. Reeves
E.W. Reuthe
A. Reynolds
S. Roberts
Mrs E.F. Rolfe
M.G. Rowan
Mrs S.M. Ruck
T.M. Ruck
S. D. Rudge

J.A. Sage
R. St. John
E.J. Salholm
D. G. Salmon
A.N.M. Sanders
R.F. Sanderson
J. Sankey
J. Scheck
M. Scheck

M.J. Schickner
J.G. Schmidt
D.G. Scott
Miss E.M. Seaman
P.J. Sellar
J.C. Seymour
M. Sharp
Miss E.M. Sheen
D. Shepherd
I.E.H. Shepherd
Mrs H.W.Sheppard
R.A. Sheppard
S. B. Sheppard
E. Simms
L.M. Simonds
A.E. Sims
Mrs J. Small
Mrs L.M.P. Small
T.R. Smeeton
A.J.L. Smith
Miss B. Smith
D.A. Smith
G.A. Smith
P.J. Smith
R.E. Smith
Dr W.E. Snell
A.J. Snowden
A.R.J. Solly
P.M. Solly
T. Spall
W. Spencer
Miss K.E. Springett
S.D.G. Stephens
C.E. Storey
Mrs B. Strange
P.J. Strangeman
A.D. Styles
R.J. Styles
D. Surrey
Surrey Bird Club
J. Swift

D.W. Taylor
Dr M.P. Taylor
K.V. Thompsett
D. Thompson
R.T. Thorp
Miss V. Thorpe
J.G. Threadgold
J.R. Threlfall
E.M. Thwaites
Miss M.J. Tilley
R.J. Tomlin
A.D. Tomlins
D. Tomlinson

J.E. Treganna
Mrs M. Tugendhat
R.E. Turley
C.F. Turner
D. Turner
R. Turnham

Mrs B.M.E. Unsworth
Mrs R. Upton
E.D. Urquhart

E. Venis
A.G. Verrall
J. Vickers

A. Vittery

D.I.M. Wallace
C. Walsh
Miss B. Wand
J. Warde
Prof. E.H. Warmington
Mrs A. Warren
D.S. Warren
R.B. Warren
Mrs P.M. Washer
G. Watkin Williams
R.D. Watson
M.G. Wells

M.J. Wells
C.W. Westwood
J.J. Wheatley
T. Wheeler
C.A. White
R.V. White
Dr P.J. Whitfield
J.P. Widgery
J.S. Wilding
A. Wilkins
J. Williamson
J.F. Willis
Mrs Wilmore
D. Wimblett

M.E.A. Winn
N. Witham
D. Withrington
Miss V. Wodehouse
Mrs E.A. Wood
J.H. Wood
K. Wood
S.B. Wood
Miss D.E. Woods
J.W. Woodward
L.F. Woollard

Index of bird names

Reference to the relevant species account is in bold type

Index of place names

This index is not a full list of all localities where each species may be found, but is a list of place names mentioned in the text.

Index of place names